The Master Architect

Frank Lloyd Wright circa 1956. Photograph courtesy of The Capital Times, *Madison, Wisconsin.*

The Master Architect

Conversations with Frank Lloyd Wright

Edited by

PATRICK J. MEEHAN, AIA
Architect

A Wiley-Interscience Publication/John Wiley & Sons/New York • Chichester • Brisbane • Toronto • Singapore

Designed by Jules Perlmutter, Off-Broadway Graphics

Library of Congress Cataloging in Publication Data:

Wright, Frank Lloyd, 1867–1959.
The master architect.

"A Wiley-Interscience publication."
Includes index.
1. Wright, Frank Lloyd, 1867–1959. 2. Architects—United States—Interviews. I. Meehan, Patrick Joseph.
II. Title.
NA737.W7W68   1984   720'.92'4   84-11931
ISBN 0-471-80025-2

Printed in the United States of America

10 9 8 7 6 5 4 3 2 1

To Karen, Ryan, Sean, and the young architects of the future—

The Four Organic Commandments:

Love is the virtue of the *heart*

Sincerity the virtue of the *mind*

Courage the virtue of the *spirit*

Decision the virtue of the *will*

FRANK LLOYD WRIGHT

Preface

Although I never had the good fortune to meet the world's premier architect, Frank Lloyd Wright, after very carefully transcribing the bulk of the material contained in this book from tape recordings and motion picture films of Mr. Wright, I feel that I have indeed met him. Since I was able to hear and, in some instances, see the image of Mr. Wright while I was transcribing, I was able to experience and feel the dynamic quality of his personality. In his preface to Mr. Wright's *Letters to Apprentices* Bruce Brooks Pfeiffer said that "when he saw the written text of something that he had said in speaking, taken down verbatim, he remarked that what was conspicuously lacking on the printed page was the twinkle in the corner of his eye." I hope the reader of this collection of conversations with Mr. Wright will find some of that twinkle captured and sustained within these pages.

In the eighteen conversations transcribed here Mr. Wright speaks of his life, of architecture, of city planning, and of culture and education with architects, apprentice and student architects (with whom Mr. Wright had always had a special rapport), close friends, notable press personalities, and real estate developers (with whom Mr. Wright often had an adversary relationship). The conversations are organized into six parts based on theme and subject matter in order to illustrate the many facets of both Frank Lloyd Wright, the master architect, and Frank Lloyd Wright, the man. Twelve of the eighteen conversations are previously unpublished. The reader should note the consistency of Mr. Wright's philosophies as expressed in these conversations spanning a time period from 1930 to 1959.

The idea for compiling a collection of conversations with Mr. Wright emerged while I was working on my first book, *Frank Lloyd Wright: A Research Guide to Archival Sources* (New York: Garland, 1983). I found that many rare audio and audiovisual related materials of Mr. Wright had been destroyed, were deteriorated beyond further use, or were just no longer available from any source whatsoever. Unfortunately, many materials that once did exist have become lost forever. The purpose of this book is twofold—first, to make accessible to a wide audience important selected conversations with Mr. Wright which cover a wide range of topical areas and second, to preserve those conversations so that they will not become lost forever as so many others have.

A book such as this would have been impossible to coordinate into an integrated whole without the help and input from a great many persons to whom I am especially indebted. Bruce Brooks Pfeiffer, Director of Archives of The Frank LLoyd Wright Memorial Foundation, assisted in the provision of Mr. Wright's drawings which appear in this volume as well as with other illustrations and permissions from both The Frank Lloyd Wright Foundation and The Frank Lloyd Wright Memorial Foundation—without Mr. Pfeiffer's enthusiasm and support for the work, this book would not have been realized as it appears. Others who provided invaluable assistance include Dr. Vernon Bryson; Emmett D. Chisum, Research Historian at the Archive of Contemporary History of the University of Wyoming; Professor George R. Collins of Columbia University; Alistair Cooke; Helga Sandburg Crile; Hugh Downs; Catherine Egan, Assistant Director of Audio Visual Services for The Pennsylvania State University; Jinx Falkenburg; Holly Fullam of the Guggenheim Museum, New York; Judy Gardner, Public Service Librarian of the College Library of the University of Wisconsin–Madison; Jeffery Garmel of the WGBH Educational Foundation, Boston; Derry Graves of The Spring Green Restaurant, Spring Green, Wisconsin; Maurice C. Greenbaum of the "Sandburg Family Trust, Frank M. Parker and Maurice C. Greenbaum, Trustees"; Vina Jacobs, Public Relations Administrator of Johnson Wax; E. Fay Jones, FAIA; Donald Kalec of the Frank Lloyd Wright Home and Studio Foundation, Oak Park, Illinois; Jan Kreher of the National Broadcasting Company; Katherine S. Lauderdale of WTTW-Chicago Channel 11; Mary Jane Lightbown of the Department of Architecture and Design of the Museum of Modern Art; Lil Melgin and Bob Weil of the Beth Sholom Congregation, Elkins Park, Pennsylvania; Leigh A. Milner, former Librarian for *The Capital Times,* Madison, Wisconsin; Lynn Nesmith of the *AIA Journal;* Bill Randour, Director of Public Relations of the Western Pennsylvania Conservancy, Pittsburgh, Pennsylvania; Phillip L. Rane, publisher of *Food Service Marketing Magazine;* Susan Sain of the Arizona Biltmore Hotel; Pauline Saliga, Assistant Curator of the Department of Architecture of the Art Institute of Chicago; Irene Schwartz of *Newsday;* Gerald J. Stashak, Vice President of *School Arts;* David N. Sternlicht of the American

Broadcasting Company; Elizabeth Stonorov; George Talbot and Myrna Williamson of the State Historical Society of Wisconsin; Mike Wallace; Professor John G. Williams of the University of Arkansas; Susan Zeckendorf; and William Zeckendorf, Jr. I thank all of these people for their help and kindness in providing me with needed materials or permissions. Finally, I thank John Wiley & Sons for making the idea into a reality.

PATRICK J. MEEHAN, AIA

Milwaukee, Wisconsin
September 1984

Contents

The Master Architect

PART
ONE

Meet Mr. Frank Lloyd Wright

Master Architect and Father of Modern Architecture

The Prophet Without Honor in His Own Land

Conversations with Others

... when you're swimming upstream you're buffeted by all sorts of events and there may be something coming downstream that's pretty formidable and may get you. Well, it worries me a little to see that the stream seems to be running upstream quite a great extent.

On August 7, 1956 National Broadcasting Company (NBC) Radio broadcast the program *Biography in Sound: Meet Frank Lloyd Wright* to a national audience. Morgan Beatty, then NBC Washington, D. C. news correspondent, provided the program's narration and conducted the interviews of Mr. Wright, Wright's acquaintances, clients, critics, architects, students, and friends. The Frank Lloyd Wright interview portion of the program was recorded at Taliesin near Spring Green, Wisconsin. Persons commenting in the program were Charlotte Partridge, the Director Emeritus of the Layton School of Art at Milwaukee, Wisconsin; Walter Bublitz, a lay leader of the Wright-designed Community Christian Church at Kansas City; Douglas Orr, the former president of the American Institute of Architects (AIA); William Zeckendorf, real estate developer; Ivan A. Nestingen, then mayor of Madison, Wisconsin; David Wright, one of Frank Lloyd Wright's sons; H. F. Johnson, for whom Wright designed and built the Johnson Wax Company at Racine, Wisconsin; T. Inumaru, the president of the Imperial Hotel Corporation; Gerald Loeb, a New York

These conversations are reproduced from National Broadcasting Company (NBC) Radio Broadcast *Biography in Sound: Meet Frank Lloyd Wright* dated August 7, 1956 with permission of the National Broadcasting Company.

financier for whom Wright designed a residence; Blaine Drake, one of Wright's former students; John Hill, a former student of Wright's and the architectural editor of *House Beautiful* magazine; Betsy Barton, author; Bruno Zevi, critic, author, and editor; Herbert Jacobs, a Wright client for two residences; H. C. Price, industrialist and client of Wright; and Charles Lilly, then registrar of the Wright-designed Florida Southern College at Lakeland. All comments and interviews were made within the program's framework of providing a review of Wright's stormy prophetic architectural career.

The Conversations

BEATTY: There he is strutting along the edge of an excavation dwarfed beneath an earth-moving machine but still a figure of majesty. See the great tufts of white hair high at the temples, the heavy jowled lined face, he wears a flowing tie and cape and if he weren't so at home among the bulldozers and the cement mixers you'd guess he was a composer or a painter. But you know he's an architect and you won't have to go far to hear him called "the greatest architect in the world."

Frank Lloyd Wright, the genius with a T-square, has been called the pacesetter of modern-day architecture, the great uncompromiser, whose buildings may startle or delight but always are true to his beliefs. We have viewed this man's work (three generations of us have) and some of us have applauded and marveled and others of us have rung our hands and accused him of creating monstrosities. Every time he has built a building, we—everyman—had something to say about it. When he built the Larkin Building in Buffalo we called it an "eyesore"—a space waster. The Imperial Hotel we called just plain "ugly." Some of his churches we called "un-Christian" and some of his homes we said we

"wouldn't live in them for free." Not only what he has done on his master's drawing board but nearly everything he has done has upset us, divided us, made us like him more or like him less. Like the hurricane's eye, this grandfatherly man of principle and determination has been the center of an almost endless stream of controversy. "It's the way of genius" you say; well, maybe so but few men of genius have quite the built-in furor of Frank Lloyd Wright.

For instance, there was, for lack of a better title, the Milwaukee caper. The Director Emeritus of the Layton School of Art (Milwaukee), Miss Charlotte Partridge, remembers that turbulant affair in 1930.

PARTRIDGE: With a great enthusiasm, I asked the Wisconsin chapter of the American Institute of Architects to co-sponsor this exhibition and lecture for the Layton Art Gallery and also, frankly, to help pay the bills because we had no money for it. Polite refusals interspersed with much less polite remarks surprised and shocked me.

One day I was stopped in the middle of the street by a gentleman architect who literally

Meet Mr. Frank Lloyd Wright

Seneca Street elevation of the Larkin Company Administration Building (1903) at Buffalo, New York (demolished 1949–1950). Photograph from Frank Lloyd Wright, Frank Lloyd Wright: Ausgeführte Bauten *(Berlin: Ernst Wasmuth, 1911).*

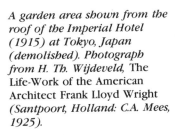

A garden area shown from the roof of the Imperial Hotel (1915) at Tokyo, Japan (demolished). Photograph from H. Th. Wijdeveld, The Life-Work of the American Architect Frank Lloyd Wright *(Santpoort, Holland: C.A. Mees, 1925).*

shook a finger in my face: "Young woman, don't you know what you are doing? You're ignorant, very ignorant." But we must have his exhibition. Milwaukee, I thought, needed it. And have it we would.

Then came his lecture "The New Architecture" and what mishaps. First, the electricity went off in the building; the building was in darkness for two or three hours. Then a phone call: "Don't worry Miss Partridge, but Mr. Wright has just been arrested because of some debt over money due." Extras on the street—"Wright Arrested"—atmosphere tense, telephones busy—it was very hectic. But, with his usual ability to rise above situations and friends at court, he was released just in time for my small dinner. The next morning, just after I reached my office, in walked Mr. Wright saying: "Will you please pay me now?" "Why? Don't you trust me?" I was a little bit indignant. "Yes, you, but not the others." Not ten minutes after he left with his check came two policemen to garnishee his payment. My glee at saying to them that we owed him no money was much brighter than their amazement. However, he was not allowed to move his exhibition out of the gallery for several weeks until after the legal matters had been settled and in his favor.

BEATTY: The friends of Frank Lloyd Wright occasionally had the last laugh but, as you can see, it has often been touch and go. One friend Mr. Wright discovered, a dozen years after the Milwaukee incident, was a Midwest clergyman who wanted to build the church of the future. A witness to what happened, Walter Bublitz of Kansas City, one of the lay leaders of the Community Christian Church:

BUBLITZ: Our pastor was that great minister, Dr. Brutus A. Jenkins, now deceased, the foremost liberal minister of his day and his liberal teachings are well accepted as standards today. Mr. Wright was the foremost thinking liberal architect of his time and it was quite natural when two such geniuses met they would fall in love with each other—they did.

Mr. Wright prepared final plans and bids were asked from local contractors. All of them refused to bid because they said they "couldn't understand the plans" of the then revolutionary type of construction. City authorities said that the design was so unusual and different in principle from recommendations in the building code that they "didn't see how they could grant a permit." Mr. Wright was asked to explain certain theories and principles in his design but Mr. Wright refused and said "the authorities should be educated enough to figure them out and disprove them if they could. If not, issue the permit." The code committee hesitated in granting the permit because the auditorium was designed to seat 1,200 persons and they were solicitous of the welfare of those persons in such a fantastic type of building. Mr. Wright then urged the committee to proceed with construction without a permit and said he did not think the authorities would chance a court test that would prove the building code inadequate for modern needs. No building permit was ever issued.

BEATTY: You're getting the idea this man Wright is, well, an individualist. He scorns the commonplace, the red tape, the details, the incompetent. He stays away from the crowd— always ahead of it, usually. And when the crowd is composed of other architects, he usually stays far away. The architecture of today, the so-called modern architecture, says Mr. Wright, is "servile insignificant refuse" or "puerile

*The Kansas City Community Christian Church (1940) at Kansas City, Missouri.
Photograph by the editor.*

nostalgia." This is hardly the kind of talk to draw cheers from the American Institute of Architects, a group composed of practically all the leading T-square and triangle men with the exception, that is, of Frank Lloyd Wright. Things have never been too harmonious between Mr. Wright and the AIA—the body professional—the paternity of the non-Wright practitioners. Some of the AIA men have had unkind words to say about the individualist from the prairie and he, not infrequently, has loosed a blast or two in their direction. In 1949 there was a flourish-filled burying of the hatchet—the AIA awarding its Gold Medal to Mr. Wright. The other day we asked for some of the details from the man who then was president of the AIA, Douglas Orr. We

also asked Mr. Wright himself for a few comments. We've taken the liberty of putting some of the two gentlemen's thoughts side by side.

WRIGHT: Well, the AIA, I have never joined because . . . they know why.

ORR: Mr. Wright has always been a lone wolf. He was not one given to joining associations when he had some disagreement.

WRIGHT: When they gave me the Gold Medal at Houston I told them frankly why—feeling that the architectural profession is all that's the matter with architecture. Why should I join them?

ORR: The proposal to award the Gold Medal

to Mr. Wright, naturally, brought differences of opinion in the profession as to the form of architecture which Mr. Wright advocated and as to his being, at times, critical of the procedures of the Institute.

WRIGHT: Oh, I would do anything they asked me for except join them to make a harbor of refuge for the incompetent . . .

ORR: Mr. Wright considered the Institute a very conservative body.

WRIGHT: . . . because I believe less and less in professionalism as I see it practiced. I think it's a kind of refined gangsterism. So, as Henry Luce said in astonishment, he said, "Are you an old amateur?" and I said "Yes, Mr. Luce, I am the oldest!" And that's the story of the AIA.

BEATTY: That is indeed the story of the AIA and if the sound of Mr. Wright's voice appeals to you, if the measured needling of his words amuses you, the outspoken sarcasm intrigues you—stand by, there's more to come. There's hardly a topic on which this man doesn't speak out be it politics or art or philosophy. One of his favorite topics is the city and from Los Angeles to New York easily offended people snarl when they hear the name of Frank Lloyd Wright—for he doesn't appreciate their home town. Los Angeles, he has said, "is the great American commonplace"; Miamians, he spoke out, "are living in houses pigs would be ashamed to live in"; Pittsburgh, "it would be cheaper," he guessed, "to destroy it." But for New York, Mr. Wright seems to reserve a special contempt probably because it's our biggest city and thus contains the most of the worst. Frank Lloyd Wright thinks cities are all washed up.

WRIGHT: Originally, the city was essential to culture. We couldn't have the culture we have today if we hadn't had the Medieval city. But the city, originally, was founded by Cain—the murderer of his brother. If you read Genesis, you'll find how, under the displeasure of the Lord, he went out and founded a city. Well, that city has been murdering his brother ever since because science has made it no longer essential to crowd; no longer essential to have your elbow in somebody's ribs and your foot on somebody's toes. Because if you go into the city today, it's becoming uninhabitable. New York, on any day, why you can get out of a taxicab and walk on the tops of the roofs of them to the place where you are going twice as fast as you can get there.

Now, I'd advocate movements that would start these Broadacre centers. And they would be, in themselves, cities and the city would be absorbed into them and you'd have a true marriage between country and town. You'd have all the benefits of town in the country and all the benefits of the country in that town because the city is a busted flush.

BEATTY: Frank Lloyd Wright booming the doom of the city. Well, a lot of city dwellers disagree. You see, he's gotten himself smack in the middle of another controversy.

One of the people who think the city is anything but a "busted flush" is William Zeckendorf. He's the president of Webb and Knapp, a multimillion-dollar real estate outfit. Tycoon Zeckendorf takes issue with architect Wright and says, "Mr. Wright ought to come back to earth or asphalt."

ZECKENDORF: The theory of permitting these cities to grow horizontally when we don't have any green belt areas winds up, as in the City of Los Angeles for a case of extreme illustration, with a fluid suburbia from which there is no escape. We've had repetitive conditions which are neither city or country nor really even good suburb. I fear that Mr. Wright's plan to abandon the cities and to run through helter skelter all over the nation with unplanned growth (which is the only end result because there's no way of controlling a national population expansion) is just a dreamy-eyed conception having no practical value whatever. I would go so far as to say that not only do I disagree with Mr. Wright but I feel that, unless we go completely the opposite of Mr. Wright's conception, the human race may soon find itself in a position of a general psychosis arising from a form of boredom emanating from a lack of capacity to change pace. I believe Mr. Wright to be a great architect who has made a tremendous and valuable contribution to his art; a man who is inspired to do good things but his ideas cannot survive and will not be adopted. Not for reasons of my own but just because they don't make sense and they're contrary to the needs of human nature.

BEATTY: What's it going to be—Frank Lloyd Wright's Broadacre City or William Zeckendorf's New York City? Controversy you want? Actually you don't have to get far from the architect's Wisconsin home, Taliesin, just go to the city where he went to school—to the lake-ringed City of Madison where they're planning a vast civic center. The City of Madison's Mayor Ivan A. Nestingen:

NESTINGEN: About the spring of 1954 there was an increasing amount of sentiment that Mr. Wright should be the architect for this project and the auditorium committee recommended, on a split vote, that his name be put on the ballot for the people to authorize him as the architect for this project.

The City Council turned down that recommendation of the auditorium committee so the pro-Wright people of Madison circulated petitions and in thirty days obtained about 7,000 signatures asking for a referendum on whether or not Mr. Wright should be the architect and that ballot carried by a vote of about 14,000 to 12,000. Officials and people to whom I've talked know of no comparable circumstance to this, whereby people, by referendum, select the architect for a public structure.

I think there are a couple of reasons why Mr. Wright was chosen. One is that here is a man that is internationally known, he has literally established the pace for innovations and new ideas in the field of architecture. And, I think that the city, the majority of people of this city, want to have a Wright-designed public structure in recognition of that genius.

BEATTY: Frank Lloyd Wright working for the people of Madison, on a public building at that! A far cry from the tempestuous Milwaukee days when he probably couldn't have won election to janitor of their big new courthouse—again, Miss Partridge:

PARTRIDGE: While he was installing the exhibit, a sensitive and intelligent reporter followed him around asking questions and taking notes. Finally, "What do you think of the new courthouse?" she asked. "Why, it will set back Milwaukee fifty years from any cultural standpoint!" "May I use this in print?" "Why yes, it's the truth!" And so the press in Milwaukee began a furious battle over the then being built nine million dollar courthouse. The fact that Milwaukee is a thrifty city and it also prides itself

Aerial view looking north from above Lake Monona of the model of the Monona Terrace Civic Center Project with towers (February 1955), Madison, Wisconsin. Photograph by Richard Vesey, courtesy of the State Historical Society of Wisconsin.

Frank Lloyd Wright (left) and Madison, Wisconsin Mayor Ivan Nestingen sign architectural services contracts for the proposed Monona Terrace Civic Center Project on July 5, 1956. Photograph courtesy of The Capital Times, *Madison, Wisconsin.*

10

The Milwaukee County Courthouse looking northwest from West Wells Street in downtown Milwaukee, Wisconsin. The Roman Neoclassic styled building was designed by the New York architect Albert Randolph Ross and was built in 1930. Photograph by the editor.

on being a cultural center, to be told it put millions into an outmoded building—the courthouse—did not make its citizens happy nor Mr. Wright very popular. His frankness, in always being so aesthetically truthful, sometimes reacts in a trying way for him but that isn't so important as the other things are.

BEATTY: It sounds like "truth against the world" doesn't it? "Truth against the world"—that was on his grandfather's shield; an ancient Druid symbol of inverted sun's rays. His grandfather, a Unitarian preacher, was one of the pioneers. This architect of America has deep roots here— deep in the green pancake-flat countryside of

the Midwest. The story really starts four score and seven years ago.

WRIGHT: I was born near here, thirty miles away, in Richland Center, Wisconsin. My father came here from the East. He was a preacher and a teacher. My mother was a teacher. They met and I was the consequence and for some reason—which I've never been able to fathom—my mother wanted an architect for a son. And, being sure that she was going to have a son, I was to be that architect. So, when I was born, in the room in which I was born, on the walls were nine of the wood engravings of the English cathedrals—engravings by Timothy

Cole. So I came into "English Gothic" and then she followed it up. I never had any other idea—that I was to be an architect. And, of course, the word was fascinating and is yet.

BEATTY: Well, before the turn of the century young Wright quit school just short of graduation from the University of Wisconsin. He had to be an architect and time was wasting. So, to the forbidding metropolis of Chicago where the first rumblings of a "new" architecture were beginning to be felt.

WRIGHT: Well, I was born an architect, grew up educated as one, and came to Chicago to Louis Sullivan with a T-square and triangle technique. Adler and Sullivan were the only "moderns" in sight at the time. They were considered revolutionary and I hungered for revolution and so I went. I took some drawings with me and he looked at them and said "All right, you'll do! You've got a good touch. How much money do you want?" Well, I was getting eight dollars; Silsbee had raised me, however, I think at that time I was getting eighteen dollars—I had been there about a year. [*Editor's note*: Wright had first worked for architect J. L. Silsbee before seeking employment with Adler and Sullivan.]. And so I said "twenty-five dollars a week" and he looked quizzically at me and he said "Well, I guess we could fix that later on!" [slight laughter from Wright] I could have had fifty or more! Now I was with Adler and Sullivan at that time like a pencil in the master's hand.

BEATTY: Louis Sullivan was the only man Frank Lloyd Wright ever called "master." It was 1888 and Adler and Sullivan were building the ancestors of our skyscrapers. It was new and daring and it was an education. This was the year of another turning point—1888—the year

he fell in love with Catherine Tobin of Oak Park, an impulsive teenager with serious thoughts occasionally narrowing her blue eyes. Within a year after they were married, as Mr. Wright put it, "Architecture was my profession, motherhood became hers." It was a fast-growing family—a big busy talented brood that was destined to be abandoned later on by a young father who never took too seriously to fatherhood. One of that brood is now an Arizona businessman who lives in a circular house on the desert designed by his father—this is the son, David Wright:

DAVID WRIGHT: I'm the third son of a family of four boys and two girls produced in my father's earlier life. We had him at mealtimes and seasonal excursions to Chicago for wardrobe outfitting. Our recollections of him in those days, however, find him mostly in the drafting room along a studio balcony editing his vast collection of Japanese prints.

Father's four boys and two girls are individualists brought up to be self-reliant. His two older sons, Lloyd and John, were associated with father at different periods in their earlier architectural development, have their own individual practices. His youngest son, Llewellyn, has a law practice. The two girls are housewives with side hobbies in art and decoration. I am what father calls "the businessman of the bunch."

Father left the Oak Park home about 1911 dedicated to architecture and not to family and established his home at Taliesin, Wisconsin. As children, and later as adults, we visited him periodically at Taliesin—at least once a year—until we all were widely distributed geographically from coast to coast. The children of Frank Lloyd Wright have a strong affection for him and great respect for his vigor, brightness in

Meet Mr. Frank Lloyd Wright

This house, which stood at 774 South Park Street at Richland Center, Wisconsin, is believed to have been the birthplace of Frank Lloyd Wright (circa mid-1800s; demolished early 1970s). Photograph by Joe W. Koelsch.

Frank Lloyd Wright's "Lieber Meister" Louis H. Sullivan circa late 1800s. Photograph courtesy of The Art Institute of Chicago reproduced by permission.

Frank Lloyd Wright's children from the Oak Park, Illinois architectural practice years circa 1909. Top, left to right: (Frank) Lloyd Wright (Jr.), John Kenneth (Lloyd) Wright, Catherine Dorothy Wright; bottom, left to right: David Samuel Wright, Frances Wright, and Robert Llewellyn Wright. Photographs by Arnold, courtesy of The Frank Lloyd Wright Home and Studio Foundation, Oak Park, Illinois reproduced by permission.

mind, and philosophy. These attributes have been a challenge to his children. Of course, his stature as an architect could hardly be an objective for us, but we are very proud to be able to call him father.

BEATTY: Taliesin—a Welsh word meaning "shining brow"—the name of the Wisconsin homestead, the scene of so much architectural triumph and personal tragedy. After Frank Lloyd Wright left his family behind him, there was another woman. At Taliesin she perished as did six others. It was murder and arson by a crazed servant. The righteous shrieked "justice has been done" but for Frank Lloyd Wright all there was was an aching emptiness.

Into his life marched Miriam Noel, a determined woman whose sympathy helped to fill the void; eventually they were married. But this union, too, had its tragedy. There were suits against him, property seized, charges against him, jail, finally divorce. Miriam Noel died soon afterward her mind and body shattered.

Frank Lloyd Wright was the darling of the sensational press, the raw material for big spicy headlines, when he finally met the woman that stands beside him today—Olga Ivanova Lazovich-Milanov of Montenegro. They chanced to meet at the ballet. The beauteous Balkan Princess and the fifty-seven-year-old poet of the drafting board. In 1928 they thrust the harassments, the debasements, the tragedies behind them and married. At last, Frank Lloyd Wright had found happiness.

Professionally, happiness was a long time in coming too. Fulfillment, recognition, they came to him deviously, belatedly. For too many years he was the prophet without honor in his own land.

They fight with Frank Lloyd Wright. They argue with him. They sometimes feel as if they're up against a stone wall for the lone wolf knows what he believes and seldom wavers. Those who know him, though, seem to get used to his honest arrogance and some of them almost enjoy it like H. F. Johnson, one of his most faithful clients, who presides over the Johnson Wax Company in a penthouse office in Racine, Wisconsin designed by Frank Lloyd Wright.

JOHNSON: His idea was that you should design a building and design the furniture to go in it because they're all one and the same thing. And, if you brought in furniture that didn't harmonize with the rest of the design of the building it's out of place. He designed these three-legged chairs here, you know, and I often asked him why he didn't put four legs on because many visitors come in and they fall off—you notice that they tip. Well, he said that "you won't tip if you sit back and you put your two feet on the ground because then you've got five legs holding you up. If five legs won't hold you, then I don't know what will!"

After our building opening, I was sitting at my desk under the skylight and more than a couple of days after, on a warm day, the tar leaked through the glass tubes and then the following day it rained and the rain came through it—hit me on the head. So, naturally, after having spent quite a lot of money for a building like this, I was pretty much upset for having rain leak in on me. So I called him up, I told him of the condition and it didn't seem to excite him at all, he just said "Well, move your chair over a foot or two!"

BEATTY: Frank Lloyd Wright has lived to see his name go into the textbooks and bound for some sort of immortality. He has lived to accept

Four-legged chair designs for the S. C. Johnson and Son Administration Building (1936) for Herbert F. Johnson at Racine, Wisconsin are similar in style to the three-legged designs. Photograph by the editor.

the honors of a grateful world, grateful for the beauty he has given us. But there were long thankless years when his buildings were ridiculed or just plain ignored. About the time of the first world war his big break . . .

WRIGHT: The Mikado decided to build a hotel to entertain or for his foreign guests. He sent a commission around the world to choose an architect. A Japanese architect went with them—I think there were three or four. Now if they'd gone around through San Francisco and had hit America first, they never would have heard of me. But they went around through Germany and in Germany they heard my praises sung and when they got to this country— straight they came to Taliesin. Well, they saw the buildings that I had been building and said "not at all Japanese but would look so well in Japan!" So, they employed me to come over and I went and there they decided to employ me to build a building.

The principle of the thing, of course, is steel in tension. I was in possession of the secret of that and I had been using it. So, here was the chance to build a building on which you could pull which hadn't existed before. So, why not make a flexible building (instead of one of those rigid things) that could ride the quake as a boat rides the wave and come through that way— and it did. Imperial Hotel was a great triumph over tragedy.

T. INUMARU: The building was just opened for business when the great earthquake struck Tokyo on September 1, 1923.

Front elevation of the main entrance lobby wing of the Imperial Hotel (1915) with reflecting pool in the foreground as reconstructed at the Museum Meiji Mura near Nagoya, Japan (1976). Photograph by Juro Kikuchi.

BEATTY: This man was there, T. Inumaru, the president of the Imperial Hotel Corporation.

INUMARU: The building began to shake like a ship in a storm. Fires were sweeping toward Tokyo and we were in the center of sheer fire and smoke. In Imperial Hotel a few things were turned over. We were standing in the center of flame and Imperial Hotel soon became the temporary home for the foreign embassies and delegations which had been destroyed.

BEATTY: The morning after the quake the telephone at Taliesin kept jangling. "The newspapers, the cables, from Tokyo," they said,

"report the Imperial Hotel a shambles, any comment?" No, no comment. Ten days later he [Wright] found out the truth. A wireless from Tokyo—"Hotel stands undamaged as monument of your genius." It had been a bad ten days.

The Imperial Hotel people went around the world to find their architect. Some clients just made a beeline for Taliesin. Others a little bit roundabout.

JOHNSON: We needed a new office building. So, I went to a local architect and had him draw up a set of plans. They were just like every other

Exterior view of the Johnson Wax Administration Building (1936) on the right side of the photo and the Johnson Wax Research and Development Tower (1944) on the left side of the photo looking from the parking lot. Photograph courtesy of Johnson Wax.

office building. I thought that we ought to have something better than the ordinary. So I went down to Chicago to see the art director of our advertising agency and he said that I should go out to see Mr. Frank Lloyd Wright—which I did. And I got acquainted with him and I was so impressed with his grasp of the functions of a building and the beauty of his designs that I immediately engaged him to design the building for us. He started insulting some of the buildings that we had in our community [Racine, Wisconsin] in the first instance and that made me sort of mad. So I tried to insult him back but it is pretty hard work!

BEATTY: And some clients never did get their buildings—like Gerald Loeb, a New York financier.

LOEB: After I knew him for a while I asked him to design a house for me, which he did. The house was to be built in Redding, Connecticut which is about sixty or seventy miles out of New York on a hilltop. He fit it to me as a bachelor and it was a perfect fit but that's why I never built the house because it didn't fit me any more as a married man and we never started another one. So that was a great loss in my life.

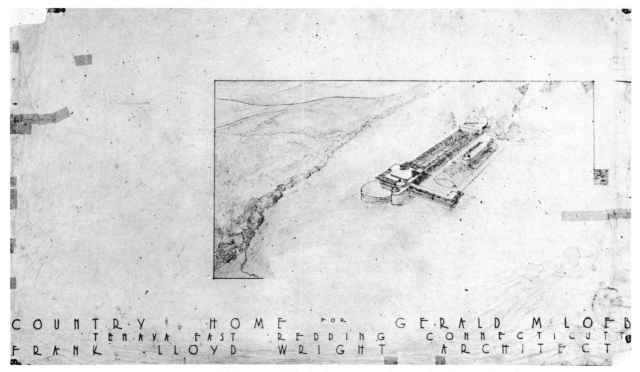

Aerial perspective drawing of the Gerald M. Loeb Residence Project (1944) at Redding, Connecticut. Copyright © The Frank Lloyd Wright Foundation, 1984.

Most architects think of a home as simply a shelter or a place to keep warm or dry or something else. Also, it always seemed to me that they sort of think that your vision is limited to looking at the four walls. But, Mr. Wright seems to be a great man for giving an atmosphere to the place. He has the ability to look up and down as well as around. I mean, in that house is where he pays as much attention to the floor, ceiling, as he does the walls. You can't hang pictures on Mr. Wright's walls either because it would be like hanging a picture on a picture. He really is completely in a class by himself.

BEATTY: Among the Wright houses, none has been more widely publicized than the Pennsylvania home of Edgar Kaufmann which straddles a waterfall. Blaine Drake, a former student of Mr. Wright's, comments:

DRAKE: This house is known as "Fallingwater." It's been highly publicized in architectural magazines throughout the world. I drove Mr. Wright down there for his discussion with the Kaufmanns at Bear Run and he described to them the way he'd like to see this house built over the waterfall. To me his description was very clear. I visualized it pretty much as it turned

Meet Mr. Frank Lloyd Wright

out. When we returned to Taliesin, Mr. Wright immediately got to work. Generally, he'd like to have a group of Fellows around him—watching and talking and having him explain what he'd do, but this time he wanted to be alone. In one day he designed the complete building and it turned out exactly as he had described it. He believes any designer or architect should have his idea firmly in mind and know exactly what

he's going to do before he does it. He has g talent but there are other men with talent to But they often give up the fight.

BEATTY: Blaine Drake is one of the architects who grew up at Taliesin drinking the wisdom of the master, learning his profession under the ruthless dedication of Frank Lloyd Wright. The Taliesin Fellowship—just what is it? A school

The Edgar J. Kaufmann, Sr. "Fallingwater" Residence (1935), Ohiopyle, Pennsylvania from Bear Run looking east during the summer. Photograph by the editor.

and yet not a school; colony of devoted men and women; a principality whose king is Frank Lloyd Wright—apprentices, they're called, not students. "They are," says Mr. Wright, "as the fingers of my hand." What about life at Taliesin? A former student remembers—John Hill, architectural editor of *House Beautiful* magazine.

HILL: Well, it's quite a wonderful life. The thing that gives it its main strength is the fact that it earns its own way. It's not a paradise where you can just go and dream beautiful dreams. It has to produce and it does produce and gets its strength there. It would be equivalent in training to four years in college, as far as a rounded picture of the arts is concerned. But it's a far more practical training, I think, because it's vital—it's living and going—it's a matter of participation rather than sitting and reading about something. Although you can say it must be a hardship to do kitchen work or weed vegetables or milk cows or something, the fact that Mr. and Mrs. Wright are directly participating in it too puts it in a different situation. I think that probably one of the greatest days in my life, although I suffered dreadfully while it was going on, was hoeing corn with Mr. Wright in about ninety-degree temperature for hours—not only was I told how to hoe but kept at it. I can remember things I learned from him at times like that, just working together at some other job maybe, and it meant a lot to me since.

BEATTY: Some merely come to visit and they're welcome providing they have something to add to the vitality of the place—philosophy or wit or music or art. Author Betsy Barton has been visiting Taliesin about every year.

BARTON: The thrilling thing about the place is that everything is new. I mean it's not monotonous—it's always different; we never have meals in the same place; the tables are always set differently; the flowers are always different. At Taliesin you're kind of never allowed to sink back and do the half-sleep that most people live in, you're always being kind of jounced into an awareness. I've seen people really completely transformed after a few months there. It's a kind of education for life, really. Mr. Wright still keeps farmer's hours—he makes his own time so that Taliesin is always run an hour earlier than the rest of the world (laughter)—to save daylight, you see. And, it's rather odd to go there for a meal if you're not living there because you're—at least I'm inclined to be—either an hour too early or an hour too late (slight laughter)—Wright standard time. But I'm surprised at the enormous hospitality. I don't know how they take care of so many guests—this huge floating population of anybody interested in art or beauty.

BEATTY: With an eye of an author and an artist, Miss Barton sizes up the man.

BARTON: He has affected everything right down to drugstores and drive-ins. His ideas have absolutely transformed our society just as much as Freud or Marx or Einstein or any one of the great geniuses but, of course, he's iconoclastic; I mean nothing is sacred and it's earthy old-fashioned American humor; a lot creative and all of the idols go crashing around (slight laughter). He's inclined to be knowledgeable about almost any subject. It's like being with somebody who has a different kind of consciousness—a lofty visionary point of view that he has really—nothing petty.

Mrs. Wright keeps feeding encouragement and stimulation into him and when I've seen him coming into the room very, very tired, after an interview or broadcast or something, she will say something to him that shocks him and picks him up and makes his cheeks red and his eyes sparkle. She is always with him. She supports him and criticizes him and watches his diet. If he's had enough meat she says, "Well now, Frank, I think that's enough," and he says, "Now mother, don't pick on me," and usually he does what she says, finally.

BEATTY: What do the experts think of him? In this country you're liable to hear voices of dissension but in Europe his stature is colossal. From Rome—critic, author, editor Bruno Zevi.

ZEVI: Wright's influence on architecture of the last fifty years is technically the greatest. In Italy the knowledge of his work conveyed the idea of American democracy much more than all the other propaganda. There is no one in Italy who does not appreciate Wright as the greatest creative mind in architecture today.

We were in front of Santa Maria della Salute, Wright was looking at this church and was thrilled. He spoke about the plastic continuity of the cupola and the base as the professional art critic could not be better. Then I said, "Mr. Wright, but you are not supposed to design the Renaissance and the Baroque architecture, and this is Baroque!" He answered immediately, "Never mind Bruno, this is good!" This showed how his sensitivity is greater than his theories. You cannot be a great architect without first being a great man.

BEATTY: And, a professional view from our own country—again, John Hill.

HILL: He produced many things that we now consider everyday—the lack of trim, any unnecessary strips and moldings and so on, recessed lights, and light coves, big glass areas.

The open plan was an effort to get rid of the closed-in confinement of an ordinary "boxlike" room and one of the means of accomplishing it was by using openings at the corners where you most expect to be confined; and that produced a corner window which, goodness knows, is all around us now and quite taken for granted. It wasn't a decision to start using corner windows, it was a decision to make the room seem, somehow, to be part of more space. The so-called ranch house is often a charming dwelling and it certainly is in a direct line from his work and represents the rather cautious transition from a conventional house toward one that is free and open. I don't think there's a building built in the last twenty years that doesn't include parts and pieces of his past work.

BEATTY: Principles are fine you say but if it costs $50,000 to put them into a house, never mind. In 1937 a young Wisconsin newspaperman bet on a long shot and it brought the genius of Frank Lloyd Wright within the range of a lot more Americans.

HERBERT JACOBS: When we got to Madison I couldn't find anything within our price range and—in a newspaperman's price range—that was what we figured would be nice to live in. So a cousin of my wife's had been out to Taliesin to visit Mr. Wright and suggested that we have Mr. Wright do something for us. He sketched out something that he thought Mr. Wright would do and it looked to me like something I didn't want to live in. But he made an appointment for us to go out there and we went along with that idea. Then, on the way out, we were—my wife and I—trying to think what is it that we can tell this great man—the architect of rich clients—what can we say to

The low hip roof projecting over the walls with wide eaves emphasizing horizontality and a closeness to the ground is a hallmark in American home design that was introduced by Frank Lloyd Wright in the design of the William H. Winslow Residence (1893) at River Forest, Illinois. Photograph by the editor.

A very early use of indirect recessed artificial lighting in residential design is in the living room area of the Frank Lloyd Wright–designed Harry S. Adams Residence of 1913 at Oak Park, Illinois. Photograph by the editor.

Frank Lloyd Wright's Frederick C. Robie Residence (1906) at Chicago, Illinois is a massive brick masonry residence with dynamic sweeping horizontal lines and cantilevered roof eaves along a single plan axis. Horizontal masses of the building appear to be suspended yet at one with the ground plane. The Robie Residence is the most famous of Wright's "Prairie" houses. Photograph by the editor.

him that would interest him in our very small case? So we put it as a sort of challenge—what this country needs is a decent $5,000 house—can you build one? Mr. Wright told us that we were the first clients that had ever asked him to build a low-cost house. He said for twenty years he had been wanting to build one but no one ever asked him to. Then he said, "Do you really want a $5,000 house? Most people want a $10,000 house for $5,000. Are you willing to give up the things that you have to give up—tile bathrooms, extra trim finish, and things like that? Are you willing to give those up? We didn't know anything about it and we said, "Sure, it's okay with us!"

And he had another pet idea he wanted to put in, namely floor heating; now very general but at that time there were no floor-heated residences in this country. The bill I paid was for $5,500 which included Mr. Wright's fee of $450. Mr. Wright is an advocate of the open plan in housing—that is, the removal of the boxes within boxes sort of thing so that you don't have many partitions. The temptation is to be together much more. I think it does something to you subconsciously. I think it did something to my children. I think it would be nice if a lot more families had that same sort of thing happen to them. Living in that house was fantastically wonderful.

BEATTY: The house that Herbert Jacobs built was the first of the Usonian houses. USONIAN—a Wright word meaning United States as it ought to be at its democratic zenith. Nowadays, Usonian houses may be seen the countrywide. You don't need a guidebook, you'll know when you see one—long, low, part of the very earth. You can practically hear the house boasting "designed by Frank Lloyd Wright." The houses

have much to boast about and so does the architect. At eighty-seven, Frank Lloyd Wright is contributing as much as ever to our skyline.

On the plains of Oklahoma, his tallest ever, an office building and apartment house commissioned by industrialist H. C. Price of Bartlesville.

PRICE: Mr. Wright said that "three floors was the most inefficient type of office building that could be built" and suggested that . . . well, first, let me say we wanted 25,000 square feet of space and he suggested that instead of having three floors with 25,000 that we have ten floors with 2,500 each and make a little skyscraper, which sounded all right. Well, to make a long story short, before we got away from there between the three floors and the ten floors we compromised and built nineteen floors.

Whatever Mr. Wright builds, he builds for a purpose and to fit a certain condition. If you asked him to build something that he did not believe was correct, I don't think he would build it! He wants to make changes as he goes along. Sometimes those changes are impractical from the matter of time or expense but, at the same time, we have never found him to make a change that wasn't for the better.

BEATTY: A skyscraper for Oklahoma but what about the city of skyscrapers—New York? Frank Lloyd Wright has never had a project in New York City, that is, until now. Ten years ago philanthropist Solomon Guggenheim asked him to design a museum, a museum that wouldn't be like every other museum. For ten years Mr. Wright battled with the city fathers and interest in the project had ups and downs. Now, at last, the construction is under way and with the usual flurry of controversy. Looking at the

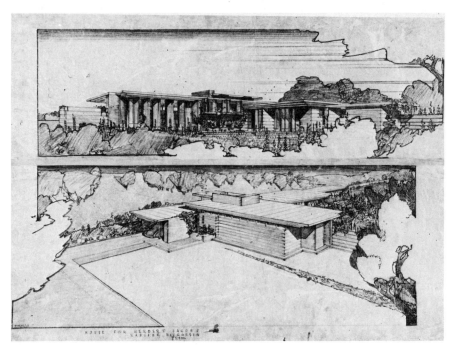

Usonia No. 1. Perspective renderings of the Herbert Jacobs First Residence (1936) at Madison, Wisconsin. Copyright © The Frank Lloyd Wright Foundation, 1954.

The Usonian House on a flat site. The Goetsch–Winckler Residence (1939) at Okemos, Michigan. Photograph by the editor.

24

The Usonian House on a steep-sloped site. The George D. Sturges Residence (1939) at Brentwood Heights, California. Photograph by the editor.

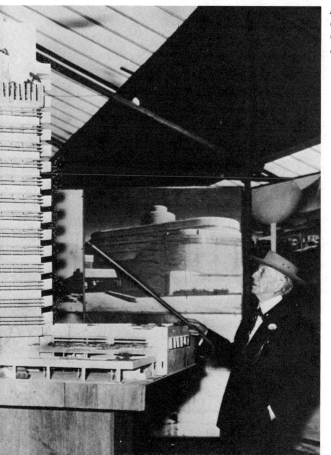

Frank Lloyd Wright points to his model of the Price Company Tower for Harold Price, Sr. (1953) for Bartlesville, Oklahoma at an exhibition of his work in 1953. Photograph courtesy of The Capital Times, *Madison, Wisconsin.*

drawings some have likened the proposed museum to a "gigantic ice cream freezer, a buffalo on Fifth Avenue"—said the August [1956] *New York Times*—"the net effect if we may say so, will be precisely that of an oversized and indigestible hot cross bun." But John Hill takes exception.

HILL: New York is not exactly what you'd call inspiration for someone like Mr. Wright. But that building will be a revelation in the museum world—I'm sure of that. The original intent was to show the paintings, there are primarily paintings in the collection, some sculpture, in an environment that people would associate with their home lives. In other words, on a scale that was almost domestic in feeling to give them a more intimate association with the things they were looking at. So that, although it is really one vast room which you can stroll slowly down and around and through, the paintings themselves will be the main interest—they're lit so that they are the jewels in a rather low-lit atmosphere. Many people have said that they felt the building was going to take the stage away from the paintings being shown in it but I think it's only because they don't have a clear picture of what it will be like.

BEATTY: We'll just have to wait and see how the Guggenheim Museum turns out. But this much is certain, Fifth Avenue, the neighborhood of the elegant baroque villas, will never be the same. No neighborhood invaded by Frank Lloyd Wright has ever been the same and that goes for some of his clients as well—Walter Bublitz of Kansas City.

BUBLITZ: Today is a far cry from that disappointing day of dedication in 1943. It was a cold day and the heating system didn't function properly and the congregation had to wear topcoats, hats, and gloves. Later, after the

Solomon R. Guggenheim Museum (1956) main entrance elevation fronting on Fifth Avenue, New York. The upper four spiral ramps of the main gallery can be seen on the right. Photograph by Rober E. Mates, courtesy of the Solomon R. Guggenheim Museum, New York.

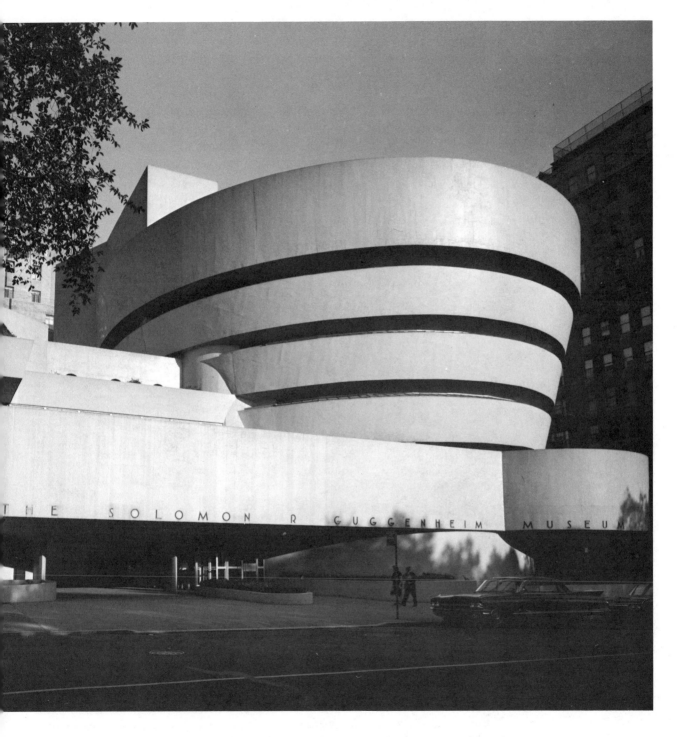

27

system was working properly, we had several days of heavy rain and water cascaded down the inside stairs of the church. But the auditorium has perfect acoustics and the radiant heating in the floors, at that time quite revolutionary, has functioned perfectly. The air conditioning that was built in the church was also revolutionary fifteen years ago and today it is a must in church design. Frank Lloyd Wright is a genius and has contributed much to American life but our experience with him has indicated, like most men of genius, he is egotistical and at times intolerant and noncooperative in his relations with others and especially those who might disagree with him. He fights for the right of free thinking for himself but the other fellow must agree with him or be cast aside. No compromising exists in Mr. Wright's thinking.

Interior view of the Solomon R. Guggenheim Museum looking down from the seventh ramp of the main gallery. Photograph by Robert E. Mates, courtesy of the Solomon R. Guggenheim Museum, New York.

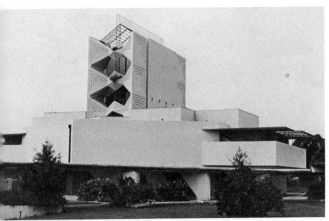

The Annie Merner Pfeiffer Chapel (1938) at Florida Southern College in Lakeland, Florida. Photograph by the editor.

The T.R. Roux Library (1941) at Florida Southern College. Photograph by the editor.

BEATTY: That sounds like the man we've met all right—no compromise—take him or leave him. Florida Southern College in Lakeland took him and they have reason to pat themselves on the back. Frank Lloyd Wright has been building them a $20 million campus. They consider it a monument to the ages and perhaps, better yet, enrollment has been zooming. The registrar at Florida Southern is Charles Lilly.

LILLY: Most interesting to watch the great architect work, how his eye takes in every minute detail. He's not by any means a tall man. He's short, chunky, dresses perhaps in a way that some folks might consider a little eccentric. When he's dealing with adults, newspapermen, photographers, the rest of us on campus, he is sometimes accused of being too abrupt but it's amazing to watch him when he's chatting with students. He never seems to tire of doing things for young people.

BEATTY: It's been the young people who keep him young, you know: the apprentices—

studious but fun loving—his children, his house guests. This man we've met is eighty-seven years old. That's the unbelievable part of it—eighty-seven and still indomitable—still a revolutionary—the pacesetter—the heretic. But what happens to the revolutionary when the war is won? What happens to the pacesetter when the rams catch up? The heretic, when the world accepts him? Until 1939 no American university thought to grant him an honorary degree. Today, Frank Lloyd Wright has a quadrant [*sic*] full of honorary degrees. Even Wisconsin, his alma mater, gave him one in 1954. Someday, perhaps, they'll even be calling him a conservative. For the stormy pioneer of Taliesin that would be ignominy and you can bet he'll never really mellow, never stop tilting at those windmills of complacency. There are moments, nowadays, breaks from the creative outpouring of the drafting room when he leans back in a comfortable chair, his surgeon's fingers exploring his watch bob [*sic*]—at last he turns introspective. Can you see him now at Taliesin,

Frank Lloyd Wright receives Honorary Doctorate from the University of Wisconsin in 1955 at a ceremony in Madison. Photograph courtesy of The Capital Times, *Madison, Wisconsin.*

Frank Lloyd Wright the arrogant prophet, turned nostalgic? Hear this man—he's doing something rare in his way of life—looking back.

WRIGHT: So many of my friends have come in here and also strangers and looked about the place and they've wondered why and how it was that a place so full of repose and quiet and in such a peaceful atmosphere there should have been such a turbulent existence. And I can't tell you any more than they. I don't know. Except I know this—that when you're swimming upstream you're buffeted by all sorts of events and there may be something coming downstream that's pretty formidable and may get you. Well, it worries me a little to see that the stream seems to be running upstream quite a great extent.

Meet Mr. Frank Lloyd Wright

Meet Mr. Frank Lloyd Wright

A Conversation with Hugh Downs

. . . early in life I had to choose between honest arrogance and hypocritical humility. I choose honest arrogance, and have seen no occasion to change—even now.

In early 1953 Frank Lloyd Wright was interviewed by Hugh Downs at Taliesin near Spring Green, Wisconsin for the National Broadcasting Company's (NBC) *Wisdom* television series. This half-hour conversation was filmed on May 8, 1953 and first broadcast over the NBC television network on May 17, 1953. Wright was so impressed with the quality of this conversation that he quickly included the edited text of it as the first chapter in his newly conceived book, *The Future of Architecture* (New York: Horizon Press, 1953, pp. 9–31). However, Wright was a perfectionist who constantly revised not only his architectural work but his literary work as well. Consequently, he had revised what was actually said during the broadcast and the revised text is what appeared in *The Future of Architecture*. The precise text of this conversation has never appeared in print.*

Jack Gould of *The New York Times* in his May 20, 1953 review of the program said:

This conversation is reproduced in its entirety from National Broadcasting Company (NBC) Broadcast *Wisdom: A Conversation with Frank Lloyd Wright* dated May 17, 1953 with permission of the National Broadcasting Company and Hugh Downs.

*Another severely edited and revised text of this conversation also appeared in James Nelson (ed.), *Wisdom: Conversations wth the Elder Wise Men of Our Day* (New York: W.W. Norton and Company, 1958, pp. 193–202).

He made an engrossing and stimulating figure on the screen as he quietly and good-humoredly discussed his work and explained his philosophy of life in general ... Hugh Downs of the NBC staff in Chicago asked direct and intelligent questions, but never intruded. As a result, at the end of thirty minutes, a viewer had a sense of having made a new acquaintance. Mr. Wright speaks softly, and in his voice there is a touch of weariness. But in his thinking and his mode of expression there is a freshness, pungency and originality that belie his years. As one who has spent much of his life in controversy, he is not one to give ground easily, but underneath many of his remarks there is an engagingly wry wit.

The NBC television network rebroadcast the program on December 1, 1957 and in 1958 Encyclopaedia Britannica Films released a film of the conversation for wide public distribution. The following is the complete unedited transcript of this most important, and Wright's best known, "conversation."

The Conversation

WRIGHT: Come in lad.

DOWNS: Hello, Mr. Wright.

WRIGHT: Glad to see you.

DOWNS: Nice to see you.

WRIGHT: What's that you've got in your hand?

DOWNS: I have a book here I'm going to ask you a question about in just a moment. I thought in the brief space of a half hour, which is the time we have, what we'd like to do, Mr. Wright, is get as clear a picture as possible, for our audience, of the essence of your thinking about American architecture and American life.

WRIGHT: In a half hour?

DOWNS: Well, as much as we are able to do it in a half hour. To launch right into it, would you identify this picture for us?

WRIGHT: The picture of the little house on Forest Avenue that I built when I was still with

Hugh Downs (left) interviews Frank Lloyd Wright for the May 17, 1953 NBC television broadcast of Wisdom. Photograph used by permission of the National Broadcasting Company.

Meet Mr. Frank Lloyd Wright

Frank Lloyd Wright's rendering of the Edwin H. Cheney Residence (1903) at Oak Park, Illinois. Copyright © The Frank Lloyd Wright Foundation, 1979.

Adler and Sullivan. I think it was built before 1893. A little tree grew up—a willow tree—between the corridor of my own house and studio. There was a continual procession around the house—where the tree grew up through the roof.

DOWNS: 1893?

WRIGHT: It seemed to interest people, yes.

DOWNS: I think many of our viewers would agree that looks like a house that could have been built last year, and I think that's as good a way as I can think of offhand to get into our subject, which we might call "Sixty Years of Living Architecture."

When did you first decide to make architecture your life work?

WRIGHT: Well, fortunately I never had to decide. It decided for me before I was born. My mother was a teacher and she wanted an

architect for a son. I happened to be the son and, of course, naturally an architect. I was conditioned by her. The room into which I was born was hung with the wood engravings of the English cathedrals made by Timothy Cole. Do you remember those? So, I was born into architecture.

DOWNS: What was your first job as an architect, Mr. Wright?

WRIGHT: Well, I think I wanted to be an architect and as near as I could get to it in Madison. We were poor. We had no money to send me to an architectural school. Madison, our home, had an engineering school and a very kind dean, Professor Conover, gave me a stipend to work for him and work my way through the course at the university and I worked my way almost through it. If I had stayed three months longer I would have been given a degree as an engineer. But, I was

Professor Allan Darst Conover (circa mid-1880s) of the University of Wisconsin at Madison provided Frank Lloyd Wright with his first professional experience in the practice of architecture and engineering. Photograph by Curtiss Artistic Photography of Madison, courtesy of the State Historical Society of Wisconsin.

anxious to be an architect and so I started out for Chicago three months before I would have graduated. And, I suppose you could say that my work for Conover, perhaps as an engineer, designing little clips and details of iron work was my first architectural job.

DOWNS: Would you say that any of Sullivan's ideas in architecture influenced you at that time?

WRIGHT: Naturally. They were influencing nearly everybody in the country.

DOWNS: How so?

WRIGHT: He was the real radical of his day and his thought gave us the skyscraper. You see, when buildings first began to be tall, they didn't know how to make them tall. They would put one-, two-, or three-story buildings on top of one another until they had enough and I remember the "lieber Meister" would come in and throw something on my table—the Wainwright building in St. Louis. He said: "Wright, the thing is tall. What's the matter with a tall building?" There it was, tall! And after that, why the skyscraper began to flourish. And, I think that all the skyscrapers you see today were the result of Louis Sullivan's initiative. And, that was his kind of mind, his type of thought you see. He saw the thing directly for what it was.

DOWNS: Most people, who are at all acquainted with your work, know the fact that your work is organic and intimately bound up with the lives of people. When did this idea first begin to take shape in your work?

WRIGHT: Well, that's pretty difficult to say. Of course, in my youth, nothing existed of the sort that I wanted to see happen. It didn't exist anywhere. It had to be made, and it happened out here in the western prairies of Chicago. The first expression, in humane terms, of what we call now "organic architecture."

DOWNS: You use the word *organic*. Is that any different from my use of the word modern architecture, in your opinion?

WRIGHT: Very different because modern architecture is merely something which may be built today, but organic architecture is an architecture from within outward, in which entity is the ideal. We don't use the word organic as referring to something hanging in a butcher shop, you know!

The Wainwright Building (1890–1891) at St. Louis, Missouri designed by Adler and Sullivan, Architects of Chicago while Frank Lloyd Wright was under their employ. Photograph by the editor.

Downs: "You use the word organic ..." *Hugh Downs as he appeared in the May 17, 1953 NBC television broadcast of* Wisdom. *Photograph used by permission of the National Broadcasting Company.*

Frank Lloyd Wright as he appeared in the May 17, 1953 NBC television broadcast of Wisdom. *Photograph used by permission of the National Broadcasting Company.*

DOWNS: I see.

WRIGHT: Organic means, in philosophic sense, entity. Where the whole is the part as the part is to the whole and where the nature of the materials, the nature of the purpose, the nature of the entire performance becomes a necessity. Out of that comes what significance you can give the building as a creative artist.

DOWNS: Well now, with that in mind, what do you try to put into a house when you design one?

WRIGHT: First of all, the family it is designed for, as a rule—not always easy and not always successful, but usually so. And we try to put into that house a sense of unity—of the *altogether* that makes it a part of its site. If the thing is successful—the architect's effort—you can't imagine that house anywhere than right where it is. It's a part of its environment and it graces its environment, rather than disgraces it.

DOWNS: A striking example of a site and house going together is, of course, Bear Run House. How did you relate the site to the house?

WRIGHT: Well, there was a rock ledge bank beside the waterfall and the natural thing seemed to be to cantilever the house from that rock bank over the fall. You see the Bear Run House came into possession of concrete and steel with which to build the house and, of course, the grammar of that house cleared up on that basis and then, of course, Mr. Kaufmann's love for a beautiful site. He loved the site where the house was built and liked to listen to the waterfall. So that was a prime motive in the design. I think you can hear the waterfall when you look at the design. At least it's there and he lives intimately with the thing he loved.

DOWNS: Tell us about your own home, Mr. Wright, Taliesin.

Meet Mr. Frank Lloyd Wright

WRIGHT: Well, Taliesin, of course, was built in nineteen hundred and eleven and a kind of refuge at the time. I was getting a worm's eye view of society and needed to get out into the country and my mother had prepared this site for me and asked me to come and take it and I did. And, of course, the countryside is southern Wisconsin—low hills—protruding rock ledges—a wooded site—and the same thing applied to Taliesin that applied later on to Bear Run. The site determined the features and character of the two houses.

Taliesin really is a stone house and it is a house of the north and it was built for the north. I

Wright: ". . . the natural thing seemed to be to cantilever the house from that rock bank over the fall." Photograph used by permission of the National Broadcasting Company.

A winter view of the Edgar J. Kaufmann, Sr. "Fallingwater" Residence (1935), Ohiopyle, Pennsylvania from Bear Run looking east. Photograph by Harold Corsini, courtesy of the Western Pennsylvania Conservancy.

The east side of Fallingwater shows the integration of both the concrete and the natural native stone materials of the building. Photograph by Harold Corsini, courtesy of the Western Pennsylvania Conservancy.

The second-floor trellis beams extend over the entrance driveway and bend to avoid the trunk of an existing tree on the grounds of Fallingwater. Photograph by Harold Corsini, courtesy of the Western Pennsylvania Conservancy.

Fallingwater: interior view of the living room area looking to the south (the water of the Bear Run flows beneath this space). Photograph by Harold Corsini, courtesy of the Western Pennsylvania Conservancy.

The first-floor dining area of Fallingwater. Photograph by Harold Corsini, courtesy of the Western Pennsylvania Conservancy.

Interior view of the guest bedroom of Fallingwater. Photograph by Harold Corsini, courtesy of the Western Pennsylvania Conservancy.

A boulder penetrates the north end of the bridgeway linking the guest wing (1938) with the main residence at Fallingwater. Photograph by Harold Corsini, courtesy of the Western Pennsylvania Conservancy.

39

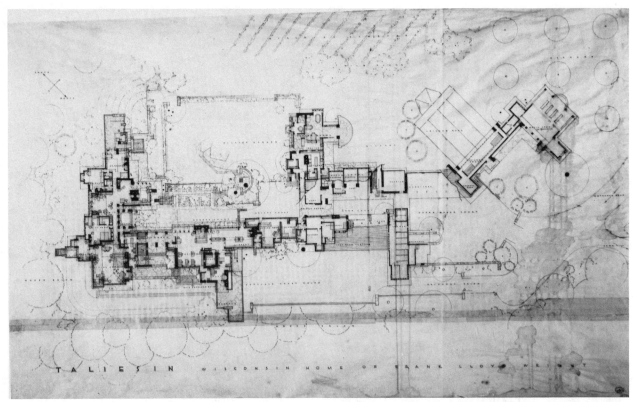

Plan of Taliesin. Copyright © The Frank Lloyd Wright Foundation, 1984.

Aerial view of Taliesin (1925ff), Spring Green, Wisconsin. Photograph courtesy of The Capital Times, *Madison, Wisconsin.*

View of the loggia entrance of Taliesin from the hill garden area. Photograph by the editor.

Wright: "... the countryside is southern Wisconsin—low hills—protruding rock ledges—a wooded site ..." View from the balcony of Taliesin. Photograph by the editor.

Exterior elevation of the kitchen wing of Taliesin. Photograph by the editor.

The living room of Taliesin. Photograph by Richard Vesey, courtesy of the State Historical Society of Wisconsin.

The living room and living room alcove of Taliesin. Photograph by Richard Vesey, courtesy of the State Historical Society of Wisconsin.

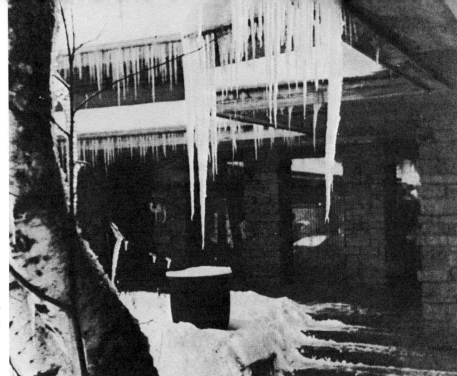

Wright: "I loved the icicles that came on the eaves . . ." Taliesin in the snowy winter. Photograph courtesy of the Frank Lloyd Wright Memorial Foundation.

Wright: ". . . built like a brow on the edge of the hill . . ." Photograph used by permission of the National Broadcasting Company.

loved the icicles that came on the eaves, and in the winter the snow would sweep up over it and it looked like a hill itself or one of the hills and it was built to belong to the region my grandfather came to when the Indians were still there about 125 years ago, and the valley was called "the valley," lovingly. It was a lovable place. And the valley was cleared by my grandfather and his sons and Taliesin is an instance of the third generation going back to the soil and really developing it and trying to make something beautiful.

DOWNS: Where did the name "Taliesin" come from, Mr. Wright?

WRIGHT: My people were Welsh, my mother's people were Welsh immigrants. My old grandfather was a hatter and a preacher and they were the cultivated element in the county,

Meet Mr. Frank Lloyd Wright

at Taliesin. They all had Welsh names for their places—my sister's home was Tanyderi, "Under the Oaks," so I chose a Welsh name for mine, and it was Taliesin—a member of King Arthur's Roundtable who sang the glories of fine art. I guess he was about the only Britisher who ever did. So, I chose Taliesin for a name. It means "shining brow" and Taliesin is built like a brow on the edge of the hill—not on top of the hill—because I believe you should never build on top of anything directly. If you build on top of the hill, you lose the hill. If you build one side the top, you have the hill and the eminence that you desire. You see? Well, Taliesin is like that.

DOWNS: In the case of Taliesin West, I wonder about some of the great contrasts between that and the other Taliesin, when it was built for the same purpose, since both are your homes. Why that difference?

WRIGHT: Well, you see the terrain changed absolutely. Here we came to the desert with these astonishing and exciting new forms. In Wisconsin erosion has, by way of age, softened everything. Out there everything was sharp, savage. Everything was armed in the desert and it was an entire new experience and so following out the same feeling for structure, the same idea of building that we had in there, it had to be absolutely according to the desert. So Taliesin West is according to its site again, according to its environment. And, the purpose, of course, is much the similar and hasn't changed much.

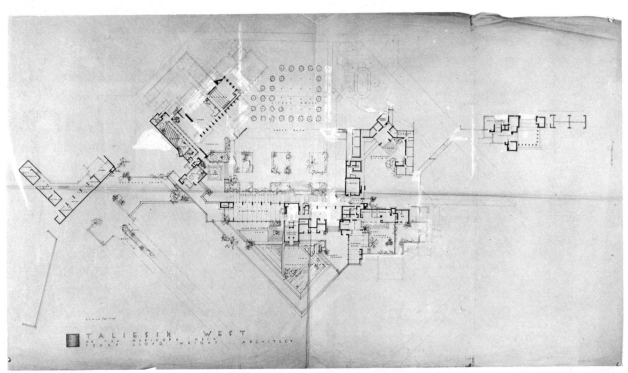

Plan of Taliesin West (1937ff), Scottsdale, Arizona. Copyright © The Frank Lloyd Wright Foundation, 1984.

Meet Mr. Frank Lloyd Wright

Entrance court to Taliesin West. Photograph by the editor.

Workroom terrace and broad steps (background) with reflecting pool (foreground) of Taliesin West. Photograph by the editor.

Exterior terrace view of Taliesin West. Photograph by the editor.

Exterior view of the terrace near the entrance court of Taliesin West. Photograph by the editor.

46

DOWNS: What is the difference between organic architecture and conventional architecture?

WRIGHT: You mean structurally, I imagine?

DOWNS: Yes.

WRIGHT: You see the old post and beam construction—you can say this is the post and beam—post and beam—was all a kind of superimposition, and if you wanted partitions, they cut, and they would butt—you see—cut, butt, and slash—and if you wanted tension, you had to rivet something to something and make a connection. It might give way.

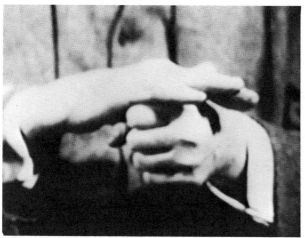

Wright: "... this is the post and beam ..." Photograph used by permission of the National Broadcasting Company.

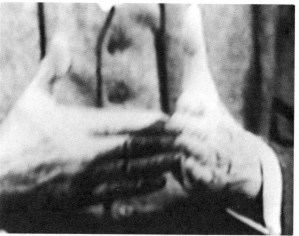

Wright: "... cut, butt, and slash ..." Photograph used by permission of the National Broadcasting Company.

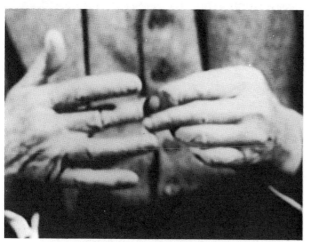

Wright: "... rivet something to something and make a connection. It might give way." Photograph used by permission of the National Broadcasting Company.

Wright: "... you could pull on the structure." Photograph used by permission of the National Broadcasting Company.

47

Well, organic architecture brought the principles together so that a building was more like this—you see—you could pull on the structure. It had tensile strength owing to steel and owing to steel it could have great spaces, and the great spaces could be protected with glass. The Orientals, of course, the Greeks, never had any such facility. If they had steel and glass, why we wouldn't have to do any thinking today. We'd be copying them. But now something had to be done with these new materials. These great new resources. And they are tremendous and because of that principle of tenuity we could use the cantilever, and into structure came this element of continuity. You see one thing merging into another and of another rather than this cut, butt, and slash. In other words, this same element of strength. That's what brought the Imperial Hotel through intact through the earthquake. That principle of tenuity and of flexibility—this—instead of rigidity which could be broken.

DOWNS: Would you recount for us some of the things which are fundamentally your own innovations in architecture?

WRIGHT: Well it would be pretty difficult and a long story too—perhaps too long for this. First of all came this new sense of space, as "reality" of the building. Then came the countenance of that space which is more or less what I termed "streamlined." That word "streamlined" got into the language, I think, about that time through my effort. Then there was the open plan. Instead of a building being a series of boxes and closets—came more and more open, more and more sense of space, the outside came in more and more and the inside went out more. That went along until we had a practically new floor plan. It had been referred to always as "the

open plan." That was the direct result. Then, of course, there were structural implications which we hinted at a little while ago. Of a building that had tenuity and instead of a building without any, it could fall apart. The houses built upon this plan are good for 300 years, I should think—several centuries.

And, in that structural dispensation, a great many new features arose, like, perhaps the most important one was gravity heat—floor heat—where the heat is in the floor beneath the slab in a broken stone bed and with a thick rug on the floor you have a reservoir of heat beneath you. So, you sit warm, you can open the windows and still be comfortable and the children play on a nice warm surface and if your feet are warm, you sit warm—you are warm.

Oh, and I think the corner window is something we should mention in connection with innovation and you can judge from what happened by way of the corner window what has happened to so many of the innovations. The corner window is indicative of an idea conceived, early in my work, that the box is a Fascist symbol, and the architecture of freedom and democracy needed something besides the box. So I started out to destroy the box as a building.

Well, the corner window came in as all the comprehension that ever was given to that act of destruction of the box. The light now came in where it had never come before. Vision went out and you had screens instead of walls—here walls vanished as walls and the box vanished as a box and the corner window went around the world. But the idea of the thing never followed it and became merely a window instead of the release of an entire sense of structure.

DOWNS: I've heard indirect lighting attributed to you. Is that . . .?

WRIGHT: I did the first so-called indirect lighting very early. I guess it's about fifty years ago. Incorporated it behind shelves, cast it on the ceiling, then burying it in the ceiling in various ways.

Doing, I suppose, nearly everything being done today. I don't know of anything new.

DOWNS: You have recently built a new church, and it is not typical of most churches in our experience. Could you tell us why?

WRIGHT: There, you see the Unitarianism of my forefathers found expression in a building by one of the offspring—the idea of unity—Unitarian. Unitarians believed in the unity of all things. Well, I tried to build a building here that expressed that sense of unity. The plan, you see, is triangular. The roof is triangular and out of it you get this expression of reverence without the steeple. The building itself, covering all, all in all and each in all, sets forth what the steeple used to say, but says it with greater reverence, I think, in the form of the structure.

And, I didn't like to build a church in the city. I sought to take it into the country and make it more like a country club in its aspects and be more interesting and inviting to the congregation. So I persuaded them to go out. We went out, but we didn't go far enough, I guess, because before we got the church built, the town came out. And we found ourselves suburban, instead of country. But if you're going to decentralize now, you've got to go far and go fast because everything is coming along. You can see decentralization everywhere now. You can see the factory going to the country. You can see the merchandiser impatient with the traffic problem moving out to the country. I think the gas station was an agent of decentralization. All these things are going on around you whether you want to acknowledge them or not. Now it has to be planned for. It's better to plan for it than it is to let it take place as the cities themselves grew. New York, for instance, is just an overgrown crazed village in plan. And so it is with all our great cities. And, what is supposed to be the growth of the city is really going to be, finally, the death of the city.

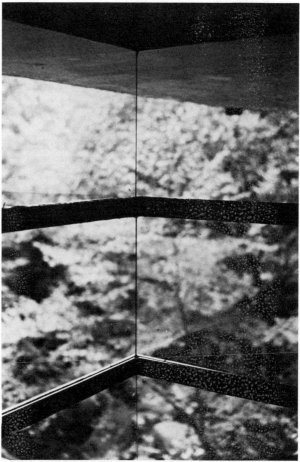

A corner window detail of the Edgar J. Kaufmann, Sr. "Fallingwater" Residence (1935), Ohiopyle, Pennsylvania. The vertical window framing element has been omitted where the glass is butted at the corner thus allowing an unobstructed view of the natural surroundings of the residence and an opening up of the interior space to the outdoors. Photograph by the editor.

Elevation view of the lobby (left) and auditorium/rostrum (right) of the Unitarian Church (1947) at Shorewood Hills, Wisconsin. Photograph by the editor.

Exterior detailed view of the rostrum of the Unitarian Church at Shorewood Hills. The large pipe organ can be seen through the elaborate glazing. Photograph by the editor.

50

DOWNS: If you were to plan and build an entire city, including the elements of shelter, work, recreation and worship, as we were just talking about, what would you intend to accomplish in doing this?

WRIGHT: Well, I think primarily the use of and sympathy with the site, the nature of the ground, and the purpose of the city or town, whatever it might be and, of course, the character of the inhabitants would be no little consideration in that connection. In other words, it would be a native, a natural performance. Organic architecture is a natural architecture. A natural architecture. Now, what would a natural architecture be? It wouldn't be some eclecticism, something you picked up somewhere by way of taste and applied to the thing. You'd go into the nature study of the circumstances and come out with this thing from within, wouldn't you? Well, it would apply to a town, apply to a city, apply to the planning of anything.

DOWNS: Even a factory? I wanted to ask— when you build a factory?

WRIGHT: Especially a factory.

DOWNS: Well, what do you consider the most important factors in this case, the building of a factory?

WRIGHT: Well, I think the human values involved. I think the lives of the workers. I don't see why it isn't a more profitable thing to make those lives happy, they'll be more productive. And, environment, as we found it to be when we built the Johnson building, results in a greatly increased efficiency on their part. If you make them proud of their environment, and happy to be where they are, and give them some dignity and pride in their environment, it all comes out to the good where the product is concerned.

The Johnson people have found that out. The Johnson people have a profit sharing system with their employees and when they got into that building, why, one of the first consequences was tea in the afternoon, and they didn't like to go home. They loved to stay in the building, be there, come early, enjoy it, charming features of a very interesting, exciting environment. And it is profitable. It does, I think the phrase is "payoff," isn't it, in our country? And the "payoff," of course, is the criterion by which everything is decided. Well, even deciding it by way of the payoff, a healthful environment in which the workers can take pride pays off.

DOWNS: Over the years, Mr. Wright, the American press and sections of your own profession have not always treated you kindly. I just wonder if you have comment about this?

WRIGHT: Well, I don't see why they should have treated me kindly. I was entirely contrary to everything they believed in and if I was right, they were wrong. Why should they treat me kindly? It was a question of time, I suppose, of their survival or mine. And in those circumstances you know what happens, don't you?

DOWNS: Something has to give?

WRIGHT: It's still happening, by the way, but not so much now. But it is true that, still, the greatest appreciation for what we've done comes from European countries and the Orient rather than from our own country. We are very slow to take things on that occurred at home. It's always been the idea of our people that culture came from abroad and it did. You can't blame them for thinking so. They didn't want to hear of its developing here in the tall grass of the western prairies. That was not exciting. In

Aerial view of the Johnson Wax Administration Building in its later construction stages circa late 1930s (Racine, Wisconsin). Photograph courtesy of Johnson Wax.

52

Exterior view from the parking lot of the Johnson Wax Administration Building (1936) on the right side of the photo and the Johnson Wax Research and Development Tower (1944) on the left side of the photo. Photograph courtesy of Johnson Wax.

53

A view from an interior balcony of the Great Workroom in the Johnson Wax Administration Building (1936) at Racine, Wisconsin. Desks and chairs were also designed by the architect. Photograph courtesy of Johnson Wax.

The consumer products sales dome in the Johnson Wax Administration Building. Photograph courtesy of Johnson Wax.

Meet Mr. Frank Lloyd Wright

fact they rather resented hearing about it in that sense. So when it had gone abroad, and it had been understood and appreciated abroad, and the Europeans came over here with it, they could sell it to the American people and they would take it from them, when they didn't take it from me.

DOWNS: Through the span of your life there have been great changes in the world,

Interior view of the pedestrian bridge which joins the Johnson Wax Administration Building (completed in April 1939) with the newer wing and tower part of the building complex, which was completed in November 1950. The roof of the bridge is constructed of glass tubing. Photograph courtesy of Johnson Wax.

economically, socially, and ideologically. Through years of war and peace, through years that spelled great hopes and great disasters for mankind. Have any of these changes influenced your work or your thinking?

WRIGHT: No, and it is a little unfortunate that my work couldn't have influenced those changes. Probably if it had been better understood, I might have had a very beneficial influence on those changes. But, I can't say those changes had any effect on my work. My ideal was pretty well fixed. I was pretty sure of my ground and my star and I saw no occasion. You see, early in life I had to choose between honest arrogance and hypocritical humility. I chose honest arrogance, and have seen no occasion to change—even now.

We are pursuing the same center line through all changes and I am confident that the principle of our work, which is its heart and center line, is really the ideology of a democracy. And if democracy is ever to have a free architecture, I mean if it is ever to have freedom, have a culture of its own, architecture will be its basic effect and condition. I believe we have the center line of that architecture. An architecture for freedom and for democracy.

DOWNS: You're a teacher, Mr. Wright. In your years of experience, what conclusions have you reached of the roles and duties of the teacher and those of the student?

WRIGHT: I'm expected to answer that now, am I? I'm no teacher! Never wanted to teach, and don't believe in teaching an art! A science, yes; business, of course; but an art cannot be taught. You can only inculcate it. You can be an exemplar. You can create an atmosphere in which it can grow. But I suppose I being

Wright: "Maybe that's the way great ideas eventually obtain—by way of abuse." Photograph used by permission of the National Broadcasting Company.

exemplar would be called a teacher, in spite of myself. So, go ahead, call me a teacher.

DOWNS: Do you feel that American architecture has progressed generally over, well, the past several years?

WRIGHT: No, I'm afraid it has not. I think that the effects have been sought and multiplied and the *why* of the effect—the real cause at the center of the thing—seems to have languished. If they once mastered the inner principle, infinite variety would be the result. No one would have

to copy anybody else. And my great disappointment, and it always is, that instead of emulation, what I see is a wave of imitation.

DOWNS: In your long life of practical and artistic endeavor, what do you consider is your most satisfactory achievement?

WRIGHT: Oh, my dear boy—the next one, of course, the next building I build!

DOWNS: Well, go on from there. What is that?

WRIGHT: I don't know. I'm not sure. But whatever it is. That would be it.

DOWNS: What would you say is the greatest disappointment in your career?

WRIGHT: Well, I think I touched on it a moment ago when I said that instead of emulation that I had seen chiefly imitation of imitation by the imitator.

DOWNS: Might that not be the price that you pay for being ahead of your time?

WRIGHT: Well, I've had to think about it a good deal of recent years. Looking back, I suppose that is the way the thing always happens. Probably it has always been so. And is a little more obvious in our day because of commercialized conditions and everybody being in a kind of free for all to pull out what he can as soon as he can and make the most of it. So I don't suppose it's any worse than it ever has been and maybe that's the way it has to come. Maybe that's the way great ideas eventually obtain—by way of abuse. Well, it's a moot question. It's not to be settled here. Nor is it to be settled by me.

PART
TWO

Creativity and the Philosophy of Organic Architecture

3 Modern Architecture

The New Architecture

There is no reason in the world why this fresh hold on architectural life shouldn't maintain its vogue and character, go on growing continually, and be the genuine liberation of creative impulse.

In 1930 Frank Lloyd Wright visited New York City and viewed the Contempora Exhibition of modern architecture being held there. While visiting, Wright took part in a radio broadcast with architect/artist Hugh Ferriss to discuss the new architecture called "modern." Throughout the broadcast Wright was optimistic concerning both the future of the new modern architecture movement and of the European architects who create these modern buildings. This optimism did not last long since Wright soon after found that modern architecture wasn't necessarily *organic architecture.*

The Conversation

WRIGHT: Architecture is really the humanizing of building; something which, perhaps, is more important to us, where we live, than anything else in the world. A real expression of ourselves is bound to appear in our architecture eventually. All the signs along the road, as I motored along through 145 towns on my way from Chandler, Arizona to New York, seemed to say "Why not now?" In fact, it seems to be coming now—with astonishing, yes with alarming rapidity—for the cornice is dead! Many years ago, it seems very long ago now,

Edited and reprinted from "Frank Lloyd Wright and Hugh Ferriss Discuss This Modern Architecture," *Architectural Forum*, Vol. 53, November 1930, pp. 535–538.

Frank Lloyd Wright circa 1930. Photograph courtesy of the State Historical Society of Wisconsin.

new ideas in art and decoration, furnishing and dress that we see—and I think one may see them now from Wanamaker's clear up the Avenue— ... in fresh new patterns, in vital forms that seem at first peculiar, are really, all of them, a serious endeavor to realize life, a better life, and more of it. And so, I would like to have everybody think of the so-called New movement and even of "modernism"—that rather awful aspect of the thing—not as a freakish effort to realize something peculiar for some few people, but the sign and often the substance of a very real awakening to what is intensely valuable in human power—that is, simply, love of life.

We are learning now that materials themselves all live—that stone has character, that brick has character, wood character; that they all have characteristics that may become alive in the hands of the imaginative artist through sympathetic interpretation in design, for I suppose we have to call him still the artist, although a more prophetic name should belong to him now that he is really finding something of this sort for himself. At any rate, this fresh life is a very practical thing with very definite meaning for Americans and the American home. And it is interesting in that while America herself, out on the western prairies, expressed these ideals in concrete form many years ago, they have gone to Europe, associated with European minds of brilliance and power, and are now coming back to us sometimes queer, sometimes refreshed, to awaken us to the realization that here is something that we need more than any other nation can need it. And we are going to have it, as one may now see for one's self.

Most of our architecture heretofore, of course, as

the thought came to some of us in our own country that architecture was a much "deader" affair than it had any right to be. It had become an academic inhibition. In America, largely, imitation practiced for profit. But if it is anything at all, it is no masquerade. Architecture is an intensely human affair, and it seems to me that the so-called New is simply an awakening to that fact—realization that it is a matter concerning us all and one that lives really where we live. So I think these new forms and these

60   *Creativity and the Philosophy of Organic Architecture*

one may readily believe if competent to sympathize at all with this new movement, has been an extraneous thing. It has been something applied to life, imprisoning life really instead of releasing it. It is the misfortune of all thought that while at one time it is a living and a becoming thing, full of color and importance, it soon becomes crystallized in becoming commercialized—standardized. And then it is the misfortune of that thought-form to become recognized as fixed, accepted by academies, formalized, and taught to the young as a kind of religion. So of course, this particular new thought, being by nature fluid matter, naturally rejects all that has gone before to choose only those matters which are living and which it sees as alive. And, knowing that the principle that works in all this is eternal, this "New" is more reconciled to let the flowers fade in order that the "Old" may be ever "New" and the "New" ever "Old." Of course, many flowers must be born only to die while this new thought is taking effect, while—I shouldn't say new field of human thought, for it is really a fresh effort only, at least in America—I say—born only to die, while all this is taking effect, going forward as one may see it going forward now. I said "only to die" hoping a little symposium, that somebody would give me incentive for "edge" so I wouldn't indulge in too much philosophy, because the world is pretty well tired of philosophy already; but they all say here that we are too much in accord to take issue.

At any rate, the watchword in this new effort is "integration." By way of the "plan factory" we have had effective disintegration applied to our country's architecture. Flotsam and jetsam came floating down ready made, practically burying all our legitimate human interest, legitimate because in architecture no less than in painting, writing or sculpture, the central interest for mankind, as it is in nature herself, is individuality. We have had little or none. As a democracy we are not particularly successful, either. I think because we have not honored, as we should, that particular principle. We have not known how. But I think the "New" movement, so-called now by nearly everyone, will unearth the fact that it is in itself an expression, a defense, a statement of that valuable thing in us which we call "individuality."

The thing to be most grateful for now, I think, is that the time is not far distant when, because of this "New" grasp on the essentials of architecture, every man will own his own house in the truest sense of the term. It will be a place where what he feels and what he likes and what seems to him beautiful and valuable may be reflected in his environment without false shame, academic let, or economic hindrance. But there is no school yet; and God forbid that this "New" should ever decline into a style or stultify itself as a school. There is no reason in the world why this fresh hold on architectural life shouldn't maintain its vogue and character, go on growing continually, and be the genuine liberation of creative impulse. Yes, it begins at the top, as all such movements do begin, with the better minds, with the more vital well-to-live of the world, undoubtedly; and, now as always, it will find its way down, eventually to reach the school and the academy. When that time comes, the danger point has been reached. It is not so far away. I hope there will be among us, with the coming decade, enough knowledge of the principle involved in the work to prevent forming anything in the way of a school, in the way of a style, in the way of any prevalent thought form, however finely felt, from taking possession of this valuable new thing, to make it either a passing fashion or an academic matter of form.

The hardest thing in this world for me to do is to make a speech against time. I had thought, when I came here and began to talk, that I was going to arouse dissension and be stimulated by my friendly enemies, and yet only friends seem to be round about me here. But they have picked me up by the scruff of the neck and, having flung me in here, are now watching me struggle, hoping that I'll be able to swim. I'm painfully conscious of not having said at all the things that I should have said, because everybody wants to know something specific about this work, and they want the thing as hard as a keg of nails. They want to talk about brass tacks and boards and all those mechanical things which are absolutely incontrovertible and leave no room for argument, and all this before they understand what it is all about anyway. I think to do that is quite impossible. I myself should have to become much more expert, much more master of my subject before I should be able to present it in such hard and fast terms as to show its "inside" without its general form and outline being first comprehended by the beholder.

FERRISS: I want to ask Mr. Wright a question. It has seemed to me that the real tradition of architecture is that a building must express the material whereof it is built, the method whereby it is built, and the purpose whereof it is built; and having that in mind, it seems to me that we aren't engaged in a really new movement. On the contrary, is it not true that men like Mr. Wright, whom we speak of as the "New"

architects, are in fact carrying on the real tradition of architecture?

WRIGHT: I think Mr. Ferriss has established an important fact. The "New" architects are "New" merely because they are more true to tradition almost than any tradition can be true to itself. It is, of course, the spirit of anything that deserves to live and all that eventually does live. This is no less true of tradition than of anything else. We have had an erroneous idea of tradition as something entirely fixed, a form fastened upon us somehow by faith and loyalty perhaps, and which eventually takes us by the throat and says "No" to pretty much everything of life we have. But tradition, too, is a living spirit. Architecture is not the buildings that have been built all over the world. These buildings are only the residue, the wreckage perhaps, thrown upon the shores of time by this great spirit in passing. This spirit lives now. To be true to this spirit is what we are all endeavoring to do, each in his way. And to be true to it we must with the materials at hand and in the spirit of our own time produce those forms which are to become characteristic and true forms of our day, as those forms we violate in the name of tradition were true to their day; or else we merely stupidly violate tradition only to keep "traditions" for selfish or sentimental purposes. Unfortunately, these forms will be new as things are with us now. But they shouldn't necessarily be so were we sufficiently developed. I heartily agree with Mr. Ferriss and I am glad he raised the point.

FERRISS: It has seemed to me that most of our practicing architects today content themselves with reproducing the external forms, the details that we find on the facades of ancient monuments, whereas the true interpretation would be to grasp the spirit which was behind those monuments and to express it as opposed to its exterior coating, or, we might say, its corpse.

WRIGHT: The things that we call "the details" and what we refer to as "ornament" are really incidental. They are minor products and come after or come along with the main theme and construction, whereas, as we are now taught and as architecture is now practiced, they have become, unfortunately, architecture itself. In other words, you can't see the trees for the wood there is in them.

FERRIS: I unfortunately find myself in such continual agreement with Mr. Wright that we have no conflict here. He and the men who think somewhat as he does stand, in short, for the expression of the spirit; that is to say, the expression of that which lives as opposed to the corpse, the crystallized and discarded forms. I think all of this which we speak of as a new movement is in fact the old urge for vital being.

WRIGHT: The New is ever Old and the Old is ever New. All we need in order to progress without so much pain and waste is the capacity to see that and a broad sense, a liberal scheme of life that will allow growth to keep this New alive all the time in a natural process of change. And now, inasmuch as we are all so completely in accord, I think we may call this discussion a failure.

FERRISS: I should like to ask Mr. Wright another question. I feel that one of the most important aspects of architecture is the effect which it has on the average man, and I'm speaking of the effect which is received by the average man unconsciously. We know that there are a few people who are keenly alert to technical architectural values, but it is not in their minds that the important result is produced. The important thing in architecture is the effect that it is having on the man in the street. I am quite sure that people, however, subconsciously, are influenced in their thoughts and actions by the kind of forms and spaces which they habitually encounter, and it appears to me that architects who are engaged in producing these forms and spaces are exerting a quite definite influence on people in general. I am wondering how aware architects are of that influence. Have you, when you have been engaged in designing a house, been concerned with whether or not it is an expression of yourself, or have you been concerned with the impression it is going to have on the beholder and the occupant?

WRIGHT: If you mean by the average man, the unspoiled man, I would say that man would be good audience—if we only had an unspoiled man—because after all he is the vital factor in the problem. It is but a demoralized audience as a rule that we have to appeal to, so to make conscious appeal to the man with the little knowledge which is a dangerous thing. Who is your "average man" really? Would be something like what an actor might experience were he to appeal to the "gallery." I think that as architects we can only look to that which shines for us, and with what intelligence we have when it comes to the essential architecture of our problems. For, after all, when a man does that, he is appealing to the true man, because inherent in all men is the same ideal, shared perhaps in greater or less degree. Usually every man who truly builds is true to himself. When we make any criterion outside of ourselves, that is to say, when we set up anything as a judge, or an objective—call it "popular opinion" or "society" or what you please—we fall into its power and lose our own, and we cease really to be the artist. Just as an actor, I'm sure, were he to have his eye on the gallery—were he to speak his lines and make his interpretation to and for the gallery—would fail, and we know he will fail. We know well that type of actor, and I think we know the type of architect who is his counterpart.

4 The Creative Mind

I believe that what we would call a creative individual would be a man who could see inside and come out with something fresh, something vital to whatever it happened to be he was doing.

The following conversation was originally broadcast by WGBH-FM radio, Boston, on December 29, 1958. It had been conducted by educator and writer Dr. Lyman Bryson a short time earlier at Frank Lloyd Wright's Plaza Hotel suite in New York.

The Conversation

NARRATOR: The Lowell Institute Cooperative Broadcasting Council presents "Frank Lloyd Wright: The Architect as Creator," Essay No. 2 in the National Association of Educational Broadcasters series "The Creative Mind" produced by WGBH-FM in Boston under a grant from the Educational Television and Radio Center. These conversations explore the creative process as it pertains to the American artist and scientist in the twentieth century.

And here is the host and commentator for "The Creative Mind," Lyman Bryson.

BRYSON: We are going to continue our series of conversations with a talk I recently had with Mr. Frank Lloyd Wright, the architect. Mr. Wright

The text of this heretofore unpublished conversation with Frank Lloyd Wright is reproduced with the permission of the WGBH Educational Foundation, Boston, Massachusetts, from the radio program entitled "The Creative Mind: Frank Lloyd Wright—The Architect as Creator." Audio recording of this conversation was furnished the editor courtesy of the State Historical Society of Wisconsin.

65

Frank Lloyd Wright circa late 1950s. Photograph by Cameron Macauley, courtesy of the State Historical Society of Wisconsin.

is a very striking type of creative mind. He's had a long life and he has succeeded in startling and bewildering and conquering the taste, not only of Americans, but of a very large part of the world, in Europe and Asia too. He's spread his ideas of design all over everywhere. He doesn't mind being paradoxical. In fact, he rather likes throwing things into other people's glass houses.

In his conversation with me he announced a number of themes which I think we'll find running through all of these talks. He has strong ideas about education, for example. He thinks we are making a rather bad mess of it in our bringing up of the young. He thinks that we

tend to suppress the creative powers they have. We tend not to develop them along natural lines. "Natural" is a great word with Mr. Wright. He thinks that all great ideas come out of nature, that all great artists depend upon nature, that his own creativity came out of his close contact with nature in his youth and the fact that he was allowed to have that.

One of the things he objects to most about the way we plan our cities and our houses is that we cut off our people from that contact with nature which would encourage and develop in us the powers that he thinks are so valuable.

He touches, also, on another theme which a

Creativity and the Philosophy of Organic Architecture

great many of our creative thinkers are interested in—the relation between restraint and freedom. That is, the necessity to be faithful to experience, to be truthful in what one reports and works with but at the same time to give scope to the imagination. In fact, we began talking about the term "the creative mind." I asked Mr. Wright if there was such a thing as a general creative mind or that it would be closer to the truth to say that creativeness shows itself in special ways and special forms of creative activity. Is there such a thing as a general creative mind?

WRIGHT: I think the word is very carelessly used as a rule and I don't think people who use it know exactly what they mean. What do you mean by creativity, Doctor?

BRYSON: I think I am reflecting an assignment rather than anything else, Mr. Wright. What I mean by it when I use it is a capacity to use the techniques of the past without being bound to the ideas of the past.

WRIGHT: Well, that would be one feature of it, I dare say. I think if you were truly creative, you would be in league with what we call nature and I think you would interpret nature very differently from the usual interpretation. I am inclined to put a capital N on the word nature because I am sure that no human mind is really capable of creating anything except as it is somehow related to the nature of the thing done and the way it's done, why it's done, and all of the other features of doing.

BRYSON: You don't mean by that, Mr. Wright, that the creative mind simply reproduces a natural object or a natural scene?

WRIGHT: That would be impossible. It can't be done except on a very low level of intelligence. No, I mean seeing into the thing rather than

looking at it and coming out with something of its characteristic nature—using the word nature again in a broad sense—as the intrinsic character of whatever is.

BRYSON: Then it is the kind of capacity to express an insight into . . . into the . . .

WRIGHT: Yes, I believe that what we would call a creative individual would be a man who could see inside and come out with something fresh, something vital to whatever it happened to be he was doing.

BRYSON: Do you think this is a widespread capacity, Mr. Wright?

WRIGHT: I think it ought to be, but I am afraid it isn't because of education.

BRYSON: That is, the capacity is there but we kill it?

WRIGHT: The capacity is there, but . . .

BRYSON: . . . discourage it?

WRIGHT: . . . we don't intend to kill it. We think we are going to develop it when we merely condition it and do not enlighten it. I imagine that enlightenment is not so simple and not easy because it's a quality of freedom that's needed and that freedom is lacking.

BRYSON: But just any freedom wouldn't do it, just complete lack of restraint or training . . .

WRIGHT: Well, a complete lack of restraint. I don't think restraint is an element in it at all. When I say freedom I mean an opening of the doors and the windows and the fresh air of nature, again using the word, comes in or he goes out or she goes out to it.

BRYSON: Do you mind if I ask you a personal question at this point? I'd like to know very much, Mr. Wright, if you can remember in your

Anna (Hannah) Lloyd-Jones Wright (1839–1923), Frank Lloyd Wright's mother, shown here in her later years. Photograph courtesy of the Frank Lloyd Wright Memorial Foundation.

own youth what happened or what series of happenings occurred which somehow enabled you to discover *in yourself* the capacity to create things in an artistic sense?

WRIGHT: I don't think you put it quite correctly because I didn't discover it in myself.

BRYSON: Did somebody discover it in you?

WRIGHT: It had been developing to the point where I've been accused of it, but personally it has not been a conscious search, on my part, until very recently when I became more self-conscious, perhaps, than I ought to be. But it was quite natural to me because of my early

training, because I chose my ancestors with the greatest of care. My father was a preacher and my mother was a teacher. Father loved music and didn't love preaching. And mother loved teaching, and always, even [in] her elder years, would bring you some backward children and have pleasure in trying to do something for them. So she put me down to the kindergarten table when I was seven. That was Froebel kindergarten. I don't know if you are familiar with F–R–O–E–B–E–L—Froebel?

BRYSON: Yes. Yes, after all I am a professional . . .

WRIGHT: Well he was a wonderful philosopher. And, of course, this thing you talk of as "creative" cannot occur without some philosophy. No artist, I think, ever lived who didn't have his philosophy. And his philosophy develops by way of what he can call, perhaps, his education or his way of enlightenment let's say. It isn't often education now. Maybe it used to be. So there it lies and in my young life coupled with this kindergartening where Froebel says it forbids the youth, the young, from drawing from nature—the appearances of nature—until they have discovered some form of the principles of form that lie back of the effects of nature. But when I had that I didn't care to draw from nature. I wanted to design using those principles and elements of nature. And that's what my mother's kindergarten did for me and I think that was where I began to be an architect. Now coupled to that was the farm experience. I was getting to be sort of a "Little Lord Fauntleroy" growing up there in a special school in Boston and I had long curls, finger curls that mothers like to put on the heads of their little darlings.

Creativity and the Philosophy of Organic Architecture

William Russell Cary Wright (1825–1904), Frank Lloyd Wright's father, shown here in his middle years. Photograph courtesy of the Frank Lloyd Wright Memorial Foundation.

BRYSON: Velvet pants?

WRIGHT: (laughter) And when she saw this going too far, why she cut those curls from the back of my head and sent me off to my Uncle James on the farm. And Uncle James took over my education at that point. I was eleven when I went up there. And every summer up to the age of eighteen I went to the farm. And I never went to school the prim term [sic] of my life because the farm was so much more fascinating *and instructive.*

BRYSON: Didn't your father's music have something to do with this too, Mr. Wright?

WRIGHT: Father's music, of course. I used to go to sleep to the strings of . . . well, I heard him play almost all of the Beethoven's sonatas. I went to sleep to them and heard him play down below on the Steinway Square these things. And music has always been to me one of the great creative arts and Beethoven probably the greatest of all the builders or the architects. Father taught me to listen to his symphony as an edifice . . . as I would see an edifice of sound. And that was very valuable, too, coupled with the kindergarten. Some music became architecture. Everything in nature was architecture. And then I got to the farm. I found out who and how I was, where nearly everything around me was concerned, which was very useful, too. And I've never found anything but useful that contact firsthand with the experiences of the struggle which we call work on the farm.

BRYSON: Well you've got three elements here. You've got a sense of structure from music and an appreciation of that kind of structure and you've got your Froebel principle structure of seeing the basic structure in natural objects before you try to make a representation of them and you've got your own acquaintance with yourself as a person. But we've only got you up to your eleventh year, Mr. Wright! Did these things just go on developing?

WRIGHT: Well now, these things didn't all happen in my eleventh year; I think you better take it up to eighteen.

BRYSON: Eighteenth year. Well all right. Oh, it was the eleventh you went to the farm.

WRIGHT: And I wasn't conscious of it myself then. It is all as natural as boxing, skating or riding or anything.

The Creative Mind

James Lloyd-Jones (1850–1907), Frank Lloyd Wright's Uncle James. Photograph courtesy of the Frank Lloyd Wright Memorial Foundation.

BRYSON: When did you start actually building? When did you?

WRIGHT: Well, I built some when I went to Sullivan, but it was 1893 when I put my name on the door, and by the way it was a plate glass . . . the first plate glass panel door that I had ever seen, in gold letters as "architect."

BRYSON: The first time you saw a plate glass door you put your name on it?

WRIGHT: (laughter) Now, let me see that was a . . . 1893. What age would I be, having been born in 1869?

BRYSON: I should think you were about twenty-four. But now in your experience you have quite specific and definite ideas, Mr. Wright, about things that gave you your basic, shall we say, education or training, enlightenment, or whatever you want to call it.

WRIGHT: I've tried to look into the nature of them now that I have grown up and turned and looked the other way occasionally, but I seldom looked backward.

BRYSON: Well, but tne experience or a man like you who has done so much for your own art, it seems to me we ought to be able to tap it somehow, use it for the development of whatever talent there is in other young people. What can we do to keep the power to do things, to create [sic] things from being killed?

WRIGHT: Only by doing them, not by telling young minds how, not by even showing them how, but by doing them for themselves. That's the basis of Taliesin as we have it now, a foundation for young architects. We have them from all over the world now. There are sixty-five of them there at the present time and all we try to do for them, and we try especially not to teach them, but open the doors and the windows of what constitutes the good life. I don't believe you can get an architect. Shakespeare said it, didn't he?—"You can't make a silk purse out of a sow's ear." So he must be a cultured individual before he will ever be able to do much with architecture. So the collateral arts, music and all the crafts and especially movement, all enter into the culture we are trying to afford. The young man wants to be an architect and all we expect to do for him is to open the doors and the windows of what you call, well let's call it for lack of a more specific term, life, as building the structure of whatever is. And again the word nature. We

70   *Creativity and the Philosophy of Organic Architecture*

want to relate him, so nearly as we can, to the very nature of the thing he would do by letting him share in the doing and we believe that a man really learns, chiefly and perhaps principally, by what he does.

BRYSON: Do you think that each man's original genius is self-corrective or does he need somebody who is older and wiser than he to point out some holes?

WRIGHT: Oh, I think we'll never have . . . I think we will never know a substitute for leadership, but leadership is what he needs and leadership doesn't necessarily imply didactic instruction. It does, perhaps, imply correction of a sort, but it does imply, most of all, exemplar—example.

BRYSON: Put him where he can see the thing properly done, done well rather, not properly?

WRIGHT: Where he is an assistant in the doing of the things superbly well. And all that's necessary is the sympathy, a feeling, the desire to do something that is beautiful and be himself something fine and beautiful.

BRYSON: Is a modern city natural, Mr. Wright?

WRIGHT: The modern city is, of course, disappearing. It was, of course, our great misfortune that we didn't have architects, genuine architects, coming over with our pilgrim fathers and most of them knew the dormitory— the London dormitory town only. And, of course, in true British fashion, they started and planned it here just as it was at home. And so far as our towns are concerned, they are still the old-fashioned feudal town and we've never planned one. We've crammed the present one with all sorts of gadgetry and the automobile is something it can't digest. They can tear down rotten spots and throw them out, improve them and they can make freeways so people can get out to the country and at first they'll serve for

getting in. But the whole idea of the gregarious nature of man in the Middle Ages is now no longer a friend of culture. The city once was the agent of culture. There was no other way of getting culture. But now it's in the way. It's in the way of the dissemination, now, of knowledge; in the way of the enjoyment of what was true and beautiful in the past. Instead of being liberated and by choice we've got somebody standing on our feet with their elbow in our ribs or pushing us around or we're pushing somebody around and there's no really real development of what we declared as the sovereignty of the individual.

BRYSON: I was thinking back to your boyhood, your years on the farm, that gave you a sense of freedom, Mr. Wright. What about all the young people who live in these outmoded and moribund places? Do they get any contact with nature?

WRIGHT: Well you've heard of the teenager, haven't you?

BRYSON: I certainly have.

WRIGHT: The teenager problem. I think distinctly it's a problem of overgregarious life. Life not with the green acres, not life where the wind blows and where a man is free to indulge his instincts according to his better nature and where everything in him is likely to be developed by, what do you call it? Suppression, oppression, all these pressures that are exerted upon youth in the name of education, in the name of parental authority, in the name of anything you like to name. But freedom is not there and he doesn't know freedom. And if he did, we wouldn't have the teenager problem.

BRYSON: How does the architect come in on this, Mr. Wright? What could a better race of architects do for us to conquer this problem?

WRIGHT: It's because we believe that the architect is primary, is the real cornerstone of any culture, of any society at any time anywhere in the world. That we need him now more than we ever needed him because we haven't had it. We've not had the enlightened architect. The architects we've had were educated in the Beaux Arts and on the old system. Architecture has meant certain fashionable things that have been admired during the centuries. Root—architecture lost its roots 500 years ago and it's very well told by Victor Hugo in his story of Notre Dame where he tells about the great cathedral and tells what happened to destroy it. And what happened to destroy the cathedral was a new tool coming into our hands which we've never yet learned how to use and that's the "machine." All we've done with machinery is to desecrate our naturehood rather than to develop it, which the machine should enable us to do. And there, I think today, is the basic problem of the architect. And the architect is the basic servant of society. But where are our architects? Most of them have gone into business now, big business. We haven't had the training ground for them. Where would they go to learn these things we're talking about? They go to a department in some university which is merely a department. Whereas it should be a basic university in itself. It should be fundamental, elemental, to what we call enlightenment and it doesn't exist. It's merely on one side as an adjunct, possibly, but only superficially and, therefore, we are high and dry practically so far as this need for the new things and the new life and the new forms that should go with all this scientific endowment. Science has really overdeveloped us. We are scientific beyond any capacity to use it.

BRYSON: Some people want us to be still more so.

WRIGHT: Yes, and, of course, it is idiotic. To me it seems fantastic.

BRYSON: But there are people, Mr. Wright, who seem to believe that you can't make an industrial society beautiful. If you're going to have the advantage of industry, you've got to have a certain amount of ugliness.

WRIGHT: That's not only treachery to the Declaration of Independence and the sovereignty of the individual, but to the nature of the human being. I think it was the nature of the human being to love and desire beauty and to do its best to live in it. Look at the civilizations that we call creative now. Those primitive civilizations were far superior, where their life was concerned in relation to nature, than we are. That whole thing has somehow been mixed up. It's gone backward rather than forward because we've had all these ways of making life artificial.

BRYSON: It's not the fault of the machine itself, is it?

WRIGHT: The machine is not at fault for anything. It's a great tool. But it's not a great tool for construction, only for destruction, unless you put it under the hand of what we were calling "creative mind architects," a man with a deep sense of structure or a sense of the elemental in human nature.

BRYSON: What is it in us, Mr. Wright, that makes so many of us respond to the . . . to the tremendous, to the tall, to the monumental, the impressive in modern architecture if it's wrong? I suspect that it is, and I'm sure you think so.

WRIGHT: The thing in itself is not wrong. But all

those buildings were dedicated to the inferiority complex and our declaration of the sovereignty of the individual demands a different sense of proportion. And I felt that when I was a young architect. So my scale in the buildings that I built has always been the human scale. People said that if I had been, instead of five feet nine, I'd been six feet three or four, that all of my buildings would have been different and they're right. They would have been.

BRYSON: Right here on Park Avenue, not more than a few hundred yards from here, Mr. Wright, we're building enormous square boxes of steel and glass. Now is this just merely enclosing office space or is this expressing something deep in our sense of design or perhaps some of them do one thing and some another?

WRIGHT: Well you see Doctor, the sense of space is what has been preserved in Paris and it made Paris the most beautiful city of the world today. We've lost it in all of our cities. We can't have it. And in most of our life we have lost it— the sense of space. Nothing is more important. And that is the sense of the new architecture, the space within becoming a reality of the building and the roof and the walls taking place accordingly. That's the new thought that we call *organic architecture* and to which I have devoted my life. If that were put into circulation where the teenager could feel it, understand it, use it, he wouldn't be a problem. We'd be listening to him and following him very soon ourselves. Education is really depriving us, as it exists, of all this virtue which I've been referring to as "creative." There will never be anything creative coming out of the education which the

The desk of the creative master architect Frank Lloyd Wright at Taliesin, Spring Green, Wisconsin circa late 1950s. Note the overall neatness of the desk and array of colored drawing pencils in the holder on the right-hand side, Mr. Wright's glasses set on top of his Taliesin stationery, the orderly stacks of publications, and the three "FLLW" signed red square tiles used to mark his buildings on the lower right hand corner of the desk pad. Photograph by Richard Vesey, courtesy of the State Historical Society of Wisconsin.

teenager will receive today in this drift toward conformity.

BRYSON: What about the drift toward science?

WRIGHT: About what?

BRYSON: What about the drift toward science or the compulsory movements?

WRIGHT: Well, that again is a drift toward conformity. Science is something you can put your hand on and something you can see and you will only see what you can put your hand on. Science is, of course, capable and will eventually join with art and religion and when they're one then we will begin to have the right kind of education. We'll have the right kind of buildings. We'll have a greatly improved method of life.

BRYSON: It's a great . . . it's a great reassurance, Mr. Wright, to have you base your belief in the future upon the natural gift of artistic power and appreciation and the natural human being . . .

WRIGHT: But broaden the word "nature," deepen it, and you're all right, I agree with you.

BRYSON: Well then you're setting out a future for the architect, as you describe it, which is as wide a sculpture of nature itself, is there . . .

WRIGHT: That's right.

BRYSON: . . . a future like that for the architect?

WRIGHT: The architect is the natural interpreter, in terms of structure, of whatever is for his people.

BRYSON: But can he help make it, can't he too, as well as interpret it?

WRIGHT: Well if he will make it he will help make it. But the interpretation is in itself creative, because the principles which he would work with and the results that would come from what he did, if he were true to what he knew, would be completely what we would call "creative."

The Philosophy of Organic Architecture

"Organic Architecture" ... is the architecture of nature ... the architecture based upon principle and not upon precedent.

In late October 1958 Wright appeared twice in the WTTW–Chicago television series called *Heritage*. Both half-hour programs were filmed the same day and titled "Part I—The Philosophy of an Architect" and "Part II—Organic Architecture." The programs consisted of two conversations between Wright and William MacDonald. The two programs were released as films in 1959 for national distribution by the National Educational Television (NET) Film Service.

Mrs. Wright recounted Mr. Wright's day filming the program in *The Capital Times* (Madison, Wisconsin), October 31, 1958:

We flew to Chicago .... He had three heavy sessions which took up all his morning starting at 9:30. Between the second and third session, he went to the Tavern Club where he, by mere chance, ran into 20 architects who had gathered for a conference. Among them were the well known Edward Stone, Alfred Shaw, John Root, Jr., and Samuel Marx .... After lunch, Mr. Wright went back for an additional broadcast saying he would return to the Blackstone [Hotel] at 2:30. It was 3 o'clock when finally a telephone message came from him—he was still working on the broadcast! "But our plane is leaving at 4 o'clock," I said.

Mr. Wright came down from the broadcast to meet Mrs. Wright at about

This heretofore unpublished conversation with Frank Lloyd Wright is reproduced in its entirety from the WTTW–Chicago *Heritage* series television programs titled "The Philosophy of an Architect" and "Organic Architecture" by permission of WTTW–Chicago Channel 11 television.

Frank Lloyd Wright (left) and interviewer William MacDonald as they appeared in conversation on the WTTW-Chicago television program Heritage *in late October 1958. Photograph used by permission of WTTW-Chicago Channel 11.*

3:30 and used the assistance of a policeman and police car with the siren blowing to drive the Wrights to the airport. The Wrights arrived at the airport at 4:55 and boarded the plane to return to Taliesin.

The Conversations

PART ONE
"The Philosophy of an Architect"

MACDONALD: At the opening of *A Testment* you state that "a philosophy is to an architect or to the mind of an architect as eyesight is to his steps."

WRIGHT: That's true. Without the knowledge of where and how and why, what's he going to do? Where is he going? What's going to become of him?

MACDONALD: This, at least from my very initial point of view, the idea of a philosophy in architecture, is a strange one, a new one. Could you explain a little bit more fully what it is that you mean by a philosophy?

Creativity and the Philosophy of Organic Architecture

WRIGHT: I'm astonished. You shock me. I think that an architect would necessarily be dependent upon his philosophy, his point of view, before he could perform. Maybe that's what's the trouble. Maybe that's where architecture or architects are all that is the matter with architecture. I think they are and probably because they have no philosophy. What is a philosophy? It is a way you think, believe, and behave concerning anything. So is there a new definition of philosophy? Is that stretching it? I don't think so.

MACDONALD: No, I don't think so. It's possible then, taking this definition, to equate philosophy . . . philosophy with principle?

WRIGHT: Philosophy, of course, is the . . . of principle based upon principle. Principle is the basis of a philosophy. Without principle—no philosophy—no foundation—foundation of a philosophy is principle.

MACDONALD: I remember your quoting Lao-tse in this statement that "the reality of a building is neither the walls nor the roof but the space within." Surely . . . .

WRIGHT: Working on that, architecturally, I had the feeling that that was what was the matter with architecture in modern times—the interior content, the sense of it as related to life is missing and had been missing for 500 years. So when I built Unity Temple in Oak Park I was aiming at making the interior of the building come through. And then I read Lao-tse. The Japanese ambassador to America sent me a little book called *The Book of Tea* and there for

Exterior view of Unity Temple (1905), Oak Park, Illinois. Photograph from Frank Lloyd Wright, Frank Lloyd Wright: Ausgeführte Bauten *(Berlin: Ernst Wasmuth, 1911).*

the first time I read this pronouncement of Lao-tse and I had written it, I had been trying to build the thing that he had said that "the reality of a building consists not of four walls and a roof but in the space within to be lived in" and that's what I've been trying to build. Well, I had thought I was something of a prophet you know and when I read this, 500 years before Jesus, as had been directly said, I was like a sail coming down . . . (laughter)

MACDONALD: (laughter)

WRIGHT: . . . and it took me days to recover. I thought—well now what? I'm not a prophet after all, this is old and then I thought well he didn't build it and I'd been trying to build it, to make it his reality. So I began to swell up again and had been there ever since!

MACDONALD: One thing in particular in mentioning the Unity Temple—one thing that I

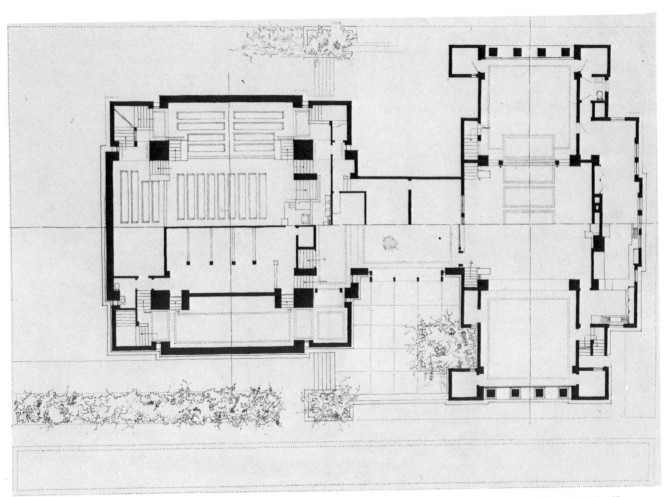

Floor plan of Unity Temple shows the main auditorium (left) and Unity House (right) with its classrooms. Copyright © The Frank Lloyd Wright Foundation, 1942, 1970.

thought of as a problem and a particular problem for the architect—is the matter of space and scale.

WRIGHT: Yes.

MACDONALD: And . . .

WRIGHT: That's where it came first to me before I had read Lao-tse.

MACDONALD: I have the drawings of the Unity Temple over here. Could we look at them?

WRIGHT: Yes, let's look at them. That was my first expression of this eternal idea which is at the center and the core of all true modern architecture. The sense of space—a new sense of space. I worked for weeks to make this circular thing becoming to the Temple—I had this then I had to get that.

MACDONALD: What is that section?

WRIGHT: That's a circular section Sunday school and social activities but here you see no walls, only features grouped about an interior. And the ceiling over all coming through so when you're inside your vision goes out to the infinite in every direction—no sense of containment only a sense of interior space protected from the exterior by features. See?

MACDONALD: I see. There's one drawing a little farther on here of the inside.

WRIGHT: Well, this shows it. Now here's a ceiling which is a flat overhead extension and you look out from the interior through these side windows here you see. You see you're conscious of the whole sense of space and here's the interior and eight comfortably seated is the audience. This is the organ. But you have no sense of confinement—no sense of being a "boxation"—of being boxed in—you are still free when you're in here and even more free

Wright: ". . . here you see no walls, only features grouped about an interior." Frank Lloyd Wright as he appeared on the WTTW-Chicago television program Heritage in late October 1958. Photograph used by permission of WTTW-Chicago Channel 11.

than out on the street because here the sense of space, distance, and all is brought within.

MACDONALD: Ya, this would be the question that it isn't a matter of a limitless kind of freedom where you just keep going off. It's a matter of a defined freedom.

WRIGHT: It's a matter of freedom within the soul of man and the sense of it in his environment brought there by a comprehension of the beauty of space. I think that is where I did this before I read the little *Book of Tea* so I was eligible. (laughter)

MACDONALD: Well, how is this same sense of . . . for a completely different purpose, how in this same sense of space and the relationship of one's self to space is this problem worked out in, for instance, the Johnson Administration Building?

WRIGHT: Yes, it's worked out in anything I ever did. That is the core of the philosophy, as you mentioned a little while ago, of my . . . what I call my architecture. Now I have no right to call it mine. But "organic architecture," which is the architecture of nature, the architecture based upon principle and not upon precedent. Precedent is all very well so long as precedent is very well but who knows when it is very bad? Now that's something to guard against in

architecture—know when to leave your precedent and establish one.

MACDONALD: Let me repeat this just to be sure that I have it exactly right—that the core of this is the sense of the space within?

WRIGHT: Yes, it's the sense of the space within as related to you, to environment, and to the past and to the future. Does that take it off too far?

MACDONALD: I'm not sure, it's . . . it's difficult to conceive of this in terms of future—to be standing within a confined—or not a con-fined—within a *defined* space and I'm not sure I quite know what you mean by future here?

Building section of Unity Temple looking at the pulpit area and general interior view. Drawing and photograph courtesy of the State Historical Society of Wisconsin.

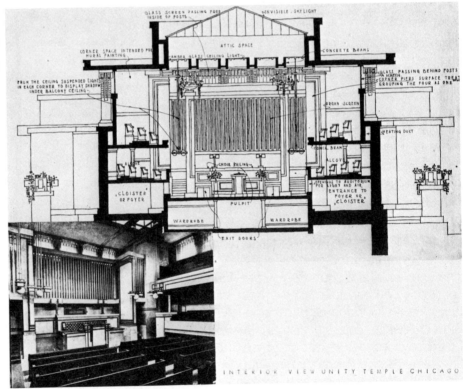

Creativity and the Philosophy of Organic Architecture

Wright: ". . . when you're inside your vision goes out to the infinite in every direction . . ." Detail interior view of art glass windows behind exterior posts of Unity Temple. Photograph by the editor.

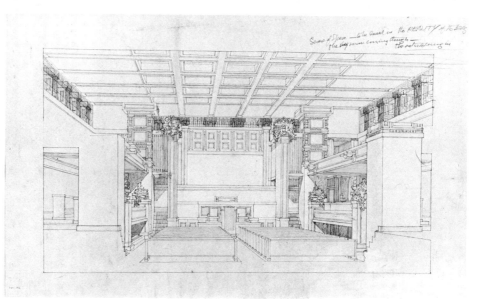

Wright: ". . . a ceiling which is a flat overhead extension and you look out from the interior through these side windows . . ." Perspective drawing by Frank Lloyd Wright of the interior of Unity Temple looking from the first-floor level toward the pulpit with the organ behind the pulpit. Copyright © The Frank Lloyd Wright Foundation, 1962.

Interior view of a corner of Unity Temple from the balcony. Photograph by the editor.

82

WRIGHT: The future is now. All that we can conceive of the future is now so that tomorrow is really today because it's all of it that we can conceive of as the future.

MACDONALD: Ah . . . I see.

WRIGHT: So we needn't worry, it's all one. It's all natural as the shining of the sun. And, that's what we need to bring home to the youngster, the young mind in America today who really doesn't know where he is or where he's going or what it's all about and there's a mystery there; and it's to him insoluble and he is more of a mystery even in the mystery that is insoluble. And if you can bring him to the sense of his relation to his environment, as a feature of it, and a necessary feature of it in his life that is something that can be becoming and beautiful in relation to it or a mere ugliness to be destroyed then I think you've done a great thing for the teenager.

MACDONALD: Well, this sort of gets us over into the problem of education.

WRIGHT: Yes.

MACDONALD: Education as opposed to culture or perhaps they're one and the same?

WRIGHT: Education, at the present time, is not on speaking terms even with culture. I doubt if many educators could explain to you the difference between education and culture—mistaking education for culture. It isn't at all culture. If you would understand—I think a simple incident, didn't I mention this to you before? The little delphinium in the garden? The Dutchmen saw it and the Dutchmen are very appreciative of growing things. They made the tulip what it is today. And they saw the little larkspur in the garden. The little larkspur appeared to them as having beautiful design and qualities but insignificant. So here the larkspur was in the garden about a foot high—maybe eighteen inches—so they find out better ones and take them and plant them under conditions that are suitable and they grow bigger and taller and better. Then they take the better ones and plant them again under conditions they've discovered to be agreeable so that from within the nature of the little larkspur comes more and more larkspur. Finally, we get what they call the "queen of the garden," the delphinium, isn't it? It's about as tall as you are and beautiful and still a little larkspur. Well now, education didn't do that—it was culture, cultivation, understanding of the character and nature of the thing that they were working upon giving it more and more of that thing that enabled it to be itself. Well now, that's what our democracy means—culture rather than education. We ought to get out of the sovereignty of the individual a greater individual; a finer member of society; richer in relation to society and to himself by way of his education, which, if it was culture, would be the case. And I think Thomas Jefferson had every idea that it would be the case to qualify the vote and prevent democracy from being democracy [sic—Wright probably meant to say "mediocrity"] rising into high places. Well, have we done it? Is it so? Is the politician a statesman? Are we in possession of the type of mind anywhere in the nation competent to prophesy peace and happiness for humanity? Didn't politics used to be the science of human happiness? It did. What is it now? It's a science of getting a job and getting into the place where the purposes are the best in the quickest and the farthest. Now where were we? I've got off of architecture, let's get back.

MACDONALD: (laughter) There is this picture here of part of the inside of Unity Temple which I'd like to show right over here. The wall planes here have an abstract quality like an abstract painting. There's a simplicity but it isn't barren. The question would be in terms of simplicity, simplicity is not simply the elimination of?

WRIGHT: No. Simplicity is the expression—directly and simply and to the point—of the nature of the thing done—that's simplicity. A barn door isn't simple it's just plain. A simple thing is a wildflower which is exquisite and beautiful and perfect in its idea of its self—that's simplicity. So in architecture it's the same. The idea of simplicity isn't necessarily plainness but it is appropriate form and character to whatever is the nature of the materials you use, the way you use them, and the purpose for which you use them. Now that was the philosophy back of Unity Temple and that's why it's worth studying

today. And it's true of all that we call "organic architecture." That was the first time when we began to talk about organic architecture that the principles making a thing beautiful and consistent instead of abhorent came into the human possession architecturally. Before that, it had been a question of precedence and style formed by men who had a certain feeling for this and a certain sense of it in relation to something that had been long before them. But it had never become indigenous; it had never become related to the life of the time—the landscape that had existed and things as they were. In other words, it had no reality.

MACDONALD: One thing you mentioned was the use of materials and . . .

WRIGHT: Yes.

MACDONALD: . . . the use of materials in the way in which they were meant to be used or quite often . . . .

WRIGHT: Well, here's a brick. [*Editor's note:* Wright picks up a brick to show MacDonald.] What is a brick? What is the nature of a brick? I've always loved brick. It's a product of the kiln of fire. It has color. It is earth sanctified by fire and put into a beautiful format to use to build with—that's the brick. Now when you build with a brick you want the building to be beautifully bricked don't you? And you select a most interesting brick that you can find and then you want to know how to use them and feel a way to put them together in the building in such a way as to make brick more beautiful as brick than it was just as a brick. Now that's where the artist comes in; in the use of material to make the ultimate effect more valuable and into it bring spiritual sense of the integrity of what is called a brick. Well now, that applies to all other materials. It applies to wood. It applies

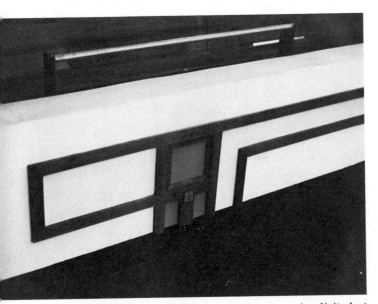

MacDonald: ". . . an abstract quality . . . a simplicity but it isn't barren." Detail of a balcony wall of Unity Temple. Photograph by the editor.

Brick, glass, and wood are integrated into an organic whole in this detail from the William Palmer Residence (1950), Ann Arbor, Michigan. In this instance, special bricks were made using a pattern which is a reflection of the residence floor plan pattern and which accommodates built-in glass for interior lighting. Photograph by the editor.

Wood, glass, and brick are integrated into an organic whole in this detail from the Maurice Greenberg Residence "Stonebroke" (1954), Dousman, Wisconsin. In this instance, similar to the Palmer Residence, special wood panels were made using a pattern which is a reflection of the residence floor plan pattern and which accommodates built-in glass for interior lighting. Photograph by the editor.

Wright: "Get the feeling of the rock in your hands or you can't build . . ." The native stone fireplace in the Andrew T. Potter Residence "Tanyderi" (1907) on the grounds of Taliesin, Spring Green, Wisconsin. Photograph by the editor.

to stone. The use of stone is a totally different sense of life from the sense of a brick. I had an old Cornish mason out at Taliesin—I used to turn the boys over to him. Occasionally he'd get one he didn't like—I remember his telling me "take him away or I'll kill him"—one of them talked all the time and didn't know how to work. And he said to them "boys get the feeling of the rock in your hands or you can't build a wall" and that's true. Get the feeling of the brick into your hands or you can't build a brick building that's worth looking at as a work of art.

Well now, that's true of our own life—the way we live. We've committed to a principle new in the world—the sovereignty of the individual. From within him and as he is, as the brick is, as the stone is, as he is will come; anything in the way of an interpretation called architecture or painting or sculpture—they're all children of architecture. It's worth having and that's what we don't know. That's what education doesn't teach and that's why education is not on speaking terms with culture because it doesn't study nature.

What does a boy go to school for? What's he sent to school to really acquire? Now, of course, the university is a trade school. He goes there to learn something about how to make a living and how to get a job or something like that instead of studying the nature of the universal—studying his nature, knowing who he is. When he comes out of the university is he on any better terms with himself? Does he know more about who he is? How he is? What he is? Because that's what the universities should teach you and he goes for and that's what culture does for him—enables him to become aware of that thing that is himself and how, eventually, to use it. Education doesn't do that.

Education now conditions this lad—conditions him according to precedent—all sorts of glorious beautiful precedents that worked in their time but may not work in this time. What was good for Dante may not be good for you Bill or me except in principle. Now the principles don't change. So long as we study the principle of the thing we're alive and useful but when we begin to study the form the principle took in that time and say that that is it then we are fools. You're fooled—nothing happens and nothing is happening today except more noise, more commotion, more violence—we're getting into a violence that's something terrifying. I had to come from the airport downtown to the hotel today. There's a series of combustions and explosions and shrieks and groans and cries that would deafen an Egyptian in the olden days (laughter) and so forth. Well, what's the use in talking about it? What have you got?

MACDONALD: Here we've got the Johnson Building . . . which again . . . .

WRIGHT: Yes. That's a good photograph; that's one of the best I've seen. What about it?

MACDONALD: Well, here would be a statement in brick . . .

WRIGHT: Yes, and glass . . .

MACDONALD: . . . of the . . .

WRIGHT: . . . a new glass form—a tube. Tubes are layed up in the wall as brick are layed up you know one above the other and that was the Johnson Building. And the Johnson Building also has a sense of space as the reality of that structure and there you can see it exemplified. You can see how materials are brought into their use according to their nature. How the building itself is planned, layed out, and it's there according to the nature of the purpose for

Creativity and the Philosophy of Organic Architecture

*This exterior night view of an entrance area of the
Johnson Wax Administration Building (1936), Racine,
Wisconsin shows the illuminated horizontal bands of
glass tubing which accent the building. Photograph
courtesy of Johnson Wax.*

87

which it was intended. You can see in it all, as it all comes together, a certain harmonious sense of the whole that you feel radiating as you would in a tree or flower or something in nature and that's what a building ought to be and so seldom is. It would be some little fraction of that but seldom is it in place in nature as a part of nature according to nature. Is this getting complex or something?

MACDONALD: No. I think it's good. This sense of the . . . this sense of the building as a whole implies . . . it doesn't imply . . . it states that the building is conceived as a whole—as one thing.

WRIGHT: Yes. Related to environment, purpose, and the character of whatever it is at the moment.

MACDONALD: And it also, I should think, would give the building itself a character.

WRIGHT: Yes.

MACDONALD: So that there would be some things which are appropriate to the building other than things which are inappropriate.

WRIGHT: Absolutely. The building is like the person. The building, if it's a good building and made according to these principles I've been enunciating, is almost a living thing like a tree; like a plant; like anything organic in nature. Seems to me when you come right down to the whole thing nature, with a capital N, is what we don't understand and what we're afraid of. We don't realize that in nature as considered as the nature of nature is all the body of God we're ever going to see and we should write it with a capital N in the sense that we use it in architecture because of that. Not that we've substituted it for God or for religion but that we know that in the character of that innate interior

Interior view of the lobby from the balcony of the Johnson Wax Administration Building. Photograph courtesy of Johnson Wax.

expression of life lies all we're ever going to know of what's called God. Does that sound heretical? Maybe it is, I hope it is. Anyhow, that's the way organic architecture sees it.

MACDONALD: And this is set up in the same sense in what you call humane architecture?

WRIGHT: That's why in organic architecture we're continually speaking of humanity. Because architecture is the primary basic expression of humanity and to say that there's nothing human in architecture is to say that there is no architecture worth looking at or considering because architecture is part of the human spirit, the human soul, and the greatest of all the tangible expressions of the human nature or the human soul. There is nothing more definite, distinct, that's come down to us from ancient times—the days of ancient civilizations—and the way they felt and thought when they built. That's the record today and that'll be our record.

PART TWO
"Organic Architecture"

MACDONALD: I wanted to start this program, Mr. Wright, by asking you about the abolition of the box.

WRIGHT: Well, you see Bill, the box has had a long and creditable history in architecture because there was no way of building a building except, practically, to make it a box or columns that form a box. But when we, in modern times, got steel we had an element, and glass, we had two elemental materials that abolish a box if wanted to abolish it. But of course architects, being educated, clung to precedent and still felt that the slab was "the thing" as they're used to say. So, you get the

U.N. [United Nations] Building. You get all these reminiscent cities of ancient architecture which, of course, was the box. But, it isn't at all characteristic of what we call "modern" or "organic" architecture. The box was a containment. It contained within everything. It was living or ought to be living. Whereas the new idea was to eliminate the box and let everything that was in go outward and associate with its environment. So environment and interior and life itself became as one. Glass and steel and architecture became what we call "modern." Now modern architecture [is] to be truly modern and [is] distinguished from just what is to be built today because anything built today is "modern." Isn't it? So, to get the real idea of the thing we've got to use some word like *organic*—means integral, of the thing, now, and preceding from the interior of it outward.

And, so there is something exterior chosen and used for effect. Therein lies the essential difference between what we call "organic architecture" and what is carelessly called, for the lack of a better term, "modern architecture."

MACDONALD: You still have walls. You still have a roof which encloses the place.

WRIGHT: Yes, but we use them differently now. We use the wall—we use the roof as shelter and we try to use it as shelter not obliterating the space but revealing the space, dedicating the space. And we use all the walls we do use in such a way as to protect and cherish the interior inhabitants of the building but not deprive them of the association with environment when that association is beautiful, and creditable, and useful. Is that clear?

MACDONALD: Ah . . . partially. Ah . . . it still strikes me as a problem. How do you bring, if I understand you correctly, the outside into the building and at the same time leave the inside free to go out?

WRIGHT: Well, here is this element of glass. We can vanish the wall in the exterior of a building and outside stands trees, perhaps a vista, perhaps water, a lake. Interior is the space of the room in which you live and inhabit. Now if you relate this interior space to this exterior sense of landscape and view and make the two one you have the beauty of both together in your life. But, as it was before, this became a room and this was a wall that divided you from this landscape, whereas now it is merely something that allows you to associate with the landscape.

MACDONALD: Well, it would seem from this that with this "organic" [architecture] choice of site would not only be extremely important but would, in part, in part at least, determine the form or forms of the building.

Wright: ". . . not obliterating the space but revealing the space, dedicating the space." Frank Lloyd Wright as he appeared on the WTTW-Chicago television program Heritage *in late October 1958. Photograph used by permission of WTTW-Chicago Channel 11.*

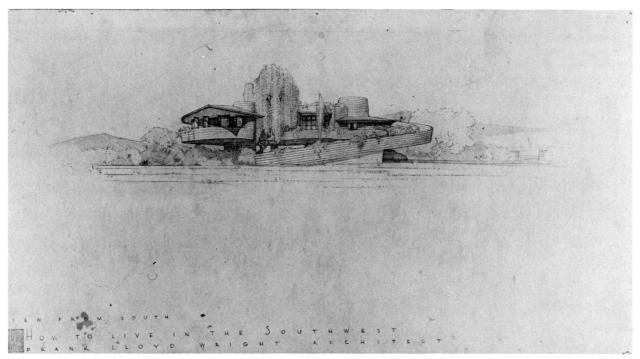

Wright: "This is a house for my son, David, which is out on the prairie and the mountains are around it ..." Rendering of the David Wright Residence (1950), Phoenix, Arizona. Copyright © The Frank Lloyd Wright Foundation, 1952.

WRIGHT: That's so. That's absolutely true. That is what happens with organic architecture. The site is all important and your sympathetic appreciation of the site and understanding of it as it appears in the building is a measure of your success as an architect, more or less. At least as your artistic claim to be one, I think, and that's entirely as it should be if our environment is to be a thing of beauty and not a thing imposed upon the landscape as an imposition.

MACDONALD: So that once an organic house was built upon a particular site, to remove the house would be to take something away from the land.

WRIGHT: Exactly. It would depreciate the landscape and to, vice versa, destroy the landscape would be to hurt the house.

MACDONALD: There are some photographs here which may help in making this a bit ... clearer.

WRIGHT: These?

MACDONALD: Not intellectually, but a bit ... clearer visually.

WRIGHT: This is a house for my son, David, which is out on the prairie and the mountains are around it, and this being the living floor, is on a level with the citrus orchards all around it

View from Maiden Lane of the V.C. Morris Gift Shop (1948), San Francisco, California. Photograph by the editor.

so they look like they belong with the house. But you don't get that in the picture.

MACDONALD: How high is the first level?

WRIGHT: The first level?

MACDONALD: Yes.

WRIGHT: That's nine feet about and this is the living floor and this is all open but the appearance of the building, when you inhabit it, is that of having the citrus orchards in the neighborhood of the lawn.

Here is another instance, perhaps not so clear, this is where there is nothing except a little street called Maiden Lane and the land itself is of no particular consequence and within becomes everything and the entrance emphasized as the human interest and then you have the wall and the street. It depends on the conditions whether you have a wall or a visual screen.

Here you have a house which really capitalized upon a beautiful site on a stream where Mr. Kaufmann loved to go and sit and I said: "Why not build your house here? Inhabit the place that you love." So, he built the house on the spot he loved on the stream and there he lived with the sound of the waterfall.

MACDONALD: Does the house go right across the stream?

WRIGHT: No, the house is cantilevered from a stone bank on one side of the stream and the stream comes down free on one side of the house.

There was an exhibition building in New York. That was a glass roof and you see its purpose was that of exhibition, interior here, and models and plans and everything, and you see the environment in which it stands.

Creativity and the Philosophy of Organic Architecture

A view of the Edgar J. Kaufmann, Sr. "Fallingwater" Residence (1935), Ohiopyle, Pennsylvania from the hill on the southeast side of the residence. The entrance driveway bridge can be seen in the lower-right corner and the large concrete cantilevered terrace which extends over the Bear Run can be seen in the lower left-hand corner. Photograph by Harold Corsini, courtesy of the Western Pennsylvania Conservancy.

93

An evening view looking northwest of the cantilevered living room and terraces of Fallingwater as they extend over Bear Run. Photograph by Harold Corsini, courtesy of the Western Pennsylvania Conservancy.

View of the steps from the main living room to the stream looking west from the entrance driveway bridge of Fallingwater. Photograph by Harold Corsini, courtesy of the Western Pennsylvania Conservancy.

Interior view of the living room area looking to the southwest from near the entry of Fallingwater. The massive native stone fireplace can be seen on the right-hand side of the view. Photograph by Harold Corsini, courtesy of the Western Pennsylvania Conservancy.

Interior view of the guest lounge or living room of the guest wing of Fallingwater (1938). Photograph by Harold Corsini, courtesy of the Western Pennsylvania Conservancy.

A quarter-circle cutout of a bedroom desk allows for the opening of a bedroom casement window in Fallingwater. Photograph by Harold Corsini, courtesy of the Western Pennsylvania Conservancy.

MACDONALD: One thing that I'd like to raise, at this point, would be the question of economy—the question of cost. Is this freedom and organic architecture something which is available to the average house buyer—in the, say, $20,000 to $30,000 house market? Or, is this something which . . .

WRIGHT: I don't think it is at all a matter of price anywhere because what I am talking about is not expensive. It isn't a question of money. It is a question of intelligence. It's a question of know-how, how to do the thing.

That's in Minneapolis, a little house on top of a hill with a great vista all around it.

And, there is the home of a dentist in . . . I think it's in Iowa. There's water coming in from a stream on the front and the house, built of stone, made of stone, brick, becomes blended in and really a part of the landscape.

MACDONALD: Is this part of what you call the "Usonian House"?

WRIGHT: That is of the Usonian House type. Usonian is a term which I borrowed from Samuel Butler. Samuel Butler wrote *The Way of All Flesh* [*sic*], the first realistic novel, and he declared the fact the Americans had no name for their country. You couldn't say the United States of America, so he suggests that we call ourselves the Usonians. The word *Usonia* having its root in freedom, unity, unity of all. So I thought it was an excellent idea. If I had been able to tell my clients in the early days when they asked me, well, "What style is this, Mr. Wright?" if I could have said "Usonian Style" they would have taken it right a way. So, after a while I began to call the thing Usonian according to Samuel Butler and handed it on to them. So now it's got back into our language. Usonian means a certain type of architecture—free architecture.

MACDONALD: One thing, sitting here looking at this photograph of a house, called into question not only the structure and texture of the house but the structure and design of literally everything in it . . .

WRIGHT: That's true. Yes.

MACDONALD: . . . the furniture, art, sculpture, the thing as a whole.

WRIGHT: Unity is, of course, the ideal in your mind when you unite interior and exterior and having made that unity a reality then you proceed to preserve it by making everything in the house and everything around about it all tributary to the one central idea or effect and out of that unity comes a great repose always. Repose, in any sense anywhere, is due to unity of sometime, somewhere, and somehow. So out of unity comes repose and out of repose comes the enjoyment of your environment, of your home as you live in it.

MACDONALD: Within this framework one thing which you've written about that I find rather

difficult to understand and that's what you call "nature pattern" and later its expansion into integral ornament.

WRIGHT: Oh yes, that's part a moot question; you see, the function of ornament and the relation to human endeavor. But it's everywhere in nature and you can't be familiar with the precedents of nature without some level of understanding of pattern because everywhere and everything nature is indulging in pattern. It seems that the geometry and the rhythm (interior rhythm) of nature manifest themselves in these various poetic forms that we see in the flowers, and trees, and everywhere as a matter of fact. I think no region of nature is exempt from pattern—even our own. We have a pattern. Your whole constitution is based upon

Exterior perspective rendering of the Malcolm E. Willey Residence (1933), Minneapolis, Minnesota. Copyright © The Frank Lloyd Wright Foundation, 1942, 1970.

Furniture designed specifically for the house in which it is to be used. The Herbert F. Johnson "Wingspread" Residence (1937), Wind Point, Wisconsin. Photograph by the editor.

Wright: "Architecture is pattern—the pattern of structure, of materials . . . and of human life as well." Frank Lloyd Wright as he appeared on the WTTW-Chicago television program Heritage *in late October 1958. Photograph used by permission of WTTW-Chicago Channel 11.*

a symmetrical pattern of some kind. So to say pattern is to say, more or less, an interior expression nature made manifest in some form peculiar to her desires or her purpose and, therefore, as we architects become educated more and more, we realize her resources and the opportunities afforded by pattern to our sense of expression of ourselves. So pattern becomes essentially important. Music is pattern—the pattern of sound. Architecture is pattern—the pattern of structure, of materials, and of practically everything in the cities and all our environment, and human life as well.

MACDONALD: Well, the pattern of the face is based on the bone structure.

WRIGHT: Yes.

MACDONALD: So that would it follow that the pattern of a building is based on the structural elements within the building?

Pattern in the roof of the Marin County Civic Center (1957), San Raphael, California.
Photograph by the editor.

WRIGHT: I think we should begin the other way around. The bone structure of the face is there according to the pattern of the face. The face is not the result of the bone structure but the bone structure is the result of the pattern of the face. So structure can form just a pattern. Pattern is the idea of the form and it is so in nature all through as it is so in architecture. Does that clear that up? Not quite?

MACDONALD: Not quite. Would it be "idea" or "ideal"?

WRIGHT: Both. The ideal of the idea or the idea of the ideal. You know? It's all wound up together, the whole thing is like this you know? [*Editor's note:* Mr. Wright interlocks the fingers of both his hands and moves his hands and arms about.] And, like this.

MACDONALD: This thing with your arms like this reminds me of the term "continuity" and also "tenuity."

WRIGHT: That's what's missing in our architecture today—the ability to think through; to begin at the beginning and proceed according to nature to the end as it was desired to be or conceived to be. A continuity, a continuous sense of what is happening. That's the basis of all good design. Without continuity, without consistency in other words, the design is merely "harimaze" as the Japanese say "mixed-up"—no beginning, no end, no order, no repose.

MACDONALD: For the design that is to be integral should have . . .

WRIGHT: To be integral it must be what we were saying.

MACDONALD: There must be a constant flow . . .

WRIGHT: . . . of continuity throughout. Continuity to whatever happens to be in your

*Pattern in the roof, windows, and ornament of the
Marin County Civic Center. Photograph by the editor.*

*Pattern in the ornament, detail, and structure of the
Marin County Civic Center. Photograph by the editor.*

mind as a necessity at the time. But I think as a necessity in the mind of the designer right at the start from beginning to end has continuity in whatever he does. The consistency, in other words, of the performance to the end and aim in mind. And that's what's lacking mostly because the Japanese have a word that's very effective called "harimaze" and when a thing gets mixed-up and too much of it they always say "oh harimaze." So nearly most of all of the designing—take cars today, take everything we do, take the buildings we build—they're all what the Japanese would call "harimaze"— mixed up.

MACDONALD: Going back to the earlier statement about materials—how have materials, as you say they helped us to eliminate the box, how have they helped in this process of the integral design?

WRIGHT: I believe Paracelsus—I think it was Paracelsus—who declared that there is no form or object in nature that's not alive. To Paracelsus, a brick would be alive. To a good architect, a brick is alive in that same sense. To a good designer or a good artist what he looks at is alive. It has a life of its own and it is that life peculiar to that thing that interests the creative artist and the creative mind because a brick has individuality—it came there by fire—stone was made by centuries of deposits of various kinds. All these things come to be according to certain conditions and arrive at a certain expression of the nature of those things.

MACDONALD: So the function of the artist, with the example in relation to the brick, is to bring out the essence . . .

WRIGHT: . . . the beauty of that material to help the significance of the thing for man's spiritual

part of you to become a reality and become more beautiful because he understands and understood what it was that brick had to give, you see. So every creative artist is an interpreter. He must see deeper. He must see nature and he must prophesy it in what he does. That's the difference between a creative artist and a mere pretender.

MACDONALD: This is perhaps aside from the point but I remember in looking through your drawings on some of them you had written down at the bottom "unit system."

WRIGHT: Yes. I found very early, in fact in kindergarten days when my mother had me at a little kindergarten table ruled with lines lengthwise and crosswise, that was the unit system. Now it enables you to proceed from this to that—from generals to particulars—by way of an ordered scale which ensures consistent proportion in whatever you do. So you have that to do your designing upon the way the cardboard perforated with holes is to the board—the cloth is to the fabric—the wove is woven on the wall. So this system becomes a kind of wall on which to weave these designs in order that the consistency in proportion may be held together as a whole. Does that make that clear? The unit system called modular—the modular system?

MACDONALD: Yes, there will be one other question and this would be directed toward the whole idea of prefabrication.

WRIGHT: This is really necessary to prefabrication. The machine is a repetitive instrument and if it can go one, two, three, four, always the same in the same track that's its great virtue. So anything that reduces a process to a standard of repeated dots or repeated

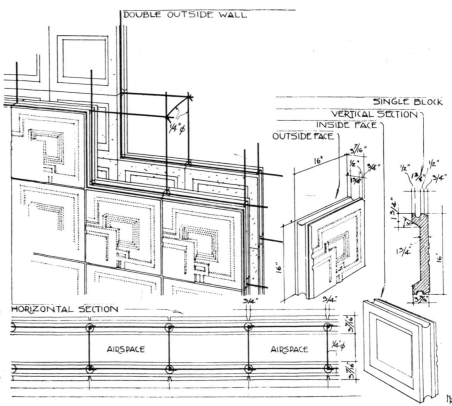

DOUBLE OUTSIDE WALL

SINGLE BLOCK

VERTICAL SECTION

INSIDE FACE

OUTSIDE FACE

HORIZONTAL SECTION

AIRSPACE　　　AIRSPACE

The Usonian automatic modular concrete block system of construction is built of shells made up of precast concrete blocks designed so that they can be made and set up at the site. Copyright © The Frank Lloyd Wright Foundation, 1954.

emphasis is mechanical and that mechanical order can be by the creative artist kept from becoming stale and dead by his imagination the way he is competent to use it. That's why the machine is a devastating instrument where human life is concerned unless the creative artist has it in his hand and is able to do this thing to save humanity from it or to save it for humanity—let's put it that way. Because without this creative imagination the machine is murderous and that I found out very early in architectural life and began to write about it. I wrote a little thesis on the subject called "The

Art and Craft of the Machine." It was the first word, I think, ever said for the use of the machine by an artist as an artist's tool. It was translated into seven languages now. But it's a great benefit and great aid to human life only if it's in the hands of the creative artist who can administer and protect humanity from its devastating results.

MACDONALD: I'd like to ask one more question in terms of this modular system and that is to ask how you get from a square or rectangular house to, as this David Wright house, a round, literally a round house?

Creativity and the Philosophy of Organic Architecture

The Arthur Munkwitz Duplex Apartments (1916) at Milwaukee, Wisconsin (demolished 1973) utilized the very early prefabricated construction system termed American System Ready-Cut developed by Frank Lloyd Wright for the Arthur L. Richards Company of Milwaukee. Photograph by the editor.

Forty years after Wright's design for prefabricated housing utilizing the American System Ready-Cut system, Wright introduced another system for prefabricated housing for the Marshall Erdman Company of Madison, Wisconsin in the design of the Walter Rudin Residence (1957) at Madison. Photograph by the editor.

Wright: "The universal thing is the natural thing."
Frank Lloyd Wright as he appeared on the WTTW-
Chicago television program Heritage *in late October*
1958. Photograph used by permission of WTTW-Chicago
Channel 11.

WRIGHT: Well, the square of course was brought in by the carpenter. There is no such thing as a square or rectangle in nature. They're all, more or less, in connection with curvature of the circle. Now the carpenter could only frame lumber together by the square—the engineer can only build a steel building with a square.

And all these habitual forms of construction are in the hands of habitual mechanics and architects and engineers who are all educated on the square. But, that was only a makeshift, it's not nature and it's not the thing that they might proceed to do with imagination, which would have a great deal more life in it.

Where were we?

MACDONALD: We've got time for just one more question and I'd like to ask you, as a final question for the program, have you any advice for the young architect?

WRIGHT: There is no source for his eirenicon to come, the only wellspring of inspiration for him—and that's nature. To study the nature of whatever it is he is interested in. What is the nature of this thumb? [*Editor's note*: Mr. Wright holds up his own thumb.] For instance. What's the nature of the nail on the thumb? Why? Why the thumb? What function has the thumb? I'm talking about interior nature. The character and purpose of whatever lives and why it lives. I'm not talking about the bees and the trees and the sound of water falling over the rocks. I'm talking about something that is continually there and present. In this thing for instance. [*Editor's note*: Mr. Wright holds up a draftman's triangle.] What's the nature of this? What's the nature of this steel T-square we have here? What makes it what it is? What is it?

MACDONALD: So the natural thing is the universal thing.

WRIGHT: That's right. The universal thing is the natural thing.

Creativity and the Philosophy of Organic Architecture

On Restaurant Architecture

An Organic Approach

. . . a man can't do much in architecture unless he gets his hands into the mud of which the bricks are made.

Frank Lloyd Wright's "On Restaurant Architecture" was originally published by *Food Service Magazine* in November 1958. The interview was the work of *Food Service Magazine* Associate Editor George Patrick. In this conversation with Patrick, Wright applies his philosophy of organic architecture to the design of a particular building type—the restaurant. Wright addresses the idea of profitability through design, his approach to the design of a restaurant, the decentralization of restaurants as well as the decentralization of other typically urban-related activities, and his design for a restaurant project planned for Yosemite Park but never executed.

The Conversation

PATRICK: Do you feel that too many people who want restaurants designed regard the profit motive as the most important one?

WRIGHT: Yes, of course, they do. If they were more aware of what it takes to make life sweet, lovely, and livable they wouldn't be the way they are.

It is a poetry question. There is no reason on earth why treating human beings shouldn't have grace and beauty, but we haven't given much attention to that. The idea is to get it and get satisfied. Good cooking—that I think we pay some attention to. But environment—well, who has it? Where is it? Where can you go in the

Reprinted by permission of *Food Service Marketing Magazine*, Philip L. Rane, Publisher, from "Frank Lloyd Wright on Restaurant Architecture: An Exclusive Interview," *Food Service Magazine*, Vol. 20, November 1958, pp. 17–21, 32.

United States today and feel that you are in a beautiful situation? Beautiful environment, beautiful furniture, beautiful service, with the accent on beauty.

Now that would redeem the restaurant and I expect to do one for William Zeckendorf in New York on the North Side. He wants it to be the finest restaurant in the world. We will call it The Zeckendorf. There we will make an attempt ourselves to show what beauty could come into a restaurant.

You know, after you have had enough of the degradation you begin to wonder if that is necessary and why it is as it is. Next you begin to think why? Then you begin to wonder if you know and pretty soon you are on the way to a plan.

PATRICK: Sir, whether planning a restaurant or anything else does an architect have the same approach to every problem?

WRIGHT: Every problem. It is not different. A man called me up at midnight from San Francisco and wanted to build a mortuary. He said, "I want the biggest architect in the world to do it for me and that is you. Have you ever built a mortuary?" And I said, "No, and I think that is my best qualification." Then I went through to get the technique of the thing so I could build a good mortuary.

Well, architecture is like that—a man can't do much in architecture unless he gets his hands into the mud of which the bricks are made. As old Charley Curtis used to say to my boys here, "There is no use for you trying to build a wall unless you get the feel of the rock in your hands." Now that is the architecture. That is everything else too.

PATRICK: You are a great exponent of decentralization. In view of the rise of interurbia, of the tremendous metropolitan traffic and

Frank Lloyd Wright's rendering of The Spring Green Restaurant (1953), Spring Green, Wisconsin as viewed from the Wisconsin River. Drawing courtesy of The Spring Green Restaurant. Copyright © The Frank Lloyd Wright Foundation, 1984.

106

*The roofed open air terrace at The Spring Green
Restaurant. Photograph courtesy of The Spring Green
Restaurant.*

107

108

A view at dusk of the entrance area from the parking lot of The Spring Green Restaurant. Photograph courtesy of The Spring Green Restaurant.

parking problems, et cetera, do you agree that the opportunities for restaurants are outside of large cities? Within 50 or 60 miles driving distance?

WRIGHT: Yes, to this I agree. We are on the way to decentralization of the city. And we are on the way because we have been forced there. The city is decentralizing itself. If the architects aren't able to accomplish what is inevitable in a law of change then nature herself will take care of it and always has.

Today the city has crowded out merchandising and all its trucking, delivering and all that, to the outside. It has also crowded out the factories with its employees and their families representing millions. The only ones that remain in the city are the clerks who occupy these red prison towers and have to be there to work with their little tap-tapping machines.

A big city such as New York is a good place to sell fish, but there are no fish in its streams you see. The fish are shipped in. And so it will be more and more as the city grows toward its ultimate twentieth-century aspect, which will arrive about twenty-five years from now. You will begin to see it then. Up to that time you won't see it much. You will see the countryside become more and more the resort of the merchant and the factory and the restaurants.

PATRICK: Do you think the same thing might happen in the suburbs eventually?

WRIGHT: Yes, the suburbs are a necessary evil and we must put up with them and with this thronging to and fro. The pattern is derived originally from the London Dormitory Town. We never got this from beauty of the English architecture. We didn't get anything but the outskirts that were already compressed and we

109

The main dining room of The Spring Green Restaurant during the daytime. The long horizontal band of windows on the left provide daylighting of the dining area as well as a view of the Wisconsin River. Photograph courtesy of The Spring Green Restaurant.

The main dining room of The Spring Green Restaurant in the evening, lit with indirect lighting. Persimmon-colored carpeting and matching chairs are the basic color of the interior. All chairs and tables are three inches lower than typical standard furnishings. Walls are buff colored native limestone or natural red oak paneling. The main dining room seats 100 persons and leads into two private dining rooms that accommodate another 75 persons. Photograph courtesy of The Spring Green Restaurant.

The cocktail lounge of The Spring Green Restaurant. Guests seated at the sunken bar on the right can enjoy a magnificent view of the Wisconsin River. Doors at the right opened into a large deck for summertime use. In 1968 these doors were removed and the cocktail lounge was extended another forty feet in order to add a dance floor. Photograph courtesy of The Spring Green Restaurant.

The cocktail lounge of The Spring Green Restaurant. A massive natural fireplace constructed of buff-colored native limestone dominates one wall of the lounge. A sunken bar on the left affords patrons a view of the Wisconsin River. Photograph courtesy of The Spring Green Restaurant.

compressed them still more. We made the thing worse instead of better.

In other words, we have given no constructive architectural thought to the problem at all. Now this is a new thing all through. Modern architecture is not the right word for this architecture. It is the new architecture. What is this life we live? It is a new life, isn't it? Didn't the Declaration of Independence put it into practical effect and proclaim the sovereignty of the individual? That's new. It needs an architecture. Organic architecture is it.

PATRICK: Organic architecture, then, is closely bound up with the trend to decentralize?

WRIGHT: Of course. Organic architecture comes out of Nature. I think we made a great mistake when we became industrialized at the expense of the agronomy. We killed off the agrarianism of the South, and now we have got the industrialization of the North and that's all we've got.

Agrarianism has to come back into this picture. The country, the grass, the green, the living ground, and the living people on the ground— all have to come back. That's why the cities are destroying themselves.

This talk of "overcrowding" makes me sick. It is silly. Have you ever gone across the country? Well, if you would take every family in the United States and put them down in Texas you wouldn't fill Texas. You could stand all the people in the world up on the island of Bermuda if it came to that so I don't know where all this talk of overcrowding comes from.

Ground, why my goodness, look at it. All you have to do is keep your eyes open when you travel and go from place to place. From hot spot to hot spot to hot spot. Well, the spots are getting too hot. Why? It is getting "overcrowded." That doesn't mean the earth is overcrowded. It only means that the present facilities and the ways of living called cities are out of date.

PATRICK: Let me pose a hypothetical problem. It is the architect's duty . . .

WRIGHT: . . . and privilege.

PATRICK: . . . and privilege to be aware of this?

WRIGHT: To be not only aware of it, but because he is aware of it, to be dedicated to it as a job.

PATRICK: Granted. Suppose then we have a restaurateur who has a little property in Chicago's Loop and on that little piece of property he wants a restaurant designed that will make money. Now where does he go for an architect?

WRIGHT: Well, if that's his chief motive there is no use talking to him. He's got to believe in his art. That is the way to make money. Give the people something better and more beautiful than they have ever seen or had.

PATRICK: This is possible even on a corner in Chicago's Loop?

WRIGHT: It doesn't matter where it is, what matters is the quality of thought you put into it. If there is room enough of course. You can't do it on top of a barrel. You've got to have space and you must have something in the way of environment. Assuming you have these, the only place to go for anything to be built is to an accomplished architect.

PATRICK: What do you think of European restaurants in comparison to those in America— architecturally?

Creativity and the Philosophy of Organic Architecture

Wright: "I electrified the Imperial Hotel ... for cooking ... and I also used electricity for the first time for heating." View of the main entrance lobby wing of the Imperial Hotel (1915) as reconstructed at the Museum Meiji Mura near Nagoya, Japan (1976). Photograph by Juro Kikuchi.

WRIGHT: Some sporadic efforts in bringing beauty into the realm of dining and wining can be found in our country but not to the degree that this has been accomplished in Europe—and especially in France where the French restaurant is the hallmark of French character.

But we might have a character and beauty of our own in our eating habits and the conviviality we practice. This seems to be gaining ground in certain sections but it is yet far behind its possibilities. Good design seems to be either besides the mark or begrudged in this realm of endeavor which remains connected to the lower elements of our civilization.

Most of the well-known restaurants

architecturally that have achieved distinction are Parisian. In all great cities there are several that have achieved distinction but really I can think of nowhere outside Paris where the atmosphere of cultivated dining for its own sake has been successfully developed as beautiful or at least charming.

PATRICK: As an architect, how do you feel about electricity?

WRIGHT: I electrified the Imperial Hotel in Tokyo for cooking. The first one in the world. That was 1919 and I also used electricity for the first time for heating in that building. I made light integral then and I made heat integral and the hotel cooked with electricity: 1919.

I had, already, in the Larkin Building in Buffalo, put in air conditioning because the building was down on the railroad tracks and the gas from the engines and all that was around it all day long. So the Larkin Building was the first air-conditioned building in the world.

You know, electricity is noiseless. The curse that has descended on American life is the roar and the scream of machinery on the road, wherever you are. You can't get away from it. Electricity doesn't contribute to that. Electricity is quiet and effective. Mrs. Wright and I were given, by Hal Price for whom I built this combination residence and office building [the Price Tower in Bartlesville, Oklahoma], a little electric cart. They use them on the golf course. We have been riding all over this place this summer and having a fine time—and no noise!

PATRICK: When you work with a kitchen in your drawings do you specify electric equipment?

WRIGHT: I think we specify all kinds of equipment according to the desire of the owner.

114

Wright: "... the Larkin Building was the first air-conditioned building in the world." View of the interior work hall of the Larkin Company Administration Building (1903) at Buffalo, New York (demolished 1949–1950). Photograph from Frank Lloyd Wright, Frank Lloyd Wright: Ausgeführte Bauten (Berlin: Ernst Wasmuth, 1911).

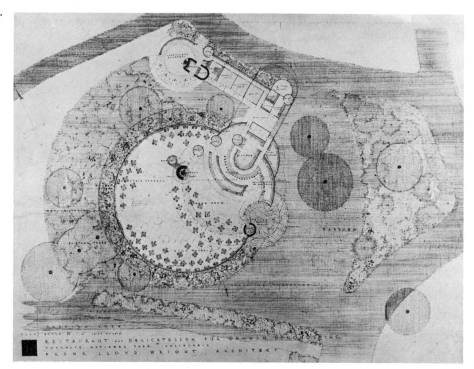

The plan of the Restaurant for Yosemite Project (1953), Yosemite National Park, California. Copyright © The Frank Lloyd Wright Foundation, 1968.

Wright: "... a little gem I hope to see built in the Yosemite." Elevation of the Restaurant for Yosemite Project. Copyright © The Frank Lloyd Wright Foundation, 1968.

They usually have some preference but if they have none then we have a preference for the cleanliness and efficiency of electricity.

PATRICK: Has the government commissioned a restaurant for Yosemite Park?

WRIGHT: Oh no, not that I know of. I drew up this restaurant for Donahoe, who wanted it built, but the government didn't like it. They said people went to the park to see the park, and not a restaurant. It is a lovely thing. It would make dining in a place like Yosemite an experience you wouldn't forget and it is not necessarily expensive—nothing about it is expensive. You can see the architectural features. It's a great simplicity.

PATRICK: I notice the series of circles for centralization. Do you do that in all your work?

WRIGHT: By no means. The carpenter invented the square and we have to use it once in a while. There is nothing in nature that is square. The carpenter doesn't know how to do anything but the square. If you hand him a plan that is hexagon he is confused and the hexagon is on the way to the circle. Square, hexagon, circle, and then especially the triangle—all those forms are architectural. These things all come out of nature that I do.

This is a little gem I hope to see built in the Yosemite because it is the Yosemite. You see, it is in the spirit of the Yosemite and people going into the beautiful atmosphere—extraordinary in every way—would find that this building "belonged." The government could only see that it would attract people's attention from the scenery. Well, so what?

PATRICK: Are you going to try this again?

WRIGHT: Oh, I'm going to build it, sure.

PATRICK: Will you go to the next administration with the plans?

WRIGHT: No, I have never in my life gone to anybody for a job. I have never turned my hand that much to ask a friend to say a word for me for a job and yet I survive. So I know it can be done. I know you don't have to shenanigan and monkey around to succeed in this country. And that it is still open.

PATRICK: Is there anything else that you would care to add?

WRIGHT: Only that architecture is the blind spot of the American people. We've got to get form, we've got to conceive the thing, as new form, an appropriate form, a life-giving form and we haven't got so much material in this country now by way of education as Thomas Jefferson thought we would have. We haven't had any of the old stock, the old staunch vision and integrity that used to be ours when we were young. Now I guess we are too successful. We haven't "succeeded" now.

This "form" is going to come from little outlying outposts, little centers of thought and feeling, that aren't afraid and that won't welsh and that will stay on the job. Now, there are lots of them. I am only one of a good many.

PATRICK: And these people are the poets?

WRIGHT: Sure. If you have the thing strong enough and deep enough, in other words, if you love it enough you will come through. That is the message I have for the young architect. I fought mine out, I didn't sell out nor will I sell out and you don't have to. That's the best I can leave the young architects of my country. Tell them you don't have to sell out.

Creativity and the Philosophy of Organic Architecture

PART THREE

Frank Lloyd Wright on the City

7 Broadacre City

...this model of the modern city of democracy is an attack upon the cultural lag of our society.

In January 1951 Frank Lloyd Wright previewed his "Sixty Years of Living Architecure" exhibition at Gimbel Brothers in Philadelphia. A model and drawings of Wright's Broadacre City were included in this exhibition. The following is the text of a recorded conversation between Wright and Oskar Stonorov (the coordinator of the exhibition and a Philadelphia-based architect) which accompanied both the Broadacre City model and photographs in this exhibition. In this ten-minute conversation with Stonorov, Wright describes his philosophy behind Broadacre City. An edited and revised text of this particular conversation was published privately for the exhibition and appeared as Palazzo Strozzi's (Firenze, Italy) *Mostra di Frank Lloyd Wright; dialogo: "Broadacre City"* (Studio Italiano di Storia dell'arte, May 15, 1951. As previewed at Gimbel Brothers, Philadelphia, Pennsylvania, January, 1951).

The Conversation

STONOROV: Mr. Wright, after wandering through your earlier buildings, people now have reached this model of the landscape of a city which you have called Broadacre City; an example of the free planning for Usonians as Samuel Butler suggested we of the United States

---

This heretofore unpublished conversation is reproduced in its entirety by permission of Mrs. Oskar Stonorov. Sound recording of the conversation furnished to the editor courtesy of the Oskar Stonorov Papers Collection of the Archive of Contemporary History at the University of Wyoming.

Taliesin Fellowship apprentices at work on the early Broadacre City Project (1934) model at Wright's temporary headquarters, La Hacienda, in Arizona. Photograph courtesy of the State Historical Society of Wisconsin.

call ourselves and you have adopted that name. Just what is the meaning of this great model of Broadacre City? For one thing, people will want to know why you put skyscrapers next to cottages on acre lots, Mr. Wright.

WRIGHT: Well, this model of the modern city of democracy is an attack upon the cultural lag of our society. The model attempts to show how more humane use of our vast leverage, the machine, could now be used to better advantage in order to free the citizen by way of his own architecture. If the machine was to be put in its proper place, now its place is the hand of the creative architect, or let us say architecture creative. To me, democracy can arrive no other way. When we realize that the right buildings for the right people in the right places will naturally form a harmonious relationship, each building, though different totally, complementary to the other—that is what you see here—then I see no reason why the habituated dweller in cities, now living upon a perch, should not come to direct association with those who live on the ground and for the ground until they too have learned to love the ground themselves for itself. The individual home on its acre, or more, together with the utility buildings of everyday American life, if made *organic,* all form a harmonious whole according to nature—either human nature or the nature of all outdoors. That's what I've aimed at here. I believe the only place for a skyscraper is in the country in its own park.

Frank Lloyd Wright on the City

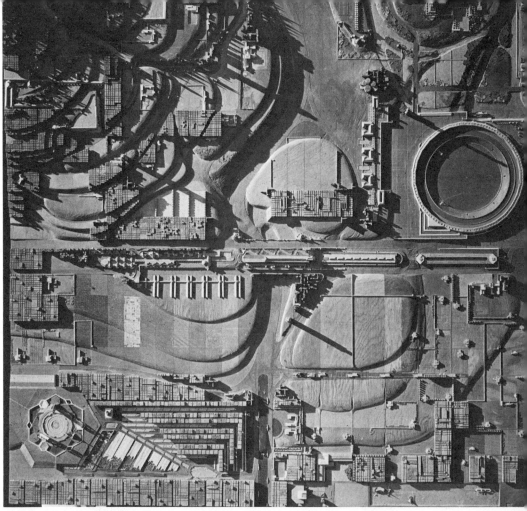

An early model of a portion of Wright's Broadacre City Project (1934). This photograph was taken at La Hacienda before the construction of Taliesin West. Photograph courtesy of the State Historical Society of Wisconsin.

Oblique view of the model of the Broadacre City Project (1934). Photograph courtesy of the Frank Lloyd Wright Memorial Foundation.

STONOROV: Mr. Wright, I would like you to make still clearer what the meaning of Broadacre City is. Am I right to assume that Broadacre City means the abolition of all artificial distinction between city, suburb, and country?

WRIGHT: Yes, you're right. This Broadacre City model means just that. It shows, too, how to end the now senseless back and forth haul. The now senseless travel to and fro of our present wasteful and wasting situation. Waste of time and life is here, in Broadacre City, ended in favor of a better use of life to understand ourselves and to cultivate leisure in the enjoyment of our own nature. That is the modern opportunity given to us by the machine and must be the aim of culture in our democracy if we ever reach that state as *organic*.

STONOROV: I take it then, Mr. Wright, that the appropriate arrangement on the land of all human activities of the twenty-four hour day, in the sense of Broadacre City, is organic planning. What, then, Mr. Wright, does the word "organic" mean in architecture itself?

WRIGHT: Well, call *organic* architecture a natural architecture. It means building for and with the individual as distinguished from the pseudo-classic order of American schools today, mainly derived from survivals of ancient military and monarchic orders. Or that later attempt at elimination and classification now grafted upon organic architecture called the "International Style" by ambitious provincials. Or, as distinguished from any personal preconceived pertinent, or impertinent, formula for mere appearance.

Organic architecture is informal architecture, architecture in the reflex, architecture seeking to serve man rather than to become, or be becoming to, those forces now trying so hard to rule over him. Here is one good reason why we may say organic architecture is the architecture of democracy.

Now, let us believe that any true concept of organic architecture, therefore of style, is the expression of character. There can then be no longer any question of the many of any "styles." But essential style must be in and of all building provided only that style be naturally achieved from within the nature of the building problem itself and always found within the very means by which the building is built. Character is the expression of principle at work from within. And, in this interior sense of Broadacre City is the free city of democracy and would inevitably arrive at style. The great city of democracy will have great style all the while as something more spontaneous and natural than the academies have yet dared preach. Nothing in the free city would be merely something exterior, forced, either in its structure or upon its people, by classic or exterior disciple. It could never be ruled by authoritarian classification and establishment. Architecture and agrarian acreage will always be seen together as landscape, as has the best architecture of the world been seen. That is to say, the great architecture which arose within the lifetime of the civilizations which they did actually express.

Now, if as a people we were ever really to understand the eternal principles of our own human nature, a basic necessary in our way of education, and we were to learn to use our machines and vast stores of material to good advantage according to a faithful sense of their fitness to humane purpose, we should—yes, inevitably we *would*—arrive at new forms and a

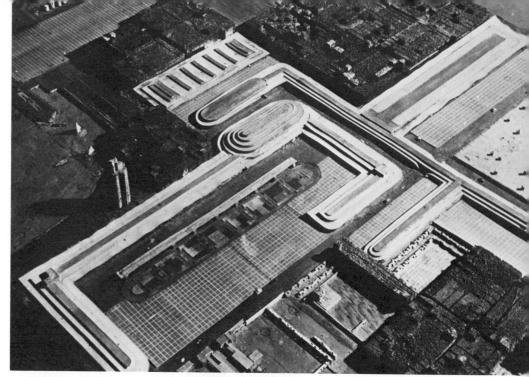

Detail of the model of the Broadacre City Project (1934) showing a roadside market. Textured block masses indicate forest areas held in trust for future generations. Treecrops to be shared by the community. Land thus reserved to go into cultivation as required by population growth. Photograph courtesy of the Frank Lloyd Wright Memorial Foundation.

Detail of the model of the Broadacre City Project (1934) showing a stadium and circus for the county fair and other pageantry. Motel for transients seen in the background. Civic center to the upper left. Sanitarium to the right. Pole announcing festivals. Photograph courtesy of the Frank Lloyd Wright Memorial Foundation.

Detail of the model of the Broadacre City Project (1934) showing a neighborhood lake and related park (foreground), civic center at the county seat showing offices across the lake, and small industries and apartments (background). Photograph courtesy of the Frank Lloyd Wright Memorial Foundation.

life modern that has true style. And perhaps, though we need not bother much about that, arrive at what, looked back upon in distance of time, might be seen as the free Usonian Style of the twentieth century but if that should ever come to pass, it could not come by miscalculated intention. It would come by honest production and long-continued experiment on our part as individuals. Style is a desirable circumstance always as we may now see. However, a "style" is always the death of "style".

Because it is chiefly concerned with integrity of structure, we may honestly say that organic architecture first grasped the integrity of this modern demand for a new and higher spiritual order of things than was accepted by authoritarians as "classic." I believe that only the mind imbued with this deeper sense of structure can perceive this fine integrity as a fundamental social necessity, demanding and creating more livable and gracious human simplicities. Perceiving anew those simples [*sic*] which were ever the necessity to a good life. But, not so to such academic substitutes for culture as now bear the authorized hallmark of these United States. War would be unthinkable to the people of Broadacre City. The black and white bipartisanship would give way to more color.

Now, while the new, swollen material means of today increasingly dam the lifeblood and emasculate the manhood of this nation, we must think of all this and keep on thinking. But if the same mechanical means now so used were used now with more intelligent self-interest to increase spaciousness, graciousness, and happiness of human living on earth; if intelligently so used to back up the enlarged sense and appropriate uses of space in our modern life that are good for organic architecture; they would automatically enable the free city to be realized. If by appropriate scientific use of the new space scale—it is human being—if used as a time scale you can see the extended highway as the horizontal line of Usonian freedom expanding consistently everywhere. Then you will see something of the modern Usonian city that is approaching you here in Broadacre City whether you like it or not.

Then if you look and can see the design of the farm itself, little or big, in its true relation to adjoining farms and to you; if you see the sizes

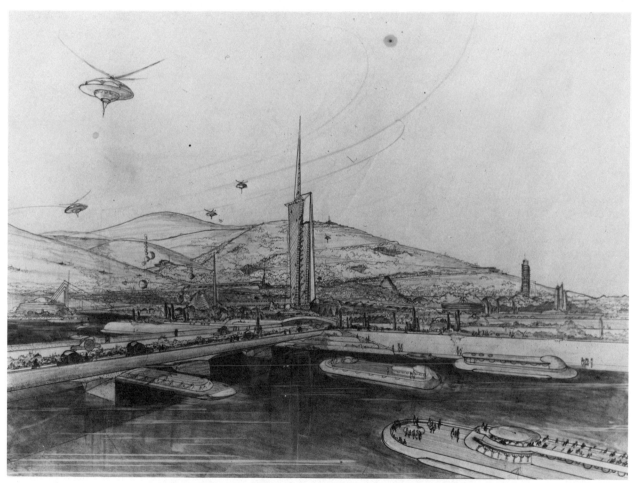

A view of the Broadacre City Project (1934–1958) showing a potpourri of Frank Lloyd Wright–designed buildings and projects including (from left to right) the first and second Pittsburgh Community Center Projects, the Huntington Hartford Country Club Project, the Beth Sholom Synagogue, the Marin County Civic Center, the Rogers Lacy Hotel Project, the Sugar Loaf Mountain Automobile Objective and Planetarium Project, the Self-Service Garage Project, the Golden Beacon Skyscraper Project, the Butterfly Bridge Project, and atomic-powered barges in the foreground. Copyright © The Frank Lloyd Wright Foundation, 1962.

An aerial view of the Broadacre City Project (1934–1958) showing a close-up of one of Frank Lloyd Wright's proposed air machines and buildings placed within a agricultural and open-space setting. An automatic overpass for the automobile transportation network of roads enables continuous uninterrupted traffic flow in four different directions. Copyright © The Frank Lloyd Wright Foundation, 1958.

A ground view of the civic center of the Broadacre City Project (1934–1958) showing vertical-bodied automobiles and helicopter taxicabs in flight. Street lights can be seen low and recessed into the curb and gutter of the roadway and are placed alternately opposite to each other on both sides of the pavement. The tower in the background (left) consists of combined apartment dwellings and commercial offices. Copyright © The Frank Lloyd Wright Foundation, 1962.

and shapes of fields all well laid out in good proportion each to each and to one and all, and can see the whole man-built occupation adapted to natural contours, tillage itself becoming a charming feature of the landscape; hedgeways, ravines, and waterways themselves becoming boundaries; if you can see all this completely rhythmic in relation to well considered, good buildings; see them all related to well-placed roads; if you can see horizontal farming, contour plowing, properly applied to crops, pastures, and animals, and all such well related to the people; if you can see these multifarious parts all contributing to a great dramatic whole in which you sense the repose of contentment and the exuberance of plenty— aesthetic, truly in the overall view from where you happen to stand—well, then you are getting a glimpse of the agrarian loving life of this *organically* planned Usonian city of our future as a democracy. No longer merely a republic. We might then boast of the culture of this nation. Our forefathers had some right and some reason to expect this culture of what they were then pleased to call—*Democracy*.

The City versus Decentralization

I think it doesn't matter very much what our realtors think any more. We should have taken them all out and shot them at sunrise years ago when the city began to go downhill.

This is an excerpt from an extemporaneous discussion broadcast by the Mutual Radio Network on February 29, 1944 as part of *The American Forum of the Air* radio program from Washington, D.C. In addition to Frank Lloyd Wright, the following people participated in this panel discussion, which quickly centered around Wright and his ideas on city planning and the city in general: Mrs. Samuel Rosenman, Chairman, National Committee on Housing; Herbert A. Nelson, Executive Vice-President, National Association of Real Estate Boards; and Mayor John J. McDonough of St. Paul, Minnesota.

The Conversation

GRANIK: Mayor McDonough, what incentive have our cities to offer suburbanites to move back into the city?

MCDONOUGH: Should not that question be: What incentive is there to keep suburbanites in the cities rather than not to have them move out of the cities? I think that we have got to prevent the better sections of the city from becoming blighted and from having the blighted area approach the better sections of the city . . .

NELSON: Mr. Mayor, what is your thought about rebuilding these areas with public housing? Do you think that that is a good thing to do?

ROSENMAN: That is a little outside the subject, Mr. Nelson. We are really talking about: Shall we rebuild the cities or shall the people be siphoned off into the hinterlands of the nation? I'd like to find out what Mr. Wright feels about that.

WRIGHT: A realtor without a financial plan would be like a hen incapable of laying eggs.

NELSON: Even architects need money.

WRIGHT: They always need money and never get it and I am not sure that it is worth having anyhow, and certainly I didn't come here from way out in the heart of this nation onto this desert strip to talk about money . . .

MCDONOUGH: How do you propose to finance the services that must be given to these people who move outside?

WRIGHT: I think that is a subordinate question and should be considered after we have got down to principles and proceeded from generals to particulars . . .

MCDONOUGH: Do you propose to put the utilities in first and have them build after?

WRIGHT: I propose to get the proper idea in the right place.

ROSENMAN: What is the proper idea?

WRIGHT: Well, I think the idea is this. The city is already an outmoded institution. Obsolescence has been the enemy of our form of civilization and we have not taken care of it as we should.

I think after this war is over and we are going to have not one thing that is of any utilitarian value, nothing really valuable. It is all going out overnight, and so our cities have gradually been going out of their own accord. They have no attention; they were never planned in the first place, and they have no planning now that is intelligent. The thing goes entirely to the beginning.

ROSENMAN: Don't you think that there are certain essentials in a city that are very costly to

Frank Lloyd Wright in December 1938. Photograph courtesy of The Capital Times, *Madison, Wisconsin.*

supply outside of the city? Just take one thing, a water supply. A water supply is a very precious thing, a very expensive thing to create. Our major cities all have adequate water supply. If you are going to create a new city you have to give it to them. You take your sewerage—it is all within the city.

WRIGHT: All details, Mrs. Rosenman.

ROSENMAN: But those are expensive equipment. If you could rebuild a new city using your old and present community facilities, couldn't you do a valuable job?

WRIGHT: What is a city?

ROSENMAN: Well, a city is a cultural center.

WRIGHT: The buildings, the streets, the water system, the sewer system? I think not. The people are the city; the people who live in the city are the city.

ROSENMAN: But the people work in the city.

WRIGHT: Unfortunately they do because they have no choice.

ROSENMAN: Well, aren't most of the industries placed within a city?

WRIGHT: Unfortunately they are but they needn't be now.

MCDONOUGH: Don't they have to have the services that the city gives?

WRIGHT: No longer.

MCDONOUGH: Why?

WRIGHT: I have built houses for people with a little septic tank and with a little Kohler plant out on a little subsistence farm and they are doing very well, thank you, and are very happy and they require nothing that the city has.

ROSENMAN: Where do they work?

WRIGHT: They have their radio, they have their schools, they have their hospitals, they have their radio and they are listening now. It is hard to believe it but I guess they are listening. And they are quite happy and I think that they have the best of it and I believe the city itself recognizes the fact. I think it doesn't matter very much what our realtors think any more. We should have taken them all out and shot them at sunrise years ago when the city began to go downhill.

ROSENMAN: Someone sells property out in the country too, so we have to be careful not to shoot them someday.

WRIGHT: It is their trick to find out where the crowd is headed, run out in front of the crowd, beat them to it, buy up the ground and then divide it up into little, small pieces of pie and sell it to them and start the inequity all over again. It is their specialty.

ROSENMAN: If we could keep from cutting the city into new slices of pie, if we had some means of accumulating the land in blighted areas of the city and reparceling it the way people really want to live and bringing some of the things that you have in the country to the city, don't you think that cities would be a proper center?

WRIGHT: I think that idea would work both ways. I think it should be done—bring the country to the city and take the city to the country—and I believe there is the city of the future. I think the city of the future is no longer a concentration. I think it is a decentralization and an integration along *organic* lines. It is our misfortune that we have never allowed ourselves to learn anything of architecture. The solution of the present-day problems is all architectural, it is all architectural.

NELSON: Oh, Mr. Wright, there has to be land planning too, now. Don't you think it is a good thing to rebuild cities by well-planned neighborhoods so that you can have the advantages of a real civilized life?

WRIGHT: Mr. Nelson, I ask you, what do you think architecture is?

NELSON: I don't think it is land planning.

WRIGHT: I think it is. I think architecture is the science of structure and the structure of whatever is, whether it is music, whether it is sculpture or painting or building or city planning or statesmanship. If we had the right kind of an architect we would have a statesman now. That is what is lacking in our present scene.

MCDONOUGH: Mr. Wright, just outside of our city is a suburban development; they have septic tanks and things like that out there and the state health department has now found it a health menace and they have demanded that they put in an effective sewage disposal system.

WRIGHT: That is simply stacking the cards against the man who is trying to be independent and it goes all down the line. I dare say if we would try to blow up this bottleneck that is our financial system, the banking system would soon crack down on us too for the same reason.

MCDONOUGH: What advantages are just outside of the city limits that aren't inside the city limits?

WRIGHT: There is very little advantage in the suburbs. The suburbs is only a moving outward toward the thing that is inevitable now, that is really modern. I don't see why you can't all see that the city is an antique, fit for collectors.

ROSENMAN: It is an antique as it is today but I think there are certain things within a city that keep people there and that the city will always be, and therefore instead of saying that everyone will want to move out to the country and have his own septic tank, or maybe two septic tanks to every house . . .

WRIGHT: The septic tank seems to have made a hit.

ROSENMAN: There will be a lot of people who will always want to live in the city. I know that every city has enough land within it so that if it were properly used, people would not have to be herded together. We have in every city of this country a lot of shabby land that pays no taxes and that is of no value to anyone. If the shack lands and if the dump lands were all counted in . . .

WRIGHT: (interposing) Mrs. Rosenman, have you ever heard of the new space scale?

ROSENMAN: The new space scale?

WRIGHT: The new space scale.

ROSENMAN: I don't think I have.

WRIGHT: The change that has come into modern life by way of the car, by way of mobilization, by way of the telephone, the telegraph, and all these things which have made ten miles as one mile used to be.

ROSENMAN: Well, that is true, but it still doesn't answer the need of the family that has to get two or three children to school in the morning, that has to get the husband to work and maybe the wife to work. They like to have a spacious life but they like to have it within a stone's throw of work and a school and I think they are entitled to have all that.

WRIGHT: Why should all this be concentrated in the city any longer? Is there a good reason for it?

The City versus Decentralization

MCDONOUGH: Yes.

WRIGHT: What is is?

MCDONOUGH: People can't afford to live out in the country.

WRIGHT: That is the point. Subsidize transportation and enable those people to go where they should go and not try to play benefactor and build for them and keep them where they are.

NELSON: You *do* have a financial plan.

WRIGHT: You dangle employment in the faces of these people. Why? They are all wage slaves. They have no choice but to go to the city to work now. They can't get their birthright, which is the ground. They can't go out there because they are employed. Is employment enough?

NELSON: You want us all to be farmers?

WRIGHT: Yes, I want us all to be part farmers; I want us to know something of farming. I would like to have us shake the dust of all this urbanism from our souls, get a little fresh air, go out and hear the birds sing and sit on the grass occasionally. I think it would be good for us all.

ROSENMAN: Don't you think that there are certain cultural things around a city? Even the town of old within a rural setting had certain social needs, people getting together. Now, some of us like to be off by ourselves but others of us like to be within a stone's throw of a neighbor where we can go in and chat and where our children can play. I really feel that the city as a meeting place and a living place is here to stay, except that those of us who want space and safety and good schools for our children are moving out because the city isn't meeting our needs; but if you gave us a choice of living in a city where we have spaciousness I think we would prefer to live in the city.

WRIGHT: But that would not prove that it was right, that wouldn't prove that it was intelligent; it might prove that it was merely unfortunate and that we had a choice of evils, which is the thing that has been presented to us now all down the line. It is apparent that we never had a choice of anything except one evil or another evil. It never occurs to us that possibly all that might change if the circumstances changed, if the conditions were otherwise, and if we do not recognize it, well, the force of overproduction itself, this imposition from above, this weight of production presuming upon consumption, this maldistribution, which is a disease—it is all going downhill and the city itself recognizes it.

NELSON: Mr. Wright, I would like to ask Mrs. Rosenman a question. She has studied city planning. Don't you think, Mrs. Rosenman, that we can make much better use of the land resources we have now in our cities?

ROSENMAN: I think so.

NELSON: About a quarter or a fifth of our privately owned land is vacant in most communities.

ROSENMAN: That is the point I was trying to make, that if we used our land properly we could bring some amenities of the country into the city and enjoy living in the city. I just can't believe that our factories within the cities and our commercial institutions are going to be scrapped. I think they are going to go on and so long as they are there people will want to live near them.

WRIGHT: I don't say they are going to be scrapped. I say they are going into the country, too. I say the city is no place for a factory if people have to live around it while they are working and there's no reason now why it should ever be in the city. It is so much better off in the country.

ROSENMAN: If a factory follows you to the country you are going to create the same situation around the factory in the country.

WRIGHT: If the factories as we have them now follow us to the country they will curse us, yes, as they curse us now, but there is no reason why that factory should ever go to the country, there is no reason why any building that we have in the city today should ever go to the country because it would be a disgrace and a stench there.

MCDONOUGH: I take it that three of us here want to preserve the cities. Mr. Wright wants to abandon the cities and move them into the country.

WRIGHT: I don't want to abandon the cities; I want the city to develop into something that is part country and part city, neither one nor the other.

MCDONOUGH: Are you in favor of rehabilitating the city?

WRIGHT: I don't know what you mean by rehabilitating.

MCDONOUGH: Rebuilding the blighted areas and making them more attractive.

WRIGHT: I believe in taking all the blighted areas and planting grass there. I think that the only salvation that any city in this nation has, looking twenty-five or ten or fifteen years ahead, even, is to plant grass over two-thirds of the area of the city, to preserve the buildings that were interesting and valuable—I don't know where you would find them; I haven't seen many.

NELSON: Didn't you build some?

WRIGHT: I have built a few but it wouldn't be proper for me to refer to them in this connection.

The Duel of the Titans

A Conversation with William Zeckendorf

Well how can you site plan in a place like New York City?

The following is a moderated, somewhat heated, conversation between Frank Lloyd Wright and real estate developer—magnate William Zeckendorf which was produced by the National Broadcasting Company for *The American Forum of the Air* television program. The program was originally broadcast by WRCA-TV in Washington, D.C. on April 22, 1956. Wright and Zeckendorf were later to meet in other such "debates" as well as to have an architect–client relationship on one of Zeckendorf's building projects—a restaurant for New York City; however, this project was never constructed.

In later years Zeckendorf wrote of his relationship with Wright in *The Autobiography of William Zeckendorf* (New York: Holt, Rinehart and Winston, 1970, pp. 241–242) and Zeckendorf quipped:

Wright I met as a supposed antagonist on a TV discussion panel where I (the builder) was supposed to be his meat. All I knew about Wright was that I liked his work. When my aides compiled a dossier of his speeches and writings, I discovered the man made profound good sense. As a result, during the TV show we ... had a great time. After the program, in order to further admire each other and ourselves, we went out to my place ... From then on we had an undying friendship.

This heretofore unpublished conversation is reproduced in its entirety from National Broadcasting Company (NBC) Broadcast *The American Forum of the Air* dated April 22, 1956 with permission of the National Broadcasting Company.

The Conversation

MODERATOR: Most of us live in cities, centers of commerce, industry, communications. Concrete and steel skylines mark our cities from coast to coast. But what of the future of American cities? How long will they last?

There are some who envision new cities, decentralized cities, away from the metropolitan areas growing in the nation's countryside where skyscrapers will stand as trees that escaped the crowded forest. Such a man is the creator of the tower standing in the rolling land of Oklahoma—Frank Lloyd Wright.

For more than half a century this country's most controversial and influential architect. From whose hand have come nearly 800 designs stimulating the minds of men throughout the world. Creating both disciples and critics wherever his work is seen.

And, there are those who foresee the continued growth and strength of today's great cities. Men who plan for even further concentration of the forces that give our present cities their vitality. Making changes where necessary. Redeveloping whole areas to ensure the better functioning of the city. Such a man is William Zeckendorf, president of Webb and Knapp, Incorporated with holdings of more than a quarter billion dollars in property, whose projects alter the face of the American cities from the land he purchased for the United Nations site in New York City westward to the Mile-High Center that dominates the skyline of Denver, Colorado.

Well gentlemen, it's a pleasure to have you here to talk about the future of the American city and may I start with that very question? I'd like, if I could, to have an answer from both of you. In your opinion, what is the future for American cities and what about New York? Such as New York? Mr. Wright, how do you feel about it?

WRIGHT: I've been pretty freely expressing

Frank Lloyd Wright greets guests at Taliesin during his birthday party on June 8, 1956 about six weeks after his meeting with William Zeckendorf. Photograph by Richard Vesey, courtesy of the State Historical Society of Wisconsin.

Frank Lloyd Wright's rendering of a view from the west of the Price Company Tower for Harold Price, Sr. (1952) at Bartlesville, Oklahoma. Copyright © The Frank Lloyd Wright Foundation, 1962.

myself concerning that. I think almost everybody knows what I feel about New York. Brother Zeckendorf, here, and his alliance with the New York real estate industry, expressed it a moment ago to me. He said that New York has substituted money for ideas and I feel that is what it's done. He can tell you what it's done better than I can. But he doesn't know much about New York, do you Zeck?

MODERATOR: Well, let's ask Mr. Zeckendorf.

WRIGHT: How far away have you been from New York and when did you come here?

MODERATOR: Let me ask his opinion of the future of New York, if I may first, and then we'll get to those too Mr. Wright. Mr. Zeckendorf, how do you feel?

ZECKENDORF: All questions, Mr. Wright, in due course.

MODERATOR: Mr. Zeckendorf, how do you see New York as the city of the future?

ZECKENDORF: I see New York as the most important triumph of man in any urban effort ever. I must say that it is very much in debt to many predecessor civilizations and, very

Frank Lloyd Wright on the City

The Mile-High Center (1954) at Denver, Colorado; I. M. Pei, architect. Photograph by the editor.

importantly, to the man sitting opposite here, Mr. Wright, in spite of the fact that he does not like the urban way of life. He does not approve of the continuance of the urban design for living as we see it—he has made an enormous contribution to it.

MODERATOR: Well, Mr. Wright, why do you think that cities are bad as such? I mean, why do you feel that way and you express yourself so vociferously along that line?

WRIGHT: Have I been vociferous?

MODERATOR: Not so far—no, no.

WRIGHT: Well, you know who founded the city don't you Zeck? Who founded New York City? It was Cain, wasn't it? Cain was the founder of the city after he had murdered Abel. He had incurred the displeasure of the Lord and he went out and founded the city and here it is yet. Here is the city founded by the man who murdered his brother and it is still murdering his brother—isn't it?

ZECKENDORF: Could be, if you feel that's murder.

WRIGHT: I think that's murder and I believe that

the time must come when justice will be done to what we call humanity. I feel that the proportions of your big cities now are inhumane. Humanity no longer is represented by your great city. I just looked at a photograph coming up where the skyscrapers grow like weeds in a garden and all extinguish each other and where man tramples on man. This is really the trampling of the herd! That's what it is really and I can see no further use for it.

MODERATOR: Mr. Zeckendorf, obviously you don't agree.

ZECKENDORF: No I don't agree. I feel that the city is the expression of man's gregarious nature. I think that . . .

WRIGHT: That it is!

ZECKENDORF: . . .and therefore a natural expression. I feel also that no great civilization has arisen anytime in history, and I stand to be corrected by you if you can name one, that did not come from urban life.

WRIGHT: Can I answer now or should I . . . ?

MODERATOR: Go ahead Mr. Wright.

WRIGHT: The answer is this. In the Middle Ages there was no means of communication whatever and culture was dependent upon crowding together in cities. You had to get a short connection in order to get anything at all. As science grew and developed our modern life and as the Machine Age came into being, what happened?—the telephone—the telegraph—now the airplane—now television. Now by all these means of communication that we have disseminated that necessity no longer exists. There's no reason for the gregarious nature of man now, which is, of course, below the belt. Humanity begins where the animal leaves off Zeck and the animal leaves off above the belt.

ZECKENDORF: I'd like to answer that.

MODERATOR: Go ahead Mr. Zeckendorf.

ZECKENDORF: I'm mindful of the tremendous difference between the civilization achieved by the nomadic tribes of our American Indians in the areas north of Mexico as distinguished from those who congregated in cities south of the border. I . . .

WRIGHT: You have splendid civilization and there have been splendid civilizations but this is not . . .

MODERATOR: Mr. Zeckendorf, will you continue sir?

ZECKENDORF: My point is that the civilizations as expressed by the Aztecs at Uxmal and Chichén Itzá; by the Mitla and Monte Alban at Oaxaca; by the Indians at Mexico City—the Toltecs—those were civilizations created by Indians of very much the same genesis as our North American Indians but who only achieved the height of their capacities under an urban existence.

WRIGHT: True.

MODERATOR: Well, do you feel, Mr. Zeckendorf, that people can work and live at their best in our present cities?

ZECKENDORF: I believe they can live and work at their best in our present cities redone. I go for what Mr. Wright says—there can be no question that the present city, which was designed for horses and buggies and sixty-foot streets in a gridiron pattern, can't take the modern conditions; it's perfectly obvious to me. I believe that we're in for a great change through urban redevelopment.

MODERATOR: But, your concept is quite different than Mr. Wright's, is it not?

ZECKENDORF: Yes, it is.

MODERATOR: What is your concept of a change in the city?

ZECKENDORF: I would like Mr. Wright's concept if I thought it was practical. I think Mr. Wright's concept is a dream existence that, in the light of several factors, if I may mention them, cannot work. Number one . . .

MODERATOR: May we first ask Mr. Wright what his idea is? I gather we are talking about the so-called Broadacre City? Is that right Mr. Wright?

WRIGHT: Well, that's not in mind. That's a model actually existing and what is in my mind is something quite superior even to Broadacre City and I think apropos concerning this matter of practical. I think what brother Zeckendorf means when he says practical is expedient. But, practical is very far-reaching and extremely difficult and expensive and requires vision. There is no vision in the present city. Once upon a time, as brother Zeckendorf has stated, the city was the cultural center of humanity and from it we have derived all of the culture that we now possess, which, unfortunately for us, makes it necessary for us now to devise, envision, and create new forms of culture which do not exist.

MODERATOR: Do you have such a form in mind sir?

WRIGHT: I have—because I believe that man's nature is in quest, even now as it always has been, of what we call the beautiful. It's a dangerous word to use now. They'll accuse you of being impractical if you talk about the beautiful. As a matter of fact, the beautiful is about the only thing that ever appeared to be practical and has been preserved and so it will be. Now I believe if brother Zeckendorf were to go afield and really see America, and not

concentrate on the centers of the cities, he'll see the city being built that I'm talking about.

MODERATOR: Mr. Zeckendorf.

ZECKENDORF: Well, in the first place, I wish Mr. Wright was as well acquainted with my interest in America as I am in his. I am acquainted with America.

WRIGHT: You have been abroad.

ZECKENDORF: I have been abroad. My family stems back to 1854 in Tucson, Arizona where they settled. My father was born there. I've dealt in forty states and I think I'm safe in saying we own more rural and semirural property than we do urban.

WRIGHT: Well, then you're safe.

ZECKENDORF: However safe, I don't know. I just want to correct your impression that I don't know America at least to some extent.

WRIGHT: Well, I assumed you were a younger fellow and had only lately come here but not sixteen years or so.

ZECKENDORF: Well, thank you for the compliment. I was one year old when I arrived and that was a little more than sixteen years ago.

WRIGHT: (laughter)

MODERATOR: Mr. Zeckendorf, you mentioned that you felt, I gather, that Mr. Wright's ideas were impractical.

ZECKENDORF: Yes.

MODERATOR: Why do you say that, sir?

ZECKENDORF: I think they're impractical not because they seek beauty because we seek beauty too in our area, in our way of trying to do things.

WRIGHT: I'll call it *style*.

The Duel of the Titans

139

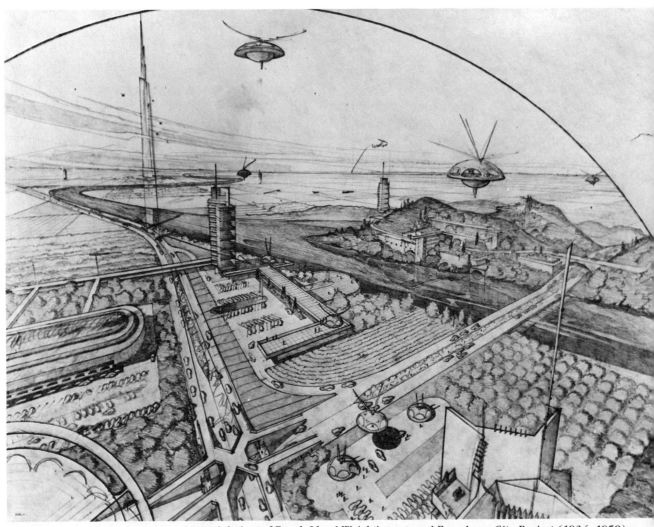

An aerial view of Frank Lloyd Wright's proposed Broadacre City Project (1934–1958) showing the Broadacre City countryside with buildings and skyscrapers surrounded by vast open spaces connected by roadways and accessible by proposed air machines. Copyright © The Frank Lloyd Wright Foundation, 1962.

ZECKENDORF: Call it what you wish. We think of it as beauty and perhaps we're mistaken. We seek it within the framework of what we consider the essential way of life. I'm mindful of the civilization, for example, that exists in India where I visited not so long ago. When Clive went to India at the turn of the century, Mr. Wright, there were 70 million people there—the turn of the eighteenth century. Without the benefit of any immigration, but having emigrated many, 450 million people live in India today emenating from the same 70 million.

Frank Lloyd Wright on the City

What worries me is this—with the curve almost vertical, due to better food, sanitation, and medical condition and the rate of growth—population is startling and shocking. I concern myself with a flat and horizontal solution, however beautiful and lovely, however desirable, that we might have one end result and that would be a maze of what I call a fluid suburbia.

MODERATOR: What does that mean Mr. Zeckendorf?

ZECKENDORF: It's a place where no matter how far you travel, no matter where you go, you only wind up where you left. I believe in the concentration of people and change of pace—very dramatic radical change of pace. I believe in the theory of the "green belt" as you do but I believe it should be rigidly controlled.

WRIGHT: I don't believe in the "green belt"!

ZECKENDORF: Well, that's fine and we can really draw lines because we totally disagree!

MODERATOR: Well, tell me this gentlemen—we've heard a great deal about possible changes in . . . some of you, I believe Mr. Wright, say that people should live and work together, is this correct?

WRIGHT: I think they should eat, sleep, and work, not necessarily together, but practically where most efficiency—not efficiency—it's a bad word—but where most usefulness and happiness comes from that operation on their part.

ZECKENDORF: I've heard you say, Mr. Wright, and read your statements to the effect that you've associated the decline of civilizations with the ascendancy of cities of the past, is that correct?

WRIGHT: That isn't correct. No, I haven't done that but I have said that the use of the city,

when these means of communication became volatile and as they are, ever present, that the necessity for the crowding, which was gratification of the gregarious in man, ended. And if while the men at the top, who had the huge investment in the city, were unwilling to let go and recognize the fact that the city had done its work they kept on with it and kept it going and by sure force and circumstance, which in our case is money in our civilization, tried to keep it there where it is. And in spite of all their efforts, in spite of everything that they do, this thing underneath and the current flowing beneath is taking the life away from the city. And you can see it when the little gas station first appeared down the road. That was the first symptom of the decay of the present city. And now you'll find it going and the people have gone already. Eventually I think there are going to be very few concentrations like New York in modern civilization.

MODERATOR: Do you feel that our cities are decaying Mr. Zeckendorf?

ZECKENDORF: I do. I think they are decaying because they are outmoded. They are obsolete and they have not kept pace with change of circumstances . . .

MODERATOR: Who should take the lead?

ZECKENDORF: Wait a minute.

MODERATOR: Oh, excuse me.

ZECKENDORF: I am very hopeful and optimistic notwithstanding that because I believe that the tremendous effort toward urban renewal, which indicates the fact that the nation at every level—national, state, and city—is alerted to the problem. Under such acts as the Title I Urban Redevelopment Act—federal, certain state laws, and city laws—that these cities are going to renew themselves and refashion themselves in the light of new circumstances. Decentralization isn't new. You're a product of decentralization Mr. Wright and I am too. We all decentralized from somewhere.

WRIGHT: Decentralization is the watchword now essential to any vision of any future we can envision.

ZECKENDORF: An inverse ratio to decentralization—let's just take the example of New York City. New York was the great "hub" of industry in this country.

WRIGHT: Was it?

ZECKENDORF: It was!

WRIGHT: When?

ZECKENDORF: It was from 1830 to 1900.

WRIGHT: It has been a great market, is that what you mean by "hub"?

ZECKENDORF: "Hub"—not only a market; it was a port; it was the greatest concentration . . .

WRIGHT: Yes, that's its greatest factor today. The greatest feature of its future is the fact that it has a port.

ZECKENDORF: May I carry the things that I indicated further?

MODERATOR: Yes, go ahead.

ZECKENDORF: It was a great industrial center as well. A port—the greatest concentration of transportation starting with the days when they went to canals through to the west which was then called Buffalo. Then the rails—now the great highways and the great airways—New York has always had that. New York, however unlike many other cities and probably known to you Mr. Wright, was one of the great manufacturing cities of the country and has lost its industry to just what you're talking about. Industry had to horizontalize. It had to go to the

periphery. It had to go to the suburbs or it had to go out into the open spaces. New York is no longer an industrial city. New York did recapture something. An inverse ratio to the decentralization of the manufacturing. New York recaptures the things that decentralization meant. Every time a factory went out to Iowa, Indiana, or down to Carolina it had to have a showroom somewhere in the midtown of New York to sell its merchandise. We want to get rid of them! We're getting rid of our manufacturing at fifty cents a foot and getting back the office space at five dollars. That's a good trade!

WRIGHT: Do you think that pressure is going to continue?

ZECKENDORF: Yes.

WRIGHT: What makes you think so?

ZECKENDORF: You speak of pressure to decentralize?

WRIGHT: No—the pressure to recentralize.

ZECKENDORF: Oh, you mean the pressure to recentralize?

WRIGHT: Yes.

ZECKENDORF: Oh, all right—I'll do it by reverse. We have the theater here in New York on a scale not known anywhere else in the United States and possibly the world. We have more music. We have more art.

WRIGHT: Those are all debatable questions.

ZECKENDORF: Well they may be debatable but I will say . . . I will take it this way. There may be parts of the world that have more than we have in any one of those things but the aggregate of the things I mention are to be found in New York in greater quantities than anyplace else.

MODERATOR: May I ask you gentlemen . . . go ahead sir.

ZECKENDORF: People don't come to New York to stay at a hotel room in a chain hotel. They come here to buy, sell, or to go to the theater or enjoy cultural activities.

WRIGHT: It's a market, yes.

ZECKENDORF: It's a market and it is a place to borrow money and loan money. However ugly that word may sound.

WRIGHT: No it doesn't sound ugly.

ZECKENDORF: It is a place where the very lifeblood of the nation generates and pulsates. It benefits the very communities in which you wish to build your towers.

WRIGHT: Little Bartlesville for instance?

ZECKENDORF: Sir?

WRIGHT: Little Bartlesville?

ZECKENDORF: Yes.

MODERATOR: Let's talk about those towers for a moment.

WRIGHT: The towns?

MODERATOR: The towns. Out of the Oklahoma plains is the Price Tower, which I gather you're quite proud of Mr. Wright?

WRIGHT: Yes, I am because it's the only use of steel in tension that you can find in the whole skyscraper industry.

MODERATOR: But does this indicate to you the kind of building that we will be seeing more and more of? Say in twenty, thirty, forty years from now?

WRIGHT: I think the advice that we've tried to give Bartlesville by the building of this tower—stay home and do your own stuff and don't impinge on Mr. Zeckendorf and New York City. Stay here—where you live—make your own town beautiful. If you want a skyscraper, it's a natural American achievement.

ZECKENDORF: Build a skyscraper on vacant land? There is where I go for your horizontal plan. I can't see the logic of a skyscraper in the open spaces.

WRIGHT: Well, the skyscraper is not in an open space. The skyscraper is in a town that can absorb the skyscraper and because it is an economic beautiful form and can cast its shadow on its own ground and be a lovely circumstance in itself in a town—every town should have one or two or three of them.

MODERATOR: Mr. Zeckendorf?

WRIGHT: Just as they have churches and steeples.

ZECKENDORF: I will grant you that if you are talking about art for art's sake.

WRIGHT: No, I'm not! I'm talking of the life of the people! The pride and joy they take in their own town and their own city—seeing the thing. They are very beautiful.

ZECKENDORF: To give a town an office building because you justify it as you would a church?

WRIGHT: Yes—I think an office building is quite as important as a church and I think it has a function and a feature that can be as beautiful as anything ever built.

ZECKENDORF: I'm sure it can be as beautiful. Should things be built for beauty alone?

WRIGHT: No—there is no such thing. Who ever saw beauty standing alone? I never have.

ZECKENDORF: I have.

WRIGHT: Oh!

ZECKENDORF: At least I have been under the illusion that I have.

MODERATOR: May I ask this Mr. Zeckendorf? I know you're quite proud of the building known as the "Helix"—H–E–L–I–X. Now, do you see

Frank Lloyd Wright's Price Company Tower for Harold Price, Sr. (1952) at Bartlesville, Oklahoma. Photograph by the editor.

William Zeckendorf's proposed Apartment Helix for a site overlooking New York's East River (1949); designed by I. M. Pei. Photograph from the January 1950 issue of Architectural Forum. Photograph used by permission of Billboard Publications, Inc., 1515 Broadway, New York, New York 10036.

144

this as the sort of building that will be more and more in use in the years to come? Will we, as we move along in time ten or twenty years, be inclined to see this kind of building go up instead of the standard oblong-type building that we now expect to see when a building is going up?

ZECKENDORF: I think it will be a contribution to construction. I don't think it will be something that will be the only form of residential construction but it will fill a tremendous need which points up an important factor. Obsolescence of residential buildings, emanating from sociological change or economic cycles, causes what might have been a perfectly attractive twelve-room apartment twenty-five years ago on Park Avenue and 49th Street to be a very impractical apartment

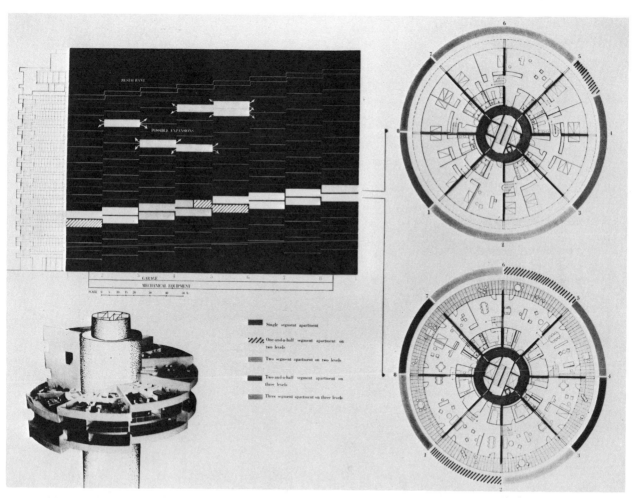

Building sections and plans of William Zeckendorf's proposed Apartment Helix (1949) designed by I. M. Pei. Sections and plans from the January 1950 issue of Architectural Forum. *Drawings used by permission of Billboard Publications, Inc., 1515 Broadway, New York, New York 10036.*

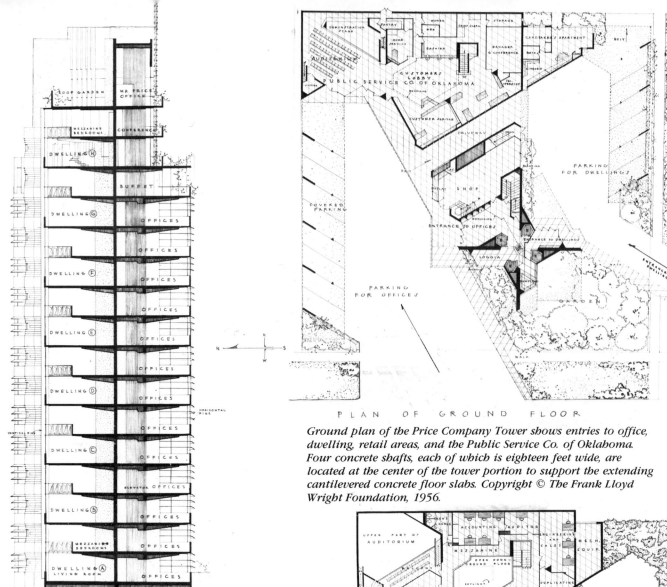

CROSS SECTION

Drawing of a section through the Price Company Tower showing a treelike structure with a steel-reinforced concrete shaft extending into the ground. Parapet walls of each floor are cast steel-reinforced concrete integral with the cantilever floor slabs. Copyright © The Frank Lloyd Wright Foundation, 1956.

PLAN OF GROUND FLOOR

Ground plan of the Price Company Tower shows entries to office, dwelling, retail areas, and the Public Service Co. of Oklahoma. Four concrete shafts, each of which is eighteen feet wide, are located at the center of the tower portion to support the extending cantilevered concrete floor slabs. Copyright © The Frank Lloyd Wright Foundation, 1956.

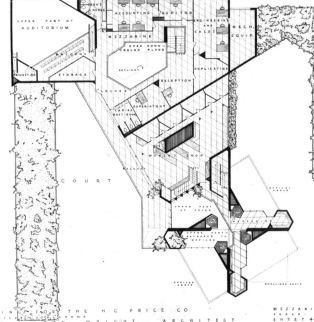

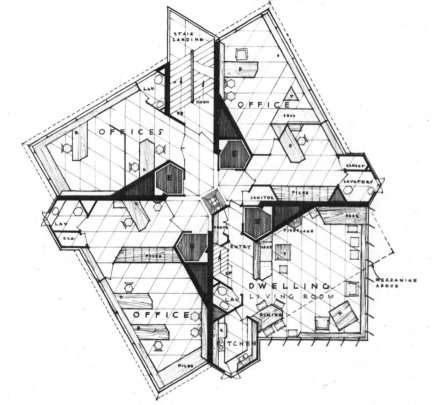

Typical floor plan of the tower portion of the Price Company Tower shows the relationship between the office spaces and a dwelling unit. Each dwelling unit occupies two levels of the tower with the living room area on the lower of the two levels and the bedrooms occupying a mezzanine above. Copyright © The Frank Lloyd Wright Foundation, 1956.

Typical floor plan of a dwelling unit bedroom mezzanine level of the Price Company Tower. Copyright © The Frank Lloyd Wright Foundation, 1956.

147

Left; Mezzanine plan (directly above the ground-floor plan) of the Price Company Tower. Copyright © The Frank Lloyd Wright Foundation, 1956.

Exterior view of the balcony of William Zeckendorf's proposed Apartment Helix (1949) designed by I. M. Pei. There is a four-foot overhang over every window, which would serve as a sunshade on the sunny side of the building. Drawing from the January 1950 issue of Architectural Forum. *Drawing used by permission of Billboard Publications, Inc., 1515 Broadway, New York, New York 10036.*

Frank Lloyd Wright on the City

because of the inroads of business and changes in circumstances. This Helix permits the breakup of a twelve-room apartment into three four-room apartments, shall we say, in one afternoon with three or four workmen because all of the plumbing is at the central core and the apartments are divided into eight equal segments.

WRIGHT: That's only a standard process. That's in the tower the same. It's in any good building the same. There is nothing original in that. Nothing interesting either.

ZECKENDORF: I'm suggesting that it is original in the sense that it is applied to a residential building. I don't know of any residential building which . . .

WRIGHT: Do you know of an office building with a residential section devoted to apartments in it?

ZECKENDORF: Ah . . . I may but I don't of any residential building or office building, as a matter of fact, where a perfect circle has been achieved for the reintegration or breakdown of apartments from large to small or from small to large with the ease that this thing ought to do it.

WRIGHT: A very simple problem.

MODERATOR: Gentlemen, may I ask this question too . . . ?

WRIGHT: I don't see anything very peculiar.

ZECKENDORF: Well, you say you don't see anything peculiar about it?

WRIGHT: No.

ZECKENDORF: Let's take an ordinary apartment house where the plumbing branches.

WRIGHT: Why take an ordinary apartment house?

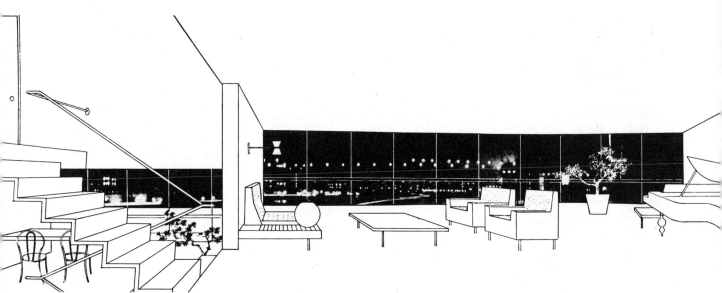

Interior view of the living room area of William Zeckendorf's proposed Apartment Helix (1949) designed by I. M. Pei. The stairway shown on the left of the drawing leads to a second level of the same dwelling unit where the bedrooms are located. Drawing from the January 1950 issue of Architectural Forum. *Drawing used by permission of Billboard Publications, Inc., 1515 Broadway, New York, New York 10036.*

149

Drawing by Frank Lloyd Wright of a main living area of a dwelling unit in the Price Company Tower. The fireplace, shown in the background, has a copper hood and is gas-fired. Copyright © The Frank Lloyd Wright Foundation, 1956.

ZECKENDORF: Well, take any apartment house you can mention that does this job! Can you name one?

WRIGHT: I don't think it's worthwhile naming any apartment house. They are all practically the same magnified or diminished. They all are committing the same sin and the same sin we want to see abolished and the Price Tower, which is a skyscraper, abolishes it! We want privacy for people. We want beauty of environment for people. We don't want to encircle them and embody them in something that they're in—like grains of wheat in a bushel.

ZECKENDORF: Do you feel that's what happens with the Helix?

WRIGHT: That's what happens with any tall building built in a city environment. It is inevitable that it should be nothing but a bushel of human beings or two or three bushels or maybe a dozen bushels. But they're all busheled. They're all . . .

ZECKENDORF: Doesn't that depend upon site planning, Mr. Wright?

WRIGHT: Well how can you site plan in a place like New York City?

Frank Lloyd Wright's interior perspective drawing showing the master bedroom opening to a planted balcony in a dwelling unit of the Price Company Tower. Copyright © The Frank Lloyd Wright Foundation, 1956.

ZECKENDORF: It can be done and I predict the city pattern will change. We'll get away from the gridiron street.

WRIGHT: But what's going to maintain the necessity for the city? Why are people going to come and crowd upon each other when they become better conditioned and more intelligent and more enlightened? The more enlightened they are, the less they are going to impinge upon one another. This is a great free country, isn't it?

ZECKENDORF: Well, I certainly hope so.

WRIGHT: What are these great spaces lying around here loose? What is this impulse to impinge upon everybody else? Your elbow in somebody's ribs and standing on somebody's feet. What is this impulse to crowd now? The basis for crowding no longer exists.

ZECKENDORF: Well, my answer is that I believe man likes a little bit of crowding, Mr. Wright, as shocking as it may sound to you. I feel that perhaps your way of life may not be the same as mine nor mine the same as our moderator here.

WRIGHT: Your way of life then is for the crowder; the man who wants to crowd.

ZECKENDORF: I like to have a man get a little bit of both. That's why I believe in the "green belt" theory and the belief that one and one equals three if two good ideas are exchanged and that cannot be had by living alone. I believe . . .

WRIGHT: Who is talking about living alone?

ZECKENDORF: Well, I mean the idea about being decentralized to the point where the whole thing is just a . . .

WRIGHT: You're talking about freedom, do you believe in it?

ZECKENDORF: I do!

WRIGHT: With a capital F?

ZECKENDORF: I believe in it with a capital F.

WRIGHT: What do you think that our Declaration of Independence meant to humanity?

ZECKENDORF: Well, sir, I believe I think what you do.

WRIGHT: The sovereignty of the individual . . .

ZECKENDORF: That's right.

WRIGHT: . . . was inviolable and that he was regarded as an independent usable beautiful unit.

MODERATOR: I must interrupt gentlemen. I'm sorry that our time is up. We hope, sir, that perhaps, at least for the immediate future, we may have a great invoke [from people] in both the city and out in the outer spaces. All right, thank you very much gentlemen. I certainly appreciate it.

WRIGHT: This was very scientific!

MODERATOR, WRIGHT, AND ZECKENDORF: (laughter)

Frank Lloyd Wright on the City

PART FOUR

With the Students of the Profession

Frank Lloyd Wright with the Apprentice Architect of the Taliesin Fellowship

Man or Machine?

The democratic principle makes of the individual the determining unit in a great harmony of the whole and denies that harmony can exist without that individual independence . . . the life of this Fellowship and the way we conduct ourselves . . . stand here dedicated to the growth of the individual.

In late 1952 or early 1953 a three-record set of 33 1/3 rpm long-playing records titled *Frank Lloyd Wright Talks To and With the Taliesin Fellowship* was pressed by Columbia Records Inc. for the Frank Lloyd Wright Fellowship and was released for national distribution at a price of $5.00 per record. Record 1 of the set included both a conversation on acoustics between Wright and his Taliesin Fellows, which was recorded at Taliesin West in April 1951, and also Wright reading from Walt Whitman at Taliesin recorded in August 1951. Record 2 of the set was a half-hour conversation on the topic "Man or Machine?" between Wright and the Taliesin Fellows at Taliesin recorded in July 1951. Record 3 included a reading by Wright of his address to the Junior AIA (American Institute of Architects), which was originally presented to that group in June 1952 (this recording, however, was made in September 1952). Record 3 of the set also included some piano improvisations by Wright recorded in the early 1950s and also a talk he gave on truth to the Taliesin Fellowship on June 18, 1950 in the Hillside Home School dining room at Taliesin.

The *Architectural Forum* magazine, in its April 1953 issue, reviewed this set of three records and concluded

"They may some day be precious... because they do this: they permit an intimacy with the fact of Wright's personality, which is vivid as his great architecture. In these records he is sometimes ornery—as in the sides which eavesdrop as he talks with fellows of his Taliesin fellowship about man and machine; at other times wryly humorous—as when he advises young architects to do the whole job of building houses: designing, contracting, landscaping, and interior decorating, because then their fees will be 40% ... But more than anything else Wright is resonantly noble."

The following is the text of record 2 of the set, which is an exchange of conversation between Frank Lloyd Wright and his apprentice architects of the Taliesin Fellowship at Taliesin in July 1951 on the topic "Man or Machine?"

The Conversation

WRIGHT: How many of you fellows believe that machinery, the introduction of it and the prevalence of machine methods throughout the world, has altered the moral status and the moral character of the world? That the moral obligation today is changed owing to these facilities? Have you ever given any thought? I'm asking because I had occasion to debate the subject not so long ago in public. Of course we know that certain circumstances alter cases but does the moral law change with facility? I mean as facilities change? Are you the same man with the same moral obligations when you're sitting in a car with a horsepower of, say 125, as you are when you're sitting in a gate behind a horse? Because there is Uncle Sam's argument—there's the political argument today—in favor of all the things that we're doing against the moral order which we professed when this nation was founded. You

see? We're justifying all that we're doing because we say—I'm using the word "we" in a colloquial way—that circumstances now put a different stress and demand a different action on the part of the individual. Now when you've got that untangled in your own mind you're fit for arguments. Has the man himself and his relation to men and his relation to himself as a man changed with machinery? Is machinery going to enter into the constitution of his soul or not? That's the question—isn't it? Does machinery make him more of a man or less of a man? That's another question—the same relationship. Does the horsepower of his engine, when he's sitting in his car, add to his stature as a man or does it detract from it? That's another question. What would you say? You've got to face it. You've got to think it out. I've no doubt and there's no argument but that humanity would immensely be better off if they knew how to

156

Aerial view of the Taliesin Fellowship Complex (1933ff) in the background, the Romeo and Juliet Windmill for Nell and Jane Lloyd Jones (1896) in the center, and the Andrew T. Porter "Tanyderi" Residence (1907) in the foreground, Spring Green, Wisconsin. Photograph courtesy of The Capital Times, *Madison, Wisconsin.*

Aerial view of the Taliesin Midway Barns and Dairy and Machine Sheds (1938–1947). Photograph courtesy of The Capital Times, *Madison, Wisconsin.*

The Taliesin Fellowship Complex, which was formerly the Hillside Home School. Photograph by the editor.

use machines for human benefit—there's no argument there. But as they are used and actually what has happened is something we're talking about now. Of course the machine is a great tool and of course it can liberate humanity but to what? What liberation?

APPRENTICE: Well, wouldn't you say that is a matter of degree? When man first had the machine he seemed to run through a period of prosperity and cultural development. So did the Egyptians and numerous other cultures.

WRIGHT: Well, the Egyptians built the pyramids with it and did all kinds of beautiful things.

APPRENTICE: I think now we are in a state where we have something which we don't quite understand and I think it's time for us to find the moral answers.

WRIGHT: That's right. It's time for us to find the moral answers to this question and that's why I brought it up this morning.

APPRENTICE: Mr. Wright, I can't see how the machine changes a man. It seems to me that the man is the same whether he has the machine or not. If he's an evil man the machine increases his ability to be evil and if he's a good man the machine increases his ability to be good. I don't think the problem is the machine. It seems to me that the problem is the man.

WRIGHT: That's right. That's what I believe but this fellow whirling down the hill by us there in a cloud of dust roaring across the bridge getting to Spring Green in seventeen minutes is just the same fellow that used to trudge over there with a bundle on the stick over his shoulder. But now he's dangerous. Now he's a menace. Now the ignorance of that man which hasn't changed, he interiorly has not developed, but he's in possession of 125 horsepower until the sparkplug goes wrong and leaves him there out somewhere about fourteen miles from nowhere to get home. But he gets the idea that that's him and with that cigar in his mouth and hat pulled down over his eyes and his hands on that wheel, he's a different individual from what he really is. He imagines himself to be something that he really isn't. Now someday the awakening has got to come. He's got to go back and pick up a lot of stitches that he dropped when he got his hands on that wheel.

Now it seems to me right, in that you have the quirks or the gists of this whole problem, and as it applies to him it applies to society—it applies to the world. The world got possession of a tremendous way of having its will and getting what it wanted before it was ready to know what it wanted or know what it was worth when it got it. So there's the mix-up and that's the confusion. You can't blame it on the machine. We can blame it on the ignorance and the unpreparedness, so to speak, because ignorance is always unprepared for anything, of the human unit.

So I think what we ought to have now are schools to teach the uses and the prohibitions that should go along with the machines. Where is it being taught? Who's learning? In fact, who's raised the question? Have you heard this question I've raised here this morning academically raised? It's been in the minds of a great many people. A lot of us have been trying to get an answer but academically I've never heard the question raised.

You see it's materialism that has the grasp on the machine now. Pure materialism has found a great means to have what it wants and to get it—even with an atom bomb. Even with the destruction of humanity it can now get what it wants. And what does it want? What really does humanity want? Of course we know the answer—three squares a day, fornication, and a good snore and above that not much else if they can get that by way of machinery more easily and more of it and better. Well, that's called the machine and that's the answer.

Come on now, there must be another side to this question? The more a man's sphere of action widens the more you see the character of that man and so machinery has brought out the weaknesses and the susceptibilities of what we call the human being everywhere, all over the world. Now we find out something about him that we didn't know before, perhaps. I'm afraid that if you were to canvass the characteristic cross section of humanity under the different names of the different nations you'd find only a small proportion in every nation even capable of proving the problem to themselves and the rest of them would be taking it as a natural thing and for granted that they should fight and lie and steal and get an advantage over their neighbor by any means possible.

APPRENTICE: Mr. Wright, I should think that when man developed the machine he had one other obligation and that was to develop his moral standards of living along with his development of machines. Now, wouldn't you say we more or less left one behind? We've developed bigger and better machines but have completely forgotten about the moral obligations that have to go along with them.

WRIGHT: That's my point. I think so. I think that's what's happened.

APPRENTICE: And if we don't make the changeover, why we've colossal machines . . .

WRIGHT: Yes, we have.

APPRENTICE: . . . and nothing to go with them.

WRIGHT: Man's moral nature dwindles as his machines increase in power. That old English moralist . . . do you remember him? . . . Sir Alfred Wallace died in England about ten years ago, I guess, and the last thing he said as he died, having written and thought on the subject all his life, was that man had made no moral progress since the days of the Egyptians. When you're out on the river in a boat, you must know whether you're going downstream or whether you've got to fight to go up, and we're now on the stream going down and it's going to take a lot of concentrated sacrifice and effort to get up where we've got to go. We said a moment ago he has possession now of a means he has not been educated to exercise. He is more deadly now and no more competent morally than he was in the days of the Egyptians.

APPRENTICE: Excuse me, sir. That sort of takes it away from the machine and puts it back to leadership, doesn't it?

WRIGHT: Yes!

APPRENTICE: Well, therefore the machine just intensifies the fact that poor leadership is really the rub and mixed up.

WRIGHT: That's right. And in the sight of the fact that education has done a poorer job, that the premiums we place upon humanity today are the wrong ones, and that if we're going to get the moral nature capable of the extensions inevitable to the use of machinery—conferred upon it by machinery—then we must have these things or we go over the brink.

APPRENTICE: Mr. Wright, what do you hold on this argument that the same thing happened to the world—and people felt the same way—with the invention of the bow and arrow and gunpowder and all the rest?

WRIGHT: It was the same problem but in a very limited fashion; so limited that it didn't come to the attention of the universe. Of course every invention that is added to man's facility for destruction has been a threat to humankind, but if each time something had been done about it . . . if there was some power that could proportion this use of the new invention to the moral nature that was using it, then we wouldn't be in the fix we're in now.

APPRENTICE: Well, after each of those inventions they seemed to blunder along again and still survive.

WRIGHT: Well, we'll blunder along in a bigger way.

APPRENTICE: Yes, a bigger way.

WRIGHT: And we may not survive. You see it's a build-up—bigger and bigger and bigger until finally what? It's pretty late now to try to get hold of this thing, but this moment, unquestionably, in the development of machine power is only relative but the problem remains the same. And now it's clear and manifest that it's gone to the point where it has exaggerated man's evil nature beyond the grasp of his better nature. I think the profit motive has been a demoralizing influence on humanity and I think that motive has made man helpless in the face of this issue of the machine. He hasn't even seen it as an issue. We're talking about

With the Students of the Profession

something he doesn't even believe in or think about much. He's not disturbed. He feels all this is grand and glorious, this bombing out a whole nation in Korea, this ability to blow up a whole continent—great accomplishment. In other words, if a man is to be allowed a greater range of action concerning his fellows, he should have given some proof of ability before that privilege is accorded to him. The argument here is whether, with these deadly extended facilities, man's nature has kept pace with his facilities and I say it has not!

APPRENTICE: Well, did it ever?

WRIGHT: What?

APPRENTICE: Did it ever keep pace with his facilities?

WRIGHT: That isn't the question! The fact that it never has is just the point we need now to make—that it must or he dies—he kills himself—he commits suicide! He's found a means to an end now he never possessed before. Unless this thing comes up now by way of the vision, the insight, and the influence of his bellwethers or his rams in the ram pasture or the universities, we might say by its educational facilities, he's gone up because nothing can restrain this power. It apparently got the best of man some time ago. It has been in the universe from time immemorial. It's been there ever since a man used a lever to pry a rock out of its place or to make an inclined plane to roll it up on the wall. It's been in the world but it's never had the importance of human life. It's never been what it is now, and it has never been morally reckoned with. And today there is this same attitude that it doesn't matter, that it is the same as it always has been, and that there is no new problem here. There is no *new* problem here; but the *old* problem has become so acute that if

the moral nature of man is not awakened to its responsibility in connection with it, we're not going to hear much more or much longer of man himself here if we don't find some way to turn this power to the good and the account of humanity. I don't see that we're going to last. Now I see nothing being done to restrain it, to put it into the category of things useful to man's good life and I don't see it anywhere. When we need statesmen, we've got only politicians and soldiers. Now that's the only thing—that's the answer we've made to it. The politician and the soldier and the machine is what we're living on. Where are the statesmen? You heard a little voice, [President] Hoover's voice, lifted here and it sounded like the voice of a statesman but that's the only one—nobody else. And you see when the thinking begins what happens? You get sent to jail or put in a concentration camp. It's already gone that far. That's the resistance now being offered to any free solution offered for this condition we're in.

APPRENTICE: Mr. Wright, I always think of our civilization as a wave that starts out as a small ripple and gradually increases in magnitude and we are all small particles of that wave. Now can we, as small particles, stop the growth of that wave before it reaches its crest and breaks and that's when you get your violence? Or does it require an external force to stop that wave?

WRIGHT: Well, as a matter of fact, I think we are the crest.

APPRENTICE: Yes, we have reached that.

WRIGHT: I think we people who think and who desire and who envision are the crest of that wave. Now I think the crest is here and I think it's time before this breaks, when we go down for another recession and stay 300 years, we did a little thinking and see if we can't stop it.

APPRENTICE: Mr. Wright, the world is . . . all of these people have gotten so much closer in the last few years and they'll get much closer in another twenty years. My point, with these primitive tribes, was that they can do it in these small societies. And when the world gets so terribly close that we will have to have a united world and talk through the United Nations, and so forth, then it will be much more solid than that.

WRIGHT: Along that line, my dear boy, I believe that only bickering and trouble exists. I think that we cannot be friends. We cannot have what you might call a "united society" until every member in it is independent and self-sufficient. That's the only free society.

APPRENTICE: Every part of our country has had that trouble. That's why the thirteen colonies got together.

WRIGHT: Yes.

APPRENTICE: They were all independent. They bickered among themselves.

WRIGHT: That's right, and now . . .

APPRENTICE: Together—it was good for them.

WRIGHT: No. When they were independent and when they lived their own life, until it was taken away from them by the seventeenth amendment, this nation had a chance to do some independent thinking along independent lines. When they gave up that independence and federalized themselves and became as one, the whole thing is helpless. Independence has gone out of the window. Independent thinking goes to jail. The individual has been decimated and so it would be with a world federation the same. It's only when a strong little independent nation—as Japan is one—as Russia is one—if England minds her own business and the

United States minds hers—then all form a society if that society has any chance to survive at all. That's the democratic doctrine as against communism, as against fascism, against all the rest. The democratic principle makes of the individual the determining unit in a great harmony of the whole and denies that harmony can exist without that individual independence. Interdependence is always a basis for squabbling, quarrels, recriminations, and a family squabble.

APPRENTICE: You don't see a disappearance of the separate nationalities then, Mr. Wright?

WRIGHT: No sir. I think that democracy in the future of the world depends more on maintaining the individuality and independence and qualities that characterize different nations and maintaining them as such. I'm not preaching nationality at the expense of unity but I am preaching national characteristics and quality as the basis for a rich human society. Now that's the democratic faith as against the communist faith. The communist says otherwise. The communist says this must all be on a question of build up, then subdivide. If it builds up again, again subdivide. Share, share alike, share and share alike—share what? Share your own soul's characteristic individuality? You can't!

APPRENTICE: The thing is you have to get together first to decide on this.

WRIGHT: On the contrary, you've got to be somebody first before you get together. That's my point! [If] You get together when you are nobody, you'll never be anybody.

APPRENTICE: People did go off and this nation did break up into smaller units and restore it more completely to the individual.

WRIGHT: This nation dropped its thesis when it

became more important as a federation than it was as an independent group of states, and so it would be with the world. If Russia were to be the whole world and if Russian ideals and Russian costumes and Russian this and that, the whole world were to be Russianized, do you think the world would be any better off? Not I. Nor do I think it would be any better off if it was all United Statesized either. I'd hate to see the derby hat crown the whole world, myself, too. I wouldn't care to see everybody rolling up his trousers because it was raining in London!

APPRENTICE: Mr. Wright, couldn't you please prove your argument, naturally on a smaller scale, but right here at the Fellowship? Each person is an individual—at least I hope so—and each person comes from a different part of the world, but we've united for a common purpose. We've all come here together . . .

WRIGHT: That's right.

APPRENTICE: . . . and we live very well together . . .

WRIGHT: We're a very shining example of what I'm talking about.

APPRENTICE: . . . not dependent upon the other.

WRIGHT: And I intended it to be so and that's the basis of this Fellowship. That's why we're a democratic institution.

APPRENTICE: And the same could be in the entire world. It isn't any different, just on a larger scale.

WRIGHT: That's on a larger scale and it's democratic. That's the faith that I call democratic and I'm grieved they don't agree with me.

APPRENTICE: Mr. Wright, even here in the Fellowship as soon as we've associated with someone for six months we pick up characteristics or . . .

WRIGHT: That's inevitable. That's legitimate. Can't find fault with that.

APPRENTICE: Well, this increased communication of the world . . .

WRIGHT: That's the danger of it! That's not the virtue of it! That's the danger of it! The danger is that the little Japanese will be wearing the derby hat when it doesn't become them; that they will put on trousers when they should wear the skirts their little legs demanded and when they all lose sight of their own natures and their own best effects and try to all be alike. There's no difference between the aesthetic point of view and the moral point of view ever.

APPRENTICE: In a way, we've come here all together to decide on an idea and we've come here for a principle . . .

WRIGHT: Now, now, now we're getting to something else. The principles that lie at the basis of human conduct are the same in every nation and that's where we should strive to put them into effect; but insofar as those affect the nature and character of the individual life of the person involved—no. Principles do not change. Go into the garden out here, go into the woods, into the forest, look at the trees; look at the flowers—there's only one principle. Let's see the individuality, see the color, see the joy of life in the expression of it. And it's the same in human life. The same thing that made that so charming to our eyes because nature loves individuality and leaves nothing undone to achieve it should teach us something as human beings because we are as natural as are other products—we don't change.

So, it's idiotic to try to impose upon all human life the sacrifice of all these qualities, these things of beauty that have grown up under

Exterior view of the two-story assembly hall wing (background) and drafting studio (foreground) of the Taliesin Fellowship Complex. These areas were formerly of the Hillside Home School (1901). Photograph by the editor.

different names—as Greek—as Roman—as Egyptian—as Italian—as Norse—as Italian—as South Sea Island—all that sort of thing. If that were to be blotted from the universe and one law for the lion and one for the ox, that would be oppression as I understand it. One law for the lion and the ox will always be oppression. It'll never be anything else. And it was that oppression that this nation was founded to refute. America exists in the world today as the first comprehensive, well-devised protest against

the thing. That's why we're here! And we have to defend it. We have to prove that this idea that we call America was right and that it had a reason for its existence.

Now, the life of this Fellowship and the way we conduct ourselves isn't ideal. We do approximate only an ideal, but we do approximate an ideal, and the ideal we approximate is that ideal. We stand here dedicated to the growth of the individual per se as

Exterior view of the drafting studio of the Taliesin Fellowship Complex. Photograph by the editor.

Exterior detail of the Taliesin Fellowship Complex. Photograph by the editor.

165

Interior view of the assembly hall of the Taliesin Fellowship Complex, which was formerly the living room pavilion of the Hillside Home School. Photograph by the editor.

such. Now there are many ways of keeping the discipline essential to becoming an individual. Now very few people can claim that distinction. You are gifted, by way of nature, with a certain personality, with a certain person. Your person is your eyes, your nose, your ears, the way you move and talk and all that. That was not your business. You got that as a gift.

Now the question is when individuality enters into this argument, what are you going to do

with it? What are you going to make of it, consciously? How are you going to bring this to bear in a direction of individuality? Now that's the artist's problem and that's where philosophy, art, and religion come to your aid and science can't help you. That's what the great artist represents in life. That's what he's for. That's his job—to increase, to make evident, and intensify this thing we call individuality. Now it's no light thing. It isn't just something one fellow has and another fellow hasn't got. It's something that is

With the Students of the Profession

Presentation area in the Taliesin Fellowship Complex. Photograph by the editor.

made consciously out of what naturally came to you and it would arise out of the essence of that thing what's called your soul, you see, becoming more and more in command of this shotgun that scatters all over a forty-acre field that's called your personality. It isn't simple. Democracy is a very high faith. The faith in the individual is a great challenge and America is that challenge to the world, you see, and it doesn't understand it any longer. America understood it in the days of the early statesmen we had. Thomas Jefferson preached it. All the great men we had preached it—how to get out, how to bring America back to its original bearings—there's only one way and that is to fight the disintegration that has come to mankind by way of overuses and abuses of machinery, abuses of his power before he knew his power or understands the nature of it, and it begins right where you are sitting. It begins right

Frank Lloyd Wright with Apprentice Architect

Dining area in the Taliesin Fellowship Complex. Photograph by the editor.

Interior of the theater in the Taliesin Fellowship Complex. Photograph by the editor.

where you are. It's you who has to do something about it. It isn't going to be done for you without any effort on your part. I doubt if this thing is going to be brought to humanity on a silver platter and humanity be asked to take it. I think he's got to fight for it and not with guns but maybe with guns—I don't know. That's the thing I'd put a gun on my shoulder and go and fight for—if I had to, I would. But I wouldn't fight for anything else. Now I believe there are ways of fighting infinitely more effective than killing somebody. In fact, I am persuaded that nobody ever got anywhere by

killing anybody. I don't think they ever ended anything except started another murder from some other direction. I think this has got to be fought out on different terms on a different kind of soil and the soil, of course, is humanity. And the fight is going to be one that's been going on, as it's been said here, it's been going on since time immemorial. And you're in it. And I think the members of the Fellowship are soldiers in the very best sense of the term if they understand it because that's your fight. That's your fight because it's my fight, and it's my fight because it's yours, as I see it.

168

Frank Lloyd Wright to the Student Architects of the University of Oklahoma–Norman

11

How are you going to know the principles that constitute a good act and a good building? Nobody knows and least of all the professors! Least of all the regents of a university or we wouldn't have the universities we have! Least of all the educational pooh-bahs—they don't know!

On the evening of May 2, 1952 Frank Lloyd Wright lectured and answered questions for about one hour before the students and faculty of the School of Architecture of the University of Oklahoma at Norman. The invitation for Wright to speak came from architect Bruce Goff, who was then chairman of the department. Goff, who was also a well-known architect and whose architecture was also firmly based in the Prairie School tradition, had known Wright for many years. More than twenty-five years after Wright's 1952 appearance at the University of Oklahoma, Goff remarked,

Ever since the first time that I heard the name of Frank Lloyd Wright it meant a great deal to me . . . it was the March 1908 issue of the Architectural Record *and the whole issue was devoted to his work and it was a very fine article . . . I was just knocked out and here was everything I liked already built! Things I'd never dream of myself, of course, it was just like entering an enchanted world that I wanted to be in. I was so carried away that I even forgot to eat lunch which was unusual! . . . . Well, who is this Frank Lloyd Wright anyway? . . . I think he helped me more than any other single thing in my life to make me realize that there was a great deal of freedom (in architectural design) once you understand more about organic architecture and develop your own feeling about it in your own way and he has been a very wonderful example to me and still is. He is still fresh and there is more* *where that came from, believe me . . . I was very fortunate in my younger days discovering Mr. Wright when he very kindly sent me his Wasmuth Portfolios [Ausgefürhte Bauten und Entwürfe von Frank Lloyd Wright, Berlin: Ernst Wasmuth, 1910 and Frank Lloyd Wright: Ausgefürhte Bauten, Berlin: Ernst Wasmuth, 1911] when I was twelve years old when I wrote to him asking what has happened since 1908 he said these had been published in 1910 and would bring me two years nearer to date!**

The letter written to Goff by Wright when Goff was only 12 years old read as follows:

Dear Bruce
It's nice to have a young friend in Oklahoma. I note your request for more recent publications of my work. I am taking the liberty of sending you gratis two portfolios which will bring you two years closer to today.
Faithfully,
FLW†

Architect Herb Greene, a former student of Goff's, attended the University of Oklahoma at the time of Wright's 1952 visit. Commenting on Wright's visit, Greene has stated,

Prepping for a visit by Wright . . . Goff carefully arranged some of the radical student work showing new directions—pre-Archigram pods, tension and freedom structures . . . Wright ignored this work like so much Edwardian wall paper, and paused to comment only at work that was blatantly influenced by Frank Lloyd Wright.‡

However, Wright must have been somewhat impressed by Goff's architecture program at the University of Oklahoma since after his 1952 visit he commented,

I myself, once upon a time, believed the function of a university to be to awaken sleepers, and the School of Architecture of the University of Oklahoma has encouraged that belief by its teachings. This is already well established by its own young architects' work, which has done more to put Oklahoma in the front rank of cultural pursuits than anything else it can show.§

This chapter presents the complete transcript of Frank Lloyd Wright's lecture and informal student question session from the evening of May 2, 1952 at the School of Architecture of the University of Oklahoma at Norman. Bruce Goff introduced Mr. Wright to the eagerly awaiting audience.

---

*From personal notes made by Patrick J. Meehan during the late Mr. Goff's talk at "An American

With the Students of the Profession

The Lecture and Conversation

BRUCE GOFF: Thirty-four years ago, when I was a little younger, I heard a very magic name—Frank Lloyd Wright—and it's still magic to me because what I saw in an old March 1908 issue of *Architectural Record* really did something to me that I've never gotten over. It made me so curious. Who could this person be that could do this beautiful work? It seemed to be what I wanted to see all my life up to then—a few short years at that time; something that I wanted to know; something that thrilled me; and I was very curious. What had this man been doing since 1908? I wrote to many magazines and books and they didn't seem to know. Finally, I got up the courage to write to Mr. Wright and I asked him if he could tell me of a publication of his work. He sent a letter saying that there was one in Germany in 1910 that he was sending to me which would bring me two years more up-to-date. From that time I've been following, with great interest, everything Mr. Wright has done and I think I can honestly say I'm one of the few people in my generation who knew him before he was fashionable to know.

STUDENTS: (laughter)

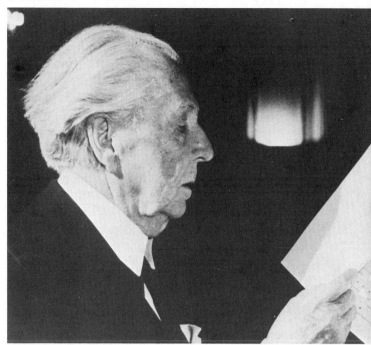

Frank Lloyd Wright studies a paper (circa mid-1950s). Photograph courtesy of The Capital Times, *Madison, Wisconsin.*

GOFF: He's certainly more than that to the students of the School of Architecture—so I'm using them. But it is fashionable these days to

---

Architecture: Its Roots, Growth, and Horizons" Conference at the Performing Arts Center in Milwaukee, Wisconsin on the evening of October 29, 1977.

†From Jeffrey Cook, *The Architecture of Bruce Goff*, New York: Harper and Row, 1978, p. 5.

‡From Herb Greene, "Recollections of Bruce Goff as Teacher," *Architectural Design* (Great Britain), Vol. 48, No. 10, 1978, p. 54.

§From "Faculty: The School of Architecture," *The Sooner Shamrock* (College of Engineering, University of Oklahoma–Norman), Vol. 15, December/January 1954-1955, p. 10 as referenced in David Gilson DeLong, *The Architecture of Bruce Goff: Buildings and Projects 1916–1974*, Vol. 1, New York: Garland, 1977, p. 228.

get on the bandwagon and say Frank Lloyd Wright is a genius. I only wish that people knew what they're saying and how true it is. I don't know much more to say and often wondered what I would say if I had to introduce Mr. Wright. It's a cryptic proposition!

STUDENTS: (laughter)

GOFF: But, anyway, he gave me a clue at dinner tonight when he told me that a man went up to talk to him one time and asked if he was Frank Lloyd Wright and he said "yes" and this gentleman said, "Well, you sure do improve with age!"

STUDENTS: (laughter)

GOFF: It's an optimum guarantee that Mr. Wright has improved with age and I'd like you to know Mr. Wright better than you know him now so I think he's the one to get acquainted with. Mr. Wright . . .

STUDENTS: (loud applause)

WRIGHT: Well, thank you ladies and gentlemen! I'm assured that this is a handpicked audience!

STUDENTS: (laughter)

WRIGHT: Somebody asked me what I thought of Gothic on the plains of Oklahoma. I was reminded of a story I've remembered my life long of old Dr. Johnson who—when asked by a very enthusiastic woman—would witness the performances of a trained dog standing on his hind legs and doing various other tricks, if he didn't think it was remarkable? "No madame," he said, "it is not remarkable but the fact that he should have done it at all is remarkable!"

STUDENTS: (laughter)

WRIGHT: And that's the way I feel (slight laughter) about Collegiate Gothic on the plains of Oklahoma.

STUDENTS: (continued laughter)

WRIGHT: Well now we're here tonight, all of us together, to consider the blind spot in American culture. And, what is it? Architecture. You see, the country knows nothing about architecture. You could go abroad, of course, and for 500 years you'd find that architecture has been lacking a soul. It's been traveling on effect. Well, of course, the tendency has always been to travel on effect. We see effects, and we like effects, we imitate the effects, and we've lived on imitation ourselves—we who shouldn't! We who made a Declaration of Independence! We who declared a new freedom for the individual perceived as such. Now we called that sovereignty of the individual "democracy" and that's what democracy means if it means anything. It means that the individual—free—finds for himself a great expression of life and his love of life which is his life. Primarily and basic in that would be architecture! Don't you know? Well, we were cheated out of it somehow and as some witty Frenchman has said, "We're the only great nation to have proceeded from barbarism to degeneracy with no culture of our own in between!"

STUDENTS: (loud outburst of laughter)

WRIGHT: Well now that's funny. You know if you realized the depth and the truth of that statement you wouldn't laugh. I laughed too when I first heard it. I think one of my clients improved on it. He said, "I remember when you quoted that Frenchman—we were the only great nation who proceeded from barbarism to capitalism with no culture of our own in between!"

STUDENTS: (laughter)

WRIGHT: Well that's better, isn't it?

STUDENTS: (laughter)

With the Students of the Profession

WRIGHT: I think it is! (slight laughter)

STUDENTS: (laughter)

WRIGHT: Well anyway it's practically true. We took for architecture what washed up on the eastern shores . . .

STUDENTS: (laughter)

WRIGHT: . . . and we've been traveling with it ever since. When I went to England last year they showed me around a bit. [They] took considerable pain to show me England. I went to the dormitory town and, of course, I saw beautiful old England which we—in America— missed. It's too bad that we never got anything of that beautiful old England! What we got was the provincial dormitory town. I learned what I was ashamed to learn, of course, that we had absolutely done nothing for ourselves—even the architraves, the windows, the carpenter work, and every detail for establishments is English provincial dormitory town—believe it or not.

Now if you want to see your own country, go to England and then discover it. Now how it got so broadcast—how it proceeded from Boston in the East, and Virginia, all over the country just the same, the same details of building and the same position, the same division of the plot, the same facing of the street, the same facades—got over the whole country, it's unbelievable! How could such a thing happen? But it did!

Well now, of course, we've got to wake up. We do have an architecture of our own and we have an architecture that belongs to this profession of freedom that we call democracy— the sovereignty of the individual which means architecture free. Now architecture free is not necessarily architecture for a fool because if you're acquainted with architecture at all, and you know architecture, you know that it's based upon principle—especially what we call *organic architecture*, which is really the architecture of democracy and that is truly our modern architecture. It's been made a monkey of, more or less, by various side issues and accidents but still the life of the thing has gone abroad and all the countries of the world—I should say much more than we are ourselves—are aware of this great thing which just happened by way of this profession of freedom which we in America established and which we call democracy—that architecture is *organic architecture*.

Well now, organic architecture is the basis from which all that we call modern architecture has proceeded. Of course it had effect and those effects have been taken, so far, as the thing itself. Well now, that's unavoidable in a nation like ours where everything goes by way of taste. Do you realize that taste is simply a matter of ignorance? Taste, as the old lady said when she kissed a cow, is just about that and it's pretty much that wherever you find it. I remember criticizing a house that had been built by a friend of mine and I didn't know the owner was standing there, but she was, and she heard what I said and she said: "Well anyhow, Mr. Wright, it suits them. It's theirs!" Well now, that was their taste . . .

STUDENTS: (laughter)

WRIGHT: . . . and by way of taste we've got everything we've got. In other words, by way of ignorance we have the architecture which we call our architecture of America today. Even the Capitol in Washington! Even that monument to Thomas Jefferson—a public comfort station— which was the best thing we could think of!

STUDENTS: (laughter)

WRIGHT: And when we wanted to honor Abraham Lincoln what did we do? What did

Wright: "*. . . a public comfort station . . .*" *The Thomas Jefferson Memorial, on the southeast side of the Washington, D.C. Tidal Basin, is a circular domed structure surrounded by Ionic columns. The central memorial room contains a bronze statue of Thomas Jefferson by Rudolph Evans. Photograph by the editor.*

we do when we wanted to honor the greatest character—let's say the greatest individual probably—the nation has produced? What did we do to honor him? Well you know, you've seen that Greek monument haven't you? The monument to the Greeks. Abraham Lincoln didn't wear a toga, did he? He wouldn't look well in one, would he? Not with those whiskers!

STUDENTS: (laughter)

WRIGHT: Well anyhow, that's what he got and I don't think of any American citizen who has fared any better.

Every great millionaire in America—every great capitalist who wanted to something for his country—what did he do when he felt the beckoning wasn't far away? Well, he cuddled

Wright: "*The monument to the Greeks. Abraham Lincoln didn't wear a toga, did he?*" *The Lincoln Memorial designed by Henry Bacon was completed at Washington, D.C. in 1917. Photograph by the editor.*

up to the past for respectability like Mellon [Andrew William Mellon] and all the rest of them and devoted his fortune to what *has* been. There's only one American millionaire that ever faced the future when he died and put his little white ally *[sic]* in what he believed in for the future. That was Solomon R. Guggenheim, who left $8 million to advance a kind of painting that everybody was laughing at—and laughing at him—and he didn't care. He believed in it and he left his fortune to the future. Can you think of another American millionaire who ever did such a thing?

Now why we are as a people so cowardly, so false true, too afraid, of course because we all are provincials! Now, you've noticed the provincial in society haven't you? You've been one yourself, maybe, in high company and society and you don't know quite how to behave yourselves. So you watch other people to see what they do with their hands, how they sit, how they behave themselves, don't you? And you do likewise, don't you? That is the provincial attitude to a culture and that is why our American millionaires and our colleges— and they are utterly provincial especially in the East . . .

STUDENTS: (laughter)

WRIGHT: . . . that is why they behave as they behave! They have no confidence in themselves! [They] do not believe in themselves! Having nothing of their own, they're quite willing to watch anybody that thinks he has something and go along. Well now that's all over.

I've just come back from Paris and Italy. The whole world—that's not an exaggeration—has concentrated its view upon what we call *organic architecture* as a true contribution to the culture of the world. We're the only ones— ourselves—who do not know it! Who do not realize that something has been born of freedom which is the most important thing that any civilization has recorded! And we treat it as though it was a street fight and record it accordingly and have no sense at home of what the thing means to the world of ours.

I've come here this evening and I could stand before you covered with gold medals and beautiful ribbons and all kinds of things and citations. Why? Just because the people from whom we expect a culture to come have looked over in our direction and seen culture developing which commands their respect— something they expected to come from this profession of freedom and haven't seen but have now seen. Why don't we see it? What's standing in the way, outside of this inevitable provincialism, which we can't help? Of course we're green, aren't we? How could we be otherwise? How do we know?

How do the people who founded this university [University of Oklahoma] know that it was treacherous to grow into the Gothic [architecture] on the plains of Oklahoma? How would they know? How would you know now? You go to Harvard—you go to these eastern colleges—you form associations—these young people who go to be educated in these things that have no longer any meaning—that no longer have any validity, and you become saturated with them. They're the only ideals that you have. The only picture that has been made for you of your own birthright. And, of course, you've been betrayed but I have an idea that you've betrayed yourself! I don't think anybody did it to you! I think you deserve what you've got! I think the kind of buildings you're living in are the kind that belong to you now and I don't think you deserve any better until you've learned better! Until you know what constitutes a good building!

Now what is it that constitutes a good building? What constitutes a beautiful atmosphere in which to live, move, and have your being? How can you grace not disgrace the landscape in which you live? What are those elements and principles? Because every great movement, every great thought that has ever been in the world was founded upon principle! Now what are the principles behind this thing we call *organic architecture*? Because they're there and organic architecture is supreme to be supreme because it is founded upon those principles and what are they? Very simple! The nature of the thing! All architecture heretofore for 500 years has had no soul! It's been lacking in soul! Why? Because it lost touch with principle. Because it no longer expressed a principle but by way of the taste—the whim—the feeling—of various artistic people became this, that, and the other. Because it lost its principle of being and lost its soul.

Now all architecture for many years has been nothing but this—cut, butt, and slash—the post and the beam—you see, like that. That's all the architecture of the Renaissance was! The architecture of the Renaissance was a facade! Nothing but a facade! By way of taste! Pilasters, effects, arches, this, that, the other, anything to make a picture! All right, now we've come to a point in architecture where it has to *be*. Where it's according to the nature of the thing. Where the thing is more like this—integral, one, one with site, one with nature, one with the material of which the building is built—and a bulding where you can ask *why* concerning everything

in it and get a good answer from the building itself! Well now, that hasn't happened in the world before—at least for 500 years! And all you hear of it is something superficial and about equal to the reporting of a slugging match in the street or a quiet fight somewhere or a baseball game. Here the whole nature and vitality of an idea of a civilization has come alive and what do you see of it? What do we see of it? The world is seeing it abroad! It's seeing it in Italy and honoring it! It's seeing it in France and the Beaux Arts and honoring it and realizing what has happened! And at home we don't know anything about it!

Well now, why is that so? Why do we know nothing of the virtue of an *organic architecture* that is the basis for a democratic culture at home? There must be some good reason! Well, I'll tell you the reason. It's education! It's the way we're educated. It's Harvard! It's Yale! It's all these superficial applications to culture instead of this development from within of the nature of a culture! We're being processed by way of education instead of developed from within by way of a culture. Well now, I suppose that that's true. I suppose that's in the realm of the otherwhere than the here. But if you think about it—if any of you are capable of thinking—getting back to first principles and asking *why*? That's the question that isn't asked in education anywhere. That is the unpopular question to ask anywhere in America! *Why*? Ask *why* the Korean War—you'll get a dozen hundred different answers! Ask *why* the university exists as present—you'll get another hundred! All rationalizations! Never the truth! Never on speaking terms with principle!

Well now, what is *principle*? I'm speaking of *principle* with a capital P and there's no getting

With the Students of the Profession

at architecture—there's no getting at this *new movement* we'll call it—I don't like the term *new movement* because it's older than Lao-tse, 500 years before Jesus—this principle we're talking about in architecture is the most ancient thing probably in philosophic thought! Jesus himself was the greatest promulgator of an organic architecture! Why and how? When he said: "The kingdom of God is within you!" And that's where the kingdom of architecture is! It's within you! It's within the nature of your situation! The nature of your environment! The nature of your site! The nature of the pile you've got to stand! The nature of what you like and what you don't like, which isn't so important as you think it is! It's in the nature of things! And it's in nature study that you're going to find out the difference between a democratic idealogy of a civilization—of a culture—and a Nazi ideal or a Communistic ideal, or any other ideal! It all lies right in that thing. Right in discovering that innate principle and nature of what is! Well that's nature study. It's the only study that's worth anything anywhere, anytime, anyhow and a university or any other institution which is not founded relentlessly upon the truth of that is not going to bring democracy to pass. It's going to miscarry the whole thing and it's doing it and of course your press reflects it. Everything we have reflects that sidestepping of the truth—sidestepping of the issue which is in the nature of principle. Well you've heard all of this before. This isn't new to your ears I'm sure. You've heard and you've read the Bible and you've been to Sunday school and you've heard these things, more or less, mouthed over haven't you? But you've never realized the meaning of them! You've never brought them home! You've never put them into effect! In other words you've never built them!

Now I had an idea early in my career—I was a very arrogant young man—in my case I was so sure of my ground and my star that I had to choose early in life between an honest arrogance and a hypocritical humility!

STUDENTS: (loud outburst of laughter)

WRIGHT: Yes, I did!

STUDENTS: (continued laughter)

WRIGHT: And I deliberately chose an honest arrogance and have never been sorry because I couldn't have served the *cause* by any hypocritical humility! But I had an idea that I was a prophet! That I had discovered something tremendously important to civilization and what was it? That the reality of a building didn't consist—did *not* consist—in the walls and the roof of that structure—not in those walls—not in that ceiling—but in the space in there to be lived in. There was the reality! Well, I built it! Unity Temple was the first time when the walls disappeared, when the ceiling went out and you saw right outside under the ceiling and when the walls became screens—features—and the whole room came through as an essential fact and truth. Well, you couldn't touch me with a ten-foot pole! I thought my God! I am a prophet! See what I've done!

STUDENTS: (loud laughter)

WRIGHT: And then I came back one day and the ambassador to America from Japan sent me a little book called *The Book of Tea* by Okakura Kakuzo. Have any of you read it? Have any of you seen that little book? Bruce has [Bruce Goff]! Have any of you seen it? No? Get it!

STUDENT: Someone over here has!

WRIGHT: Yes! Hurrah for you!

STUDENTS: (laughter)

WRIGHT: Well, I read it. In it I read this—the reality of the building does not consist of the four walls and the roof but in the space to be lived in!

STUDENTS: (laughter)

WRIGHT: All right, I came down like a sail coming down.

STUDENTS: (loud laughter)

WRIGHT: Why . . . after all . . . 500 years before Jesus—Lao-tse! What to do now? Where to go from here? (slight laughter)

STUDENTS: (laughter)

WRIGHT: I couldn't destroy the book . . . I mean . . .

STUDENTS: (loud laughter)

WRIGHT: I knew I couldn't hide! I knew the damned thing had to come out!

STUDENTS: (continued laughter)

WRIGHT: So I vegetated for several weeks. This was up there in the country at Taliesin. I went out and worked on the roads and began to think things over and, of course, like all human nature—indestructible—I began to think oh well here now, I built it! And I built it before I knew anything about this idea. I think I'm one up on Lao-tse. I think after all (slight laughter) I'm a great man! I can . . .

STUDENTS: (outburst of loud laughter)

WRIGHT: I can go on with it because while he only had the idea, I had it and built it! So I began to swell up again!

STUDENTS: (laughter)

WRIGHT: And ever since I've been all right!

STUDENTS: (loud laughter and applause)

WRIGHT: Well, you see we live by ideas. We don't live by science. We don't live by the tools.

Don't you see? We can't live by the tool box. Now we can use the tools but the idea is the same and until we have ideas and until we know the value of the idea—until we protect, champion, and defend the idea as a democratic essence—we haven't got a democracy. You can talk about teamwork, you can talk about this and that, you can beckon forth and stride forth, and you can do everything imaginable . . . because nothing will reward life in a democracy except allegiance to and practice of the essential nature of the idea. Now that's the great message I've brought to you here tonight and I have a right to bring it because my life has been devoted to it and I haven't perked my colors at home or abroad. And I tell you plainly and sincerely that nothing is worth a man's time—and that means a woman's—except his search for the beautiful and an attempt to establish it in human life by way of the human being and education. There is the secret we missed as a nation. You go out into our villages and what do you see? Ugliness. We hear about public service—corporations—what do they do to the country? They give us this life but they blot out our landscape! Poles—wires—ugliness everywhere! Service stations—what are they? The shops—the stores—they try to be beautiful. They would be if they knew how! If somebody would tell them and that's why we need architects! This nation needs architects more than it needs anything else and it needs the knowledge of architecture which is basic to the culture—basic to a civilization.

Architecture is the mother art out of which the others must come or to which they must come or we do not have a culture—not of our own. So, do you realize that only one-tenth of all the buildings built in America today have an architect at all? And out of that ten percent probably one-tenth have an architect, really, who is a good architect and he's getting scarcer and scarcer by way of the education he receives! Instead of being cultivated and developed from within—this way—again it's the old problem—the old mistake of getting obsession by way of effect—effect—seeing effects and taking them and putting them on this way, you see? That's practically what the young—the youth of America—are doing in school today everywhere and not only here but abroad. But it's changing abroad more rapidly than here. It's changing a little here. You have a different condition here by way of Bruce Goff and his helpers. You're getting a little deeper in and a little nearer the truth! But ordinarily it's still superficial. Ordinarily it's still on the surface. Ordinarily it still misses the core and essence of the truth in the development of a culture. I don't know why it is that we at home seem so obtuse when it comes to admitting and developing and exposing something so manifestly right! That's no pun! But we must wake up to the fact that now we do have the center line for a culture for democracy which is *organic architecture* and which alone can bring us home to the thing that our forefathers regarded, hoped for, and prophesied. I think if Walt Whitman, Tom Payne, and Thomas Jefferson, even Franklin, George Washington, were to take a look at us today I don't know what they would feel! Confusion certainly; disillusionment a little bit; they couldn't understand how it all happened!

Well now, here on the wide western prairies—I've always thought of the Middlewest as the cradle of democracy—you've heard the phrase— and here in the Middlewest as anywhere in this nation we will find and establish those truths of being and that element of beauty which justifies human existence if it's ever to be done anywhere. That I believe. I believe the East has gone so far and is so involved now with the other side of what it imagines to be the other side that you can't hope for it there but you can hope for it here. I think that is the liberty, the beauty, and the privilege of our position in the Midwest. We are free . . . we have been more foolish—it isn't that we haven't been monkeys too—but we haven't taken it very seriously I believe and hope anyhow that we haven't and we can shoot it now and we can go straight to the thing that has meaning and significance.

Where is an instance where you cannot build a building that hasn't some social significance? You cannot put two sticks together but that you express something—either that or this or this or that or whatever you do! Every building you build has a certain social significance. Now take the United Nations Building in New York City, for instance, which is the latest fiasco. What have you there? Two party walls standing up like this—symbols of division—the apotheosis of the New York party wall! As a symbol for the unification of the world! How ridiculous!

Well, you see what I mean.

Now you build a building, you build a house, you build anything—it has significance. No man can build anything and hide! You've got him when he builds! You know what he knows! You know that he is that thing or he isn't any better! You know he doesn't know any better! Don't you? When he builds what he built! Yes, well now we got him—this boogeyman that's the death of American culture will get you if you don't look out!

When you build you've got to build now not by way of your own taste, not by way of what you think is pretty and charming but you got to know something! Now how are you going to know something? How are you going to know the principles that constitute a good act and a good building? Nobody knows and least of all the professors! Least of all the regents of a university or we wouldn't have the universities we have! Least of all the educational pooh-bahs—they don't know! I'll venture to say the pooh-bahs of Cornell or Harvard wouldn't know a good building from a bad one! And all the other presidents of universities I think could be put into the same category and so would all the teachers, the professors, the experts! There is a lamentable lack of perception—an understanding—where buildings are concerned and that's why I've started this discourse by saying we're going to talk about the blind spot in American culture, which is building! Think it over. I doubt if any of you could go through your own village and say what was good and what was bad. Well now, that's terrible! Isn't it? What are you educated for? What is the basis of an education? You go to school—what for? For nothing other than—as I can see it and as I understand it—to learn about yourself and learn who you are, what you are, how you are—don't you? Or do you go to get some technical knowledge to make a living? Well that isn't a university. That's something else. That isn't even high school. That's a trade school. Now if all education is going to descend to a level of a trade school and you can learn nothing about the nature of the human soul and learn nothing about these things I've been talking about, well, you aren't educated! Would you call Harry Truman an educated person?

STUDENTS: (laughter)

WRIGHT: Would you call any of our senators

educated people? Eisenhower? No, none of them! Not the kind of education this nation needs to be saved from the brink of failure because we're pretty close to failure—ladies and gentlemen—pretty close. We have become militaristic, we have become imperialistic, we've become everything we were not intended to be by the founders of our nation. How did we get that way? You think education is innocent? I don't. I know better. I know that education is something that develops the man from within and that the kind of education we've had is plastered on him from the outside and can't get results!

Only by way of experience, only by way of working upon one's self can we get the difference between a horse, a cow, a chicken, and a pig, and a human being! The difference is just there. The difference lies in a house that's not a sty—in a house that's not just merely a place to eat, sleep, and take your shoes off and be comfortable but a place that has an atmosphere of beauty, of repose, of charm, of quality that belongs to the spirit. How many American homes have it? I go into them here, there, and everywhere and I do feel a love and a quality that might, were it enlightened, result in the thing I'm talking about. But who's going to give it to them? Who's going to take these children? Who's going to show them the road and tell them how to make these distinctions and how to build them and establish them in their lives and get that result which really is culture?

Now a civilization is not a culture. A civilization is merely a way of life and a culture is the way you try to make it beautiful! Now we have a civilization that's gone so far but what have we done to try and make it beautiful? That would

With the Students of the Profession

be a culture and we haven't got one. So we're back to where we started! Well, I'm here this evening to try and assure you that we have found ourselves by way of freedom—by way of the profession we have made as a nation—we have found the center line of a democracy and the center line for a culture of our own and we can't neglect it and let it die.

Now, anything you want to ask an old veteran in the field? If you let me get away from here without a lot of questions it'll be just too bad for you! Me too! So what I've said must awaken in your brains some remonstrance? I suppose I've insulted you, haven't I? I don't mean to but probably I have. Now is your time to resent it! How do you feel about all of this? Have I been telling you the truth?

STUDENT: Yes.

WRIGHT: Good! All right now where do we go from here? Somebody must want to know how to build a $3,500 house?

STUDENTS: (laughter)

WRIGHT: Usually they want me to design a house for them. One price of admission and I refuse!

STUDENTS: (laughter)

WRIGHT: I'll do anything I can do to elucidate—clarify. I'm accused of befogging the issue and being very complex. Have I been very complex tonight?

STUDENT: Well, I'm going to ask one question. You said that Gothic is out of place on the plains of Oklahoma and I'd like to know your ideas about the ranch house—the ranch-type house here.

WRIGHT: Yes, I've heard that term!

STUDENTS: (loud laughter and applause)

WRIGHT: The ranch-type house! You used to have a bungalow, do you remember?

STUDENT: Yes sir.

WRIGHT: We don't have bungalows any more, do we?

STUDENT: I don't know, sir. I don't know if I can exactly define a "bungalow."

WRIGHT: (laughter) It'll be the same as a ranch house two or three years from now!

STUDENTS: (laughter)

WRIGHT: I think what they're calling a ranch house is pretty nearly straight Frank Lloyd Wright. Does that sound redefined?

STUDENTS: (laughter and loud applause)

WRIGHT: You know they'll do anything to avoid giving it an honest name!

STUDENTS: (laughter continues)

WRIGHT: In America you know culture is a bastard and it cannot have a name. Think that one over!

STUDENTS: (slight laughter)

WRIGHT: And it is true. All American culture today has been a bastard and it has been denied a name except a fictitious one. Now to give it an honest name isn't necessary. We don't have to name it at all if only we would do it! If only we would build something significant. I think that the ranch house is a pretty good way in the right direction. It's low and broad and habitable and it belongs, usually, where it's built—doesn't it? All right, so far so good. It's usually hardly a keg of nails and that kind of thing but they haven't learned yet how to develop it. You see, people who build ranch houses are usually people who favor horses, cows, and animals and they haven't quite learned yet how to modify the place in which they live just to get out of it some charm. Now what the ranch house usually lacks is charm. How would you define charm, anyway? What is charm? It isn't the same for everybody, I guess. What would you call a charming house? Something that picks you up and makes you feel like music—that you're somewhere that you love to be. What is that quality? You all know it in various conditions somewhere, somehow, don't you? Did you ever experience charm?

STUDENT: Yes sir!

WRIGHT: Good! How many of you have experienced charm? Don't be so backwards in acknowledging something. You'll really hurt yourselves, most of you. Most of you are charming aren't you? Can be! Well, it's that charm—that quality. It's a quality! It's something you should find wherever you go! Something your village should have and, by the way, if you allow your villages to be villages and not try to imitate cities, which are dead anyway! You know there isn't a city in the United States today of over 100,000 inhabitants that's solvent! And, moreover, not one that can subsist on its own birthright for three years! These are statistics—facts! They're all vampires. They're living on a countryside and on the villages! Well what a charming thing the American village could be if it would only be content to be a village and not what I call a sanitary slum!

STUDENTS: (mild uproar of talking)

WRIGHT: That's what housing is in America—a sanitary slum! What would be individual and charming and portray or express the individual who lived in that place and who owned it and who contributed to the neighborhood—plenty of plantings—room, elbow room—not on the street—well, what's the use? You'll get there someday! So be an American village that really is a place to live in. They have them in Europe you know! See a Swiss village—see a French village south of France—see an English village, but in the old sense not the dormitory towns we copied. But look at all those things and they have the charm and we have none! Now what happened to it? Do we care? No, I don't think we do. I don't think we know enough to care! We don't know what's the matter with us.

I'm here tonight (slight laughter) trying to tell you some of the things that are the matter with you and the result will be that you'll think that it's really what's the matter with me! That's the usual American reaction!

STUDENT: Sir, you say that our educational system is hindering the students that go to school nowadays and who try to find expression from within. Take myself for instance, I never did—up until the time I got into architecture school—but now I'm trying to find myself and, as you say, I want to do things to help but I don't really know what to look for in the educational system.

WRIGHT: I know. [There are] millions of people in your fix!

STUDENTS: (laughter)

WRIGHT: The best thing you can do now to get started is to ask *why*. *Why* is the thing that way? *Why* is this shape such as I see it to be—do I like it? I wonder *why* I like it? What has happened? See? Begin to dig in and answer *why*—you'll begin to form an opinion—a feeling of your own. You'll begin, if you ever build a house for yourself, to respect those feelings which are really now, by way of questioning, related to principle. You'll know *why* a thing is done—you'll know *why* you like it or *why* you don't like it. We don't ask *why*—

Frank Lloyd Wright (left) autographs a book for a student at the University of Oklahoma at Norman on May 2, 1952 as architect Bruce Goff (right) watches. Photograph courtesy of E. Fay Jones, FAIA.

we accept a fashion. Everything tends to be a fashion. Here we have organic architecture, which is now becoming a fashion because of modern architecture. Modern architecture is going toward the gutter as a fashion soon. Why? Because people don't ask *why*? They don't reason about the thing. They don't look the so-called gift horse in the teeth! You'd soon find out if you get into the habit of asking *why*. You'd see if a thing was good or bad but until you know *why* it's good or *why* it's bad what hope have you? Who are you? You know the old saying about a sucker that was born every minute? You're one of them!

STUDENTS: (somewhat reluctant laughter)

STUDENT: Mr. Wright, if we are to understand the views of our contemporaries by reasoning or logic—and after all that's the only manner in which we can study their views and their inspiration plays such a great part in the field—

then it's our job to encourage the modern themes in culture and architecture.

WRIGHT: Oh, my dear boy! You know because a thing is modern is no recommendation for it! It's got to be more than modern! It's got to be good! Now a thing, just because it's modern, isn't necessarily any better than what was bad! And a good deal of modern architecture makes me sick! But a good deal of modern architecture that is good is right and on the right track and is going in the right direction but it needs to be criticized. It needs to be looked at close and you can't take it just because it's modern! Because I know modern architecture which is nothing but the old clichés and which is the old thought come back again and we've tried by organic architecture to eliminate the box and to liberate the human spirit in the building and relate it to its environment. So the box comes back and it's modern architecture. Those are the things you have got to get at by asking *why*. I can't recommend anything . . . than to always question what it is.

You're living in an era now when everything is more or less phony. You can't get the truth regarding anything from newspapers. You can't get it from Sunday school. You can't get it in the colleges. How are you goint to get it? By simply pouring into the nature of the thing itself and finding out *why* and not being satisfied with

any fancy peacocking around! Well, I think you've had enough! I certainly have!

STUDENTS: (loud applause as Mr. Wright starts leaving the room)

WRIGHT: (Mr. Wright turns around while leaving the room) Ladies and gentlemen, one last word—don't forget that *why!*

STUDENTS: (continued applause as Mr. Wright exits)

With the Students of the Profession

Frank Lloyd Wright with the Student Architect of the University of California–Berkeley

I understand you're all students here tonight. That makes it unanimous—I'm one too. I am not a professional. I am an amateur like you—quite proud of it . . . One of the few that has escaped!

In April 1957 Frank Lloyd Wright was invited to the University of California–Berkeley to give a number of lectures and seminars to architecture students as a guest Bernard Maybeck Lecturer in architecture. Part One of this chapter is the text of one such lecture delivered on April 24, 1957 followed by a student question and answer period.

It was during this Berkeley trip that Wright's creative genius became focused on the design of a new government complex for Marin County, California*

A meeting was arranged with him privately at the Grant Avenue offices of the Frank Lloyd Wright Foundation in San Francisco on April 26, 1957 . . . four [Marin County] supervisors . . . along with the entire Civic Center Committee met with Frank Lloyd Wright and his associate, Aaron Green, that day and heard his lecture in Berkeley that night, and the Marinites came away convinced apostles of Louis Sullivan's "Spiritual

This heretofore unpublished lecture, seminar, and conversation is published by permission of the University of California–Berkeley, College of Environmental Design/Department of Architecture. Copyright © 1984 Frank Lloyd Wright Foundation.

*From Evelyn Morris Radford, *The Genius and the County Building: How Frank Lloyd Wright Came to Marin County, California, and Glorified San Rafael*, unpublished dissertation submitted to the Graduate Division of the University of Hawaii in partial fulfillment of the requirements for the degree of Doctor of Philosophy in American Studies, August 1972, pp. 128–130.

Child." Wright is reported to have said, "So Marin County wants an architect!"... Wright's suggestion that the building should reflect the personality of the county was the magic that settled the issue. Marin County had an architect.*

The following morning, April 27, Wright conducted an informal seminar with the Berkeley architecture students which was structured as a question and answer session with the master. His rapport with these young architects was great. Part Two of this chapter is the text of that memorable seminar.

The Lecture, Questions, and Seminar

PART ONE
The Lecture and Questions

WRIGHT: Ladies and gentlemen, let's make it that, I understand you're all students here tonight. That makes it unanimous—I'm one too. I am not a professional. I am an amateur like you—quite proud of it.

STUDENTS: (laughter)

WRIGHT: One of the few that has escaped! Well, this is rather a surprise tonight for me. I thought I was scheduled for three or four appearances but this is an extra one. And inasmuch as we're all students here together it doesn't so much matter.

Why don't you make up your minds about what you most would like to hear me talk about and let some questions come to me from the floor and let me answer them for you. I think in that way we can round out a more profitable evening than if I were to try and talk to you and tell *you* what I think you ought to know. Because I know a lot of things you ought to know!

STUDENTS: (laughter and applause)

WRIGHT: So, who'll start this ball rolling?

STUDENTS: (laughter)

WRIGHT: Who doesn't know all there is to be known about architecture?

STUDENTS: (laughter)

WRIGHT: If so, let him stand and utter himself. What bothers you most—you young students—you young America?

And, by the way, I've just come from Arizona from a combined meeting of the teenagers of the state concerning a building for the capitol of Arizona. A building I was dissatisfied with as a taxpayer. And, with a special know-how, went after the architects because of the sidewalk-happy building they were trying to put over on the future of Arizona. Think of politicians being allowed to judge who and how a state capitol that would represent the state for 300 years to come—how and what it should look like. Isn't it a goody like having the politicians choose your ministers for you in the churches? Isn't it something like having them say who'll build your house for you? How more should they say who'll build the great edifices for you that are going to characterize your *future*? Well now, we've started off on the wrong foot!

STUDENTS: (laughter)

WRIGHT: But it does seem to me ridiculous—I think criminal—that the very things that are permanently characteristic, that are going to circumscribe what our sense of beauty is now and in the future should be a political matter or in some way connected with real estate investment. Now that's something you youngsters are here to consider.

Frank Lloyd Wright studies the program at his Mile-High Illinois Skyscraper Project presentation and testimonial dinner at Chicago in 1956. Photograph by C. A. Thompson, courtesy of The Capital Times, *Madison, Wisconsin.*

I believe the future of these United States, architecturally, does not lie with the architects now. I think the architects are not going to determine what that future is going to be beyond a few years hence. There must be coming from us—to us—something out of democracy in the way of a freedom which has its basis in nature. The study of nature not the study of anything or any system of any synthetic system of knowledge ever promulgated. It must be original.

It must be out of the nature of our freedom; out of the nature of our ideal—the sovereignty of the individual. What does that mean? Our forefathers conferred upon us this ideal of the sovereignty of the individual. Well now that means, of course, doesn't it, an aristocracy? It doesn't mean the common man supreme—this is only for a moment—an innate aristocracy not an aristocracy conferred upon the man by some power from without—something he develops from within his own life by way of his own soul and own sense of things. There is the aristrocracy they wanted. The aristocracy they heralded by the Declaration of Independence, by our constitution, by what we ourselves have set up in the light of the whole world and we aren't living up to it, not architecturally. And if we don't architecturally we aren't going to do it any other way because architecture is the essential cornerstone of a culture. Now you can have a civilization, such as we have, without a culture. In fact it's said of us—we're proud— that we're the only great nation who proceeded directly from barbarism to degeneracy with no culture of our own!

STUDENTS: (laughter)

WRIGHT: That's always good for a laugh but God help us—it's true! Now we're on the way to one, *perhaps*, but are we going to get it without an architecture of our own? We can't. Go back down the line—study history, analyze, don't keep comparing all the time. Don't compare this with that and that with this and tell of the other. See what it is that you're looking *in*—you're all trying to look *at*. Compare this thing with that thing and that with this and the other—you never go deeper than the surface that way. But the moment you take the thing that you look at—take it apart—take it so you can look into the nature of that thing—you'll learn, you'll grow, [you'll] get your feet on something after a while.

And I want to give you something now that'll be worth the evening if I don't succeed in saying anything else. I was in Wales lately. The National University of Wales got the notion they wanted to hang a hood on my shoulders. My grandfather was a Welsh immigrant. My mother was ten years old when she came away from Wales. But I don't imagine many of you know much about Wales—Stonehenge was Wales—King Arthur was Wales—and there is an old Welsh wisdom coming down [in] a book called *Mobinogion*. The *Mabinogion* is a saying in threes—in triads—they're very famous in Wales—the triads of the *Mabinogion*. Well now the definition of a genius—you know a nation has a genius—a man is a genius—a genius means the essential virtue and character of the individual. So, the definition of a genius for you all—a genius is a man who has an eye to see nature. A genius is a man with a heart to feel nature. And a genius is a man with a boldness to follow nature. There is the wisdom that's come down and never have I heard, or will you ever hear, a more appropriate definitive definition of what constitutes human genius.

Now of course, it doesn't strike the circle completely for you because it doesn't define too the meaning of the word *nature* as it was used in the *Mabinogion*. *Nature* with a capital N, of course, doesn't mean horses, cows, and plants, and trees, and birds you know only. It means the very intrinsic character of whatever is. It means what's there inside. It means this ability not to see at but to see in and once you get that habit of thought, once you get your feet planted on that course, in that direction, they'll call you "a genius" and they'll probably be right.

So, that is what is lacking now in our present situation in America. That's what's the matter in our educational circles. That's what's the matter with our architecture. That's pretty much what's the matter with our civilization. It's a civilization without a culture. We're living in a field in a time when great advantages—magnificent advantages—all becoming disadvantageous for the lack of the prophetic genius who can see into the nature of the thing, analyze it, and make it beneficial.

To illustrate what I'm saying now all you need to do is look at the cars out in the street. What are they? What is the nature of the car? It's mobile, isn't it? Isn't mobility the nature of the car? What's mobile about the present car except the name?

STUDENTS: (laughter)

WRIGHT: And maybe the engine because the engine isn't so bad. The engine's pretty good! But look at the design of it! Now you could take it from there. They look as though they're engendered to fight each other in the street.

STUDENTS: (laughter and applause)

WRIGHT: Well, are they mobile? You know fish

With the Students of the Profession

are mobile when they have to go in one another like this. If you were to accent the corners of a fish like a platform and then put a guard on the corner how many fish would be lying on the surface dead in harmony?

STUDENTS: (laughter)

WRIGHT: And it's still an old lumber wagon trying to digest four wheels!

STUDENTS: (laughter)

WRIGHT: But it doesn't need too! There're no ruts now in the roads. You don't have to have four wheels running in a rut. Well now what's the matter? I'm using this as an illustration. What's the matter with the mind that can produce, consume, use, and approve those cars?

Now take it from the car to your buildings, to your house—the place that you live in. They're not very much more sensible. They're the old box with compartments in the box. They're the old steel framing of the nineteenth century and that was what gave us all these upturned bridges, you know. You see them everywhere around here with great high steel overheads instead of the low beautiful arch the way it is combined with the landscape and don't hang upon a paint brush and a pot of paint for their life. Yet they go on building the other ones—for what?

Well, I could go on here the whole evening through taking one thing after another . . . get to your clothes . . . you wouldn't be very much better off.

STUDENTS: (laughter)

WRIGHT: And so it goes all down the line. There's lacking in everything we do, in the way we do it, that knowledge of *nature*—that ability

to construct, to conceive first of all and then construct, and then use the way of life that really is according to genius.

Well now, it sounds very simple—it sounds easy—but let's get back for a moment to what we meant by nature. Now when you speak of nature, you, of course, think of out of doors and you think of oceans, and perhaps the cosmic system. And all of that is nature but it's only one small phase of nature. *Nature* is all there is that any of you will ever see of the body of God. Now that sounds like heresy, perhaps, here. But the more you think about it the less you'll see heresy in it and the more you'll begin to understand that the study of nature is the study of God himself.

Now when you do violence to anything—to do anything inviolate to your sense of propriety, to your sense of honor, to your sense of what is beautiful, which is the most important thing for us now in the world, I think—truly beautiful— whenever you do violence to anything of that sort you commit murder in the first degree. And that's the murder that matters. It doesn't have to matter so much how many people are killed as it does matter how much ugliness people have to suffer from as long as they live.

Well architecture . . . the mission of an architect and of architecture is to help people understand how to make life more beautiful, the world better we're living in, and to give reason— rhyme—meaning—all that mean beauty to whatever is. Somebody asked me the other day: "Well what do you mean by architecture?" Well, what I mean by architecture is the structure of whatever is. Your structure—the way you're put together. It's interesting to see how you're built. You know you're built from the

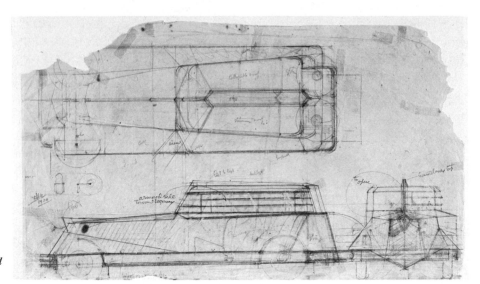

Sketch of a proposed automobile with a cantilevered top designed by Frank Lloyd Wright in 1920. Copyright © The Frank Lloyd Wright Foundation, 1962.

Sketch of a proposed automobile designed by Frank Lloyd Wright in 1958. Copyright © The Frank Lloyd Wright Foundation, 1962.

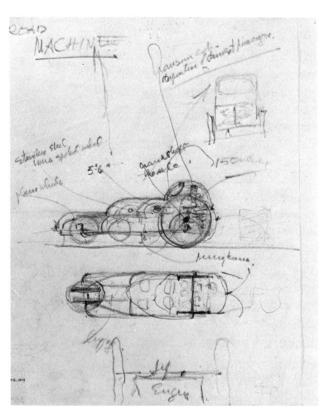

190

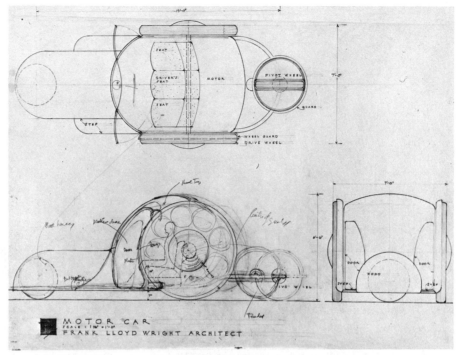

Refined drawing dated 1959 of Frank Lloyd Wright's proposed automobile of 1958. The vertical body of the automobile is balanced between two large wheels with steering by tiller and power applied from a power plant at the rear directly to the axle of the large wheels. The fuel supply and engine weight ensure gravity of the automobile while the front smaller spherical wheel ensures vehicle stability and allows for short turns. If a taxicab, the driver is above as in a hansom cab as shown in the drawing. Copyright © The Frank Lloyd Wright Foundation, 1962.

inside out! You're built on a spine. Your ribs come out, your arms extend, your fingers droop!

STUDENTS: (laughter)

WRIGHT: Well now that's twentieth-century architecture!

STUDENTS: (laughter)

WRIGHT: Now the old architecture is the old box built up with a post, you know, framed, riveted together. It was nothing but a frame and then from that they went inside and did the rest. Well now that's what we call nineteenth-century architecture and that's all we've got. New York has no other building except the one I'm building now on Fifth Avenue.

STUDENTS: (laughter and applause)

WRIGHT: I don't think you have one in San Francisco at all.

STUDENTS: (laughter)

WRIGHT: Maybe you have—maybe you can find one but I haven't seen it. Now why? Why

The Solomon R. Guggenheim Museum (1956), New York, looking southeast from the intersection of Fifth Avenue and East 89 Street. The museum portion of the building is on the right and its administration offices are on the left. Photograph by Robert E. Mates, courtesy of the Solomon R. Guggenheim Museum, New York.

does this study of nature which would have given us this building sixty years ago and did but we didn't know? And we kept right on building the old way and we're keeping right on, now, building in the old way calling it the new way just because it has a new look about it. It was just the same, essentially, as the old way. Now what are we going to do about it? You want [to be] an architect—you want to build buildings—father wants one—Uncle Henry or Aunt Patty has got a million or two and wants to move into a beautiful place— what's she going to do? Going to hire and architect, isn't she? What's he got? And try and find out where he got it! And that's the situation we're in. That's why we need good architects now more than we need anything else—even doctors.

You—the body quality—is rather vigorous but so confoundedly ignorant and the system—our physique—has improved to such an extent that we're liable to be overpopulated in a very short time. But we haven't got a grasp on that thing which would give us salvation, nobility, strength of faith in human character and human nature. And give us cities, buildings, homes, examples of the beautiful construction and way of life that the world has ever seen. Now why shouldn't we have those? What's the matter?

We've got the makings, we've got the way with all the know-how to build anything. We can build a building a mile high from the inside out—twentieth-century construction—we can't build it with nineteenth century. Now that isn't the only thing, nineteenth-century construction there standing in our way to prevent. No, because there is a larger finer sense of beauty come from these interior sources of knowledge. It's no longer the old recipe. It's no longer the

Interior view of the exhibition ramps of the main gallery of the Solomon R. Guggenheim Museum. Photograph by Carmelo Guadagno, courtesy of the Solomon R. Guggenheim Museum, New York.

Interior view in the gallery portion of the Solomon R. Guggenheim Museum looking up at the ninety-two-foot-high skylight dome at the apex of the building. Photograph by Robert E. Mates, courtesy of the Solomon R. Guggenheim Museum, New York.

old things that you had to stick on to get an effect. It's now something you've got to grow, cultivate.

You know *culture* is a greater word than education and yet today education isn't even on speaking terms with culture. Every one of you would know what I'm talking about and agree with me; but it isn't. So you've got to do a little figuring for yourself—independent—and you can only do it not by comparing one man with another man—another building with another building. You can only do it by getting at the meaning of each building in itself so far as you're able to. And at first you won't be able to to do very much. Looking *in* isn't so easy as looking *at*. And it's a nice easy thing to roam and look at and look around and compare this with that. Well, that's what your education is amounting to. Do you believe it? You're getting conditioned into a habit of mind by something that is not constructive. I won't say it's destructive except as it stands in the way of construction. Now when construction is needed then it's in the way.

We want fresher minds and that's why I've gone to the young minds in Arizona with its capitol. I believe that still in the young minds is a freshness and its susceptibility to fragrance, to beauty, to rhythm, to just proportion that doesn't exist after you've been educated beyond the school and percolated through God knows how many millions of ill-conditioned, ill-designed buildings. It's like putting something through a sieve and it isn't an appropriate method. So you've got to be rebels, to a certain extent. You've got to stand up for what you feel. An analysis by proper something or other, I guess, is no substitute for the inheritance of a sense of proportion. If you haven't that there isn't much

that an architect can do to enlighten. Not much that I can do; I don't know who can do much for you. But if you do have that . . . if you do have that sense of proportion and will take care of it, nourish it, let it grow, you'll become strong and useful and this country will be immediately affected by what you know, who you are, and what comes from you. Well now that's pretty serious talk and I didn't intend to give it to you but I guess I got time so I exuded at the pause.

Now is anything more simple now? Is there anything you want to learn children—young America—that I can tell you? Part of the long trip . . . I've come a long way. I'd be happy to . . .

STUDENT: What would you suggest, Mr. Wright, as a part of the field of architectural education? Architectural education—what do you feel about architectural education?

WRIGHT: I don't believe in it!

STUDENTS: (loud laughter and applause)

WRIGHT: Perhaps a . . . perhaps you don't quite understand what I mean.

STUDENTS: (more laughter)

WRIGHT: I mean that we don't need architectural education so much as we need architectural culture. Now the difference between *culture* and *education* is tremendously important in the arts. Now you can't get an architect the way you get a business man. You can't get an architect the way you get a scientist! An architect is a creative artist first of all! If he isn't, for God's sake call him something else! That's what I'd wish they'd do to most of them right now.

STUDENTS: (laughter)

WRIGHT: You see an architect is primarily a basic poet. And, whether you were taught so or not, the poet has always been and will always be an unacknowledged legislator of this universe. Have you been taught that? How many of you believe it? Not many . . .

STUDENTS: (slight laughter)

WRIGHT: . . . all of you will the more you develop. The more you'll grow and the more humanity you possess—and what they call wisdom—the more you'll subscribe to that. Now we want, today, the poet. We want the poetry of life. We want that quality which I've been telling you about—the world should describe it as *genius*. And it comes . . . it's going to come to us from that unspoiled, faithful nature of the individual which has been made free by our Declaration of Independence. You're all free . . . this whole room full of youngsters that you are. There isn't one of you that has anything standing in your way to be one of those discoverers, promulgators, enrichers of humankind, instead of one of these parasites.

Still . . . what are these heavy charges? You'll find out not only the good nature—the good faith— aren't even going to last you see because the meaning of nearly everything is lost. It isn't like the car alone. It's everything else. Look at the buildings you're in. Look at even the continuity here on the way down. Look at anything you've got. Look at anything anybody's got where education treads today. Education is in it's slump and education is in a fix. And education, until it comes to terms with culture, you're going to have no architecture. You're going to have no poetry. Nothing you really know is going to have any real fragrance, flavor—no.

There's something I've wanted to say but I've forgotten what it was!

STUDENTS: (laughter)

WRIGHT: Now, anything else? Where'd we get off the track here?

STUDENT: Mr. Wright, how does the economy, being in architecture, what can we do about it? Often we bring culture up and sell it to people who don't think about anything else but how much they're going to get out of this building when it's built.

WRIGHT: I'm awfully sorry—but my goodness boy—come down here . . .

STUDENTS: (laughter as the student approaches Wright and one student comments: "The wrong end too.")

WRIGHT: I'm not sure if it was the wrong end too in the first place! [Wright is referring to the design of the building which they are in]

STUDENTS: (loud laughter)

STUDENT: What can you do with the economy of . . . with the money when you design something for someone? They always cut it down, down, down until it gets to a place they can afford it and it's nothing. Actually, you start from a very nice building and they say well cut this part down and cut that part down; that's expensive and that's expensive. Well what would you do then?

WRIGHT: This lad wants to know what to do about money matters!

STUDENTS: (laughter)

WRIGHT: There's money enough to do the right thing. I think he wants to know why do it at all and that's my point. If you haven't got money enough to do it, why try to do it? And you're always worried about spending that money wisely for as much as you're entitled to. People come to me and ask me: "Well, Mr. Wright, I want a house to cost $50,000." I said: "Are you sure you want at $50,000 house? Because if you do, I can give you one but if you want a $75,000 house for $50,000 you can't do it!"

STUDENTS: (laughter)

WRIGHT: That's one economic strong point. Now we don't always know how much you can get for $40,000, $50,000, or even $15,000 but I'll try because every building we build is a first experiment and in certain particulars on a broad base of experience. But there's no reason to worry about the money. You've got so much money; money enough to give you what you want to get. If you haven't got the money enough to give you what you want you won't get it! So what?

STUDENTS: (laughter)

WRIGHT: I see no particular injustice there . . . because you can always get what you can afford—somehow, someway. We used to say around the farm where I grew up that there are so many ways to kill the cat aside from choking it to death with hot butter!

STUDENTS: (laughter)

WRIGHT: Well, does someone want some more enlightenment?

STUDENTS: (laughter)

WRIGHT: Yes?

STUDENT: Mr. Wright, when you said look into nature when you find your answer in terms of architecture, I'm curious as to what did you see in nature to give you a manifestation in The Illinois? What did you see that made you create this mile-high tower?

WRIGHT: Have you ever seen nature build tall?

STUDENT: Yes.

WRIGHT: How does she do it?

198

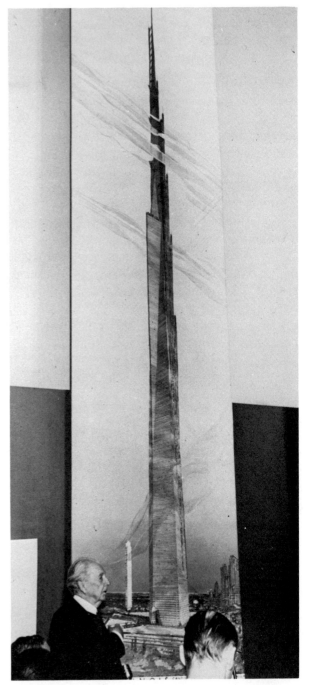

Frank Lloyd Wright presents his design for the Mile-High Illinois Skyscraper Project at a testimonial dinner at Chicago in 1956. Photograph courtesy of The Capital Times, *Madison, Wisconsin.*

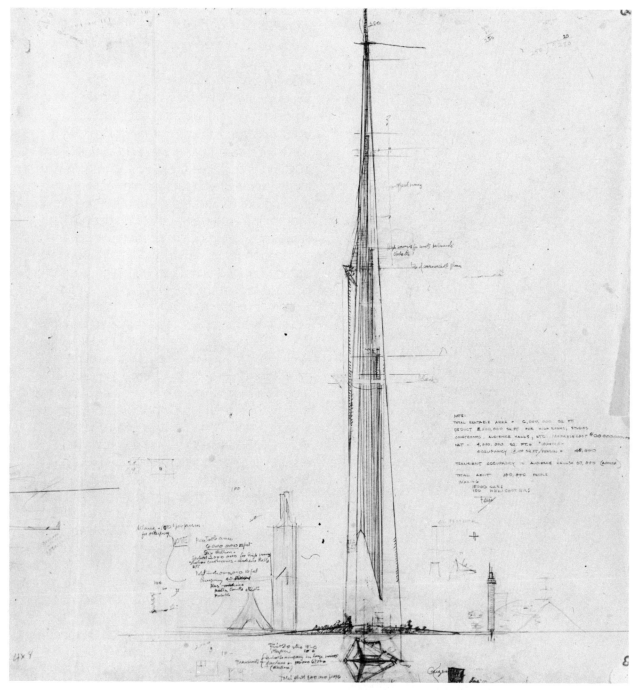

Early sketch by Frank Lloyd Wright of the Mile-High Illinois Skyscraper Project (1956), Chicago. Copyright © The Frank Lloyd Wright Foundation, 1957.

199

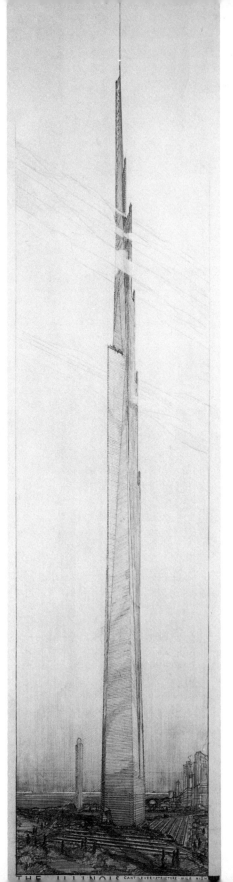

STUDENT: (no response)

STUDENTS: (laughter)

STUDENT: I've never seen it done with a . . . steel.

STUDENTS: (loud laughter)

WRIGHT: Well, you see me doing it!

STUDENTS: (loud laughter continues)

WRIGHT: You can see nature doing it right there—it's doing it the way you're built. That building is built just the way you're built with a central spine. If you look at the section you'll see it going down into the ground like the great tap root to find either bedrock or hardpan. That spine rises to the center of the building and the foundation tapers down within a reasonable distance of bedrock. Then the spine is driven into the rock and there you have . . . I think I can explain it to you easiest by . . . you've seen a rapier haven't you? A fancy blade or a sword and a handle about the width of your hand. Well now, if you were to take that blade and stick it in the ground and tamp the ground around it—go away and leave it—no wind will ever blow it over. Nothing would ever affect it. It would stay. Well this is only a larger scale, that's all. Because it has the same innate resistance to destruction being a tripod you know. That's another feature of this building. You've never heard of a tripod—a tall tripod—have you? Did you ever think of that? Where on earth is there a tall tripod? Nowhere. Now it's the natural thing for a very high building because when—in any one direction—force is exerted against it it has a broad base like a foundation resisting any thrust, that can possibly occur from any direction, upon it. Now that's only one of the features which, taken together, nature would use if she wanted to build something extremely tall—perfectly natural.

Frank Lloyd Wright's presentation rendering of the elevation of the Mile-High Illinois Skyscraper Project. Copyright © The Frank Lloyd Wright Foundation, 1957.

Now that's true in modern architecture—what we call *organic architecture. Organic architecture* is the architecture from the inside out. That's *organic architecture*—therefore twentieth-century architecture. Now the way, we've said, the Empire State Building was built—it's already gone too high . . . and, as a matter of fact, you can't build that building. Compared to this it would be like a hunk of lead. This light, strong, the exterior is all suspended from the central core the way your flesh is carried on your back. It's a perfect expression of the way the natural principle of construction works. And the more you analyze it the more you'll see it to be true.

But in order to analyze it you've got to know something about the principles of architecture that are natural. You've got to know what is the *nature* in architecture and what is just man's foolishness; what is just man's ignorant makeshift. The world is full of makeshift, of ignorance, just as the car is full of it; just as everything you have is full of it. We need this reference to nature in order to come through with something for the future better than the thing we've got now! And, as a matter of fact, I don't think much of it the way it is now.

That means it'll do!

STUDENTS: (applause as Wright leaves the room)

PART TWO
The Seminar

WRIGHT: The architect deals with sublimated sciences—many sciences—but they are not the main thing that is essential to the birth of the great thing he should do. Now if he got the great thing he should do straight and got the centerline of it where it belongs in his consciousness and he put his heart there where his mind is employed—in education only—then I think we'd begin to have beautiful, a beautiful architecture of our own. I don't think we'll ever have it so long as we're depending upon education "as is" for it.

STUDENT: Mr. Wright, do you think that it is possible that some of the civilizations that you refer to were controlled by one or two men or a small clique who could direct public taste and in a democracy isn't it almost governing in mediocrity of taste? Is this something that we can affect?

WRIGHT: Yes, I think right now we're in a drift toward mediocrity because we've had no inspiration that has taken effect. We have become more and more at the mercy of quantity—quantity production—instead of the isolated instance which could become a great inspiration to others. In other words, I think we're now drifting toward the supremacy of the common man. I think the common man is getting the idea that this nation was not only dedicated to him but devised for his special benefit and everything that is necessary to develop him in his freedom is rather resented by him. I think he looks upon the superior individual or the superior thing with a jealous eye instead of looking upon it with gratitude and ready with emulation. No, the sentiment is changing.

Now our forefathers, of course, believed we were founded—believed they were founding—a young green shoot in a direction of a genuine aristocracy. Study Adams, Jefferson—study our forefathers—you'll find that was in their minds;

that the aristocrat would arrive provided you gave man an equal chance at self-improvement and by way of their own efforts they could become and be ruled by the bravest and the best but it hasn't worked out that way.

I have many friends abroad, in Italy especially—Italy has given me everything it had in the way of an honor I guess—and the Italians feel sympathetic to us. I think the best friend, the warmest friends we have—when I say "we" I mean our experiment here—are in Italy. Now the Italians feel that we are going to wind up in the lowest form of socialism the world has ever seen. Our very best friends feel that way. Now why? And I think architecture is suffering from the same malady—virtually.

I believe that quantity has entered into architecture. I think that the old practitioner who came down the hard way, loved the thing he did, you know, with all his heart and his soul and had to build it in spite of hell and high water. We don't have many more. We now have a Skiddings, Owe More, and Sterile and so on. We have all these commercial enterprises and where does their inspiration come from? The boy in the backroom is all they've got and that's pretty much the commercial drift toward quantity. Now you talk about quantity production to anybody today and they will take quality if you can put it in but that's up to you. If you love it enough to put quality into it, put the feeling for beauty and the love of it into it, that's your business. Ha, they'll take it but they don't ask for it—that's extra.

STUDENT: In getting this morass of mediocrity whenever anything really distinguished you've done—the entire population likes it. How do you account for that?

WRIGHT: I don't blame the population for this. The population still has a heart. I'm blaming the powers that be. The powers that pay off. The men who get into the saddle and tell you what to do and the men that you work for as architects and you'll work for them and how. They *don't* come to you and say: "Now here's my problem I like your quality of mind—I believe that you have something that can do for me the thing I want done—now the price, well, first of all let's see what we can have, let's see what's appropriate, let's see what you've got on your mind for this and then let's see how much it will cost and if we can build it we'll build it and if we can't we'll change it and tone it down." How many men come to you like that? That's the way they ought to come. They ought to come to you as they'd come to a prophet. They ought to come to you as they'd come to a great artist—a great interpreter of life—in every problem. I don't care how small it is and if they came that way this place wouldn't look like it does. Our cities wouldn't look the way they do.

But there is another harassing problem that you have to meet and it's the city. I don't think any of you, so far as I heard of you—learned anything from any of you—have really addressed yourself to the problem. And what is the problem? The city—urbanism—every little village in America trying to be a big city or a city. Everybody in America leaving the farm, leaving the small village and getting to the big city if he can.

Arizona—just now I'm in a row over there. [They're] trying to build a sidewalk-happy skyscraper in a slum down there in town in order to enhance the values of real estate; betraying Arizona and her beauty and her character for the next 300 years—three

With the Students of the Profession

architects—and I butted in and said: "The hell with that. I'm a dissatisfied taxpayer!"

STUDENTS: (laughter)

WRIGHT: "... and more than that boys, I have the special knowhow and I'm on to you and you're not going to get away with this if I can help it!"

Not belonging to the AIA, and I told you last night why. And I wanted to belong and I'm wearing your "Gold Medal" but I don't join you because I always felt you never practiced what you called "ethics." In sixty years, every time I've ever had a job there hasn't been a time when there hasn't been a group or someone trying to get it away from me. That's only a minor thing. I could put up with that.

STUDENTS: (laughter)

WRIGHT: But it goes further! It goes to the point where you're now, in order to keep up with the supply of draftsmen, asking the most foolish and idiotic questions of any young man who wants to become an architect that doesn't have anything to do with the case at all. I couldn't answer those questions myself. If I wanted to be an architect now I'd be shut out in practically every state in the Union. Why? Because the questions don't concern the principles connected with the practice of architecture. You're not concerned with whether that young man understands architecture or not—whether he has anything to give of quality—whether he himself has character—what his background is—how he came down the line. No, here's some trick questions and they're so framed that he can't answer them if he's any good. If he's a freak of some kind, that education produces by way of information, he may get by—and there's your "architect"! Well, no it isn't! It isn't even

honest! The whole thing is dishonest. And, I've refused to join your profession and become one of you. I'm one of you, of course, I can't help being one of you just as you're one of me. But I've refused to join the profession of architecture because I will not consciously help make a harbor of refuge for the incompetent! Now there's the answer.

You still, now I don't want to use the word "you" advisedly because "you" applies to hundreds of thousands of you and also the country, have not waked up to the fact that the old bridge engineer's post and girder construction riveted together and standing up there is passé and was at least fifty years ago—perhaps a hundred. Now it always was temporary wasn't it? These damn bridges that ruin the country—those ugly things. Go to any city and see those top train bridges—steel posts riveted—put together—all that gives them life is paint. You got them all over the Bay, haven't you? How many millions does it take to keep one of those damn things standing?

Well, there you are in your architecture the same. There is not one building in New York City ... not one, except the one I'm building now, that is twentieth-century architecture. [Editor's note: Wright was referring to the Guggenheim Museum.] They're all nineteenth. They're all steel frame work riveted or welded—welded made it easier to keep it—they're all there, outside frames built inward like this. That's New York. That's San Francisco. That's all of your cities. They don't know anything else until now. Twentieth-century architecture begins inside. Somehow or other nature stands in architecture more strongly upright and more beautiful too. No, I wouldn't say more beautiful than the human frame—the human anatomy.

Crown Hall constructed in 1956 at the Illinois Institute of Technology at Chicago; Ludwig Mies van der Robe, architect. Photograph by the editor.

Now, how are we built? How are you built? You're built from the inside out. You're built on a spine aren't you? Your structure is an amazing thing of scientific beauty if you want to analyze it scientifically.

Look at a tree. How does nature build tall? Suppose she built that tree from the outside and tried to put an inside on it. It's all silly. It's all without sense and yet it's good practice and yet here is Mies van der Rohe trying to take that steel frame and make it architecture and thinking about nothing but the frame—the frame—the frame.

Le Corbusier, who's he? He's a painter not an architect! He sees this outside facade. He's a facade man too. They're all facade men. They're all sidewalk happy. They don't even see nature. They don't see the tree. They don't see you. They don't see anything from the inside out. Well now, I don't know why it's so damn difficult to begin inside and go out!

STUDENT: Mr. Wright, may I interrupt you for just a moment?

WRIGHT: Yes.

STUDENT: I've heard you or read some of your writings where you said the same thing you just said about Le Corbusier.

WRIGHT: Yes.

STUDENT: I've often wondered, up to now, whether you really believed that but I believe now that you do.

WRIGHT: I believe it *absolutely* and I refuse to revise.

STUDENT: Many of us think that he has a great feeling for form and space and that, not because he is my idol or god, I just think we kind of oversimplify a bit.

WRIGHT: I don't think I have. I think I've done him altogether too much credit.

STUDENT: Really?

WRIGHT: Yes. I saw a little thing he squealed into *Life* magazine. I saw that he hadn't criticized me and couldn't understand why I criticize him. Did you get my answer?

STUDENTS: (laughter)

WRIGHT: I said I had a grandson who was thirteen years old and I criticized him but he didn't criticize me.

STUDENTS: (laughter)

WRIGHT: I've seen Corbu come in. Everything, every step, everything he did without acknowledgment of it of any kind. Picking it up ready made and he has not added one thing since. Not one thing and yet he has galloped all over the place with something he didn't make.

STUDENT: He's had some of the problems you've had exciting others and finding great resistance.

WRIGHT: Well of course he has! Anybody would have that's trying to do anything.

STUDENT: But he has tried and may have succeeded in doing something.

WRIGHT: But he's not genuine! And if you look at the latest *Forum* [*Architectural Forum* magazine] and see "Corbu in the Desert"—is the title of it—and if you can look at that devastation of a national genius by way of an utter ignorance of what constitutes architecture or ethics or anything and not revolt—you're hopeless!

STUDENT: Well, I happen to agree but at this point I think you still want to give the devil his due.

WRIGHT: I don't think the devil has any due!

STUDENTS: (laughter)

WRIGHT: You know I don't really think so.

STUDENT: How about Mr. Maybeck? I didn't hear your talk last night but you dismissed him very briefly as quoted in the press.

WRIGHT: Who?

STUDENT: Bernard Maybeck, the old gentleman in Berkeley here.

WRIGHT: My dear fellow, I never knew him. I've never seen him.

STUDENT: Well, I've wondered because he has done some pretty nice things you ought to know about, maybe.

WRIGHT: The only thing I've seen of his was the monumental tribute to Rome out there in . . .

STUDENT: You did see his church here in Berkeley? Maybe before you leave you should?

WRIGHT: They tell me he's done a Christian Science Church that was sincere and suppose . . .

STUDENT: I'd think you'd enjoy it.

WRIGHT: . . . but I've never met him either so I don't know your Bay Region very well except by way of . . .

STUDENT: Well, I think we can do better.

WRIGHT: Well, there are a lot of you that are doing well I imagine, aren't you?

STUDENT: (laughter) We thought so.

WRIGHT: Who are you following now?

STUDENT: We're still following Mr. Maybeck with some respect, not idolizing him, but we still respect him a great deal. I think we're following Wright this morning.

WRIGHT: I wonder!

STUDENT: You talked about soul and to me that sort of rang the bell that closed in all the definitions that I wanted to know about your type of work—your approach to it. It's the soul that people don't know about, that don't feel, that don't see.

WRIGHT: No, they don't see. It's the soul that's inside out . . .

STUDENT: But they all talk . . .

WRIGHT: . . . the outside in is the cliché you get from those who get modern architecture from America, 1910 or earlier, and then came over here with it. When Bauhaus was closed and Huey Long folded up we got this thing now and I don't think it's right; I don't think it's cricket. I think we've been so too easily had and too easily fooled.

STUDENT: I don't think that people are as intelligent as you think they are.

WRIGHT: I always hope that they are more intelligent than I think they are.

STUDENT: (laughter) They could be.

WRIGHT: But architecture seems to be the blind spot of the nation because it's subcutaneous you see. Architecture isn't exactly subterranean but it is subjective beyond all the other arts. Now painting is something a boondoggling [*sic*] can do as a child—you know very well. Little children do it best, don't they? I think they do. But architecture is something you've got to get of a concordance of faculties. You've got to have a union there of pretty nearly all of the human faculties that go to make things—create—concede—produce. Now that's why an architect should be . . . should always have a capital A; he is the man that is the formgiver for his people—for his civilization—and if he's empty God help them. And that's what's happened—he's empty and God help his people!

STUDENT: I'd like to have answered a question down here. In my mind, I think that the hunger for this thing, whatever it is, is still there and I . . .

WRIGHT: I'd like to believe it.

STUDENT: . . . I'm sincere in this because I think I see young men, younger than myself, and . . .

WRIGHT: Yes sir, that's where you'll find it—in the young man.

STUDENT: . . . and I've seen them come out of school with a very rigid approach and I hope, in a humble way, that I have been able to work on them and I've seen those men change and it's been a wonderful experience and I've talked to groups of minor lay and one of the most exhilarating things is trying to reach a lay group of people. People who . . . well for instance an optimist club, this was a pretty tough hurdle—I haven't worked on my own group. But to talk to a group of Optimists about your work and as much as I know about your life and your readings and to try and develop in these men at least some glimmer and actually . . . you've had the experience, I'm sure, and some of the others here too . . .

WRIGHT: Sure.

STUDENT: That's why I feel that the hunger exists and that it can be settled.

WRIGHT: I don't know. It's there and I know you're right but I know that it is blind if it isn't led and when it is educated it is ruined. That's the only reason I'm taking boys in with me. I could make money you know! I could become a rich man quite easily! I could be doing $7 million during the next three or four years and I could have had riches to almost any degree and I prefer to open the doors and the windows to these youngsters who do have this feeling

With the Students of the Profession

you're describing and I have tried to prevent it from being spoiled, of being destroyed. I've tried to turn that thought away from what they would have received in college, what they would have received in school. Because how do they get their teachers? Gentlemen, what constitutes a teacher? What are the qualifications for teaching? "Being"—aren't they? Can you get a teacher out of somebody that isn't a "being"? And isn't "being" what he teaches? You can't! My God, what a country we would have now if men like Charles Evans Hughes—we'll say a lawyer inspired by the principles of the law that put man above roots and make law made for man not man made for law, you see—what if a man was inspired by that great sense of the thing he did and would open the door of his house and say: "All right you fellows who want to practice law come on in and be one of my family, let's work at it together." Well, that's Taliesin. Now the Supreme Court of Wisconsin has ruled that we are not educational. We are not. We're cultural and they don't know the difference!

STUDENTS: (laughter)

WRIGHT: Because we are making money and self-supporting and not asking anybody to help support it which is suspected as being a sly old fellow having found a way of getting his work done for nothing. So come in here now boy and pay up—pay taxes—we want back taxes—we want $120,000 from you. So . . .

STUDENT: Mr. Wright, do you believe that one of the causes of the lack of creativity in architecture today, as practiced throughout the world, might be the scission between the architectural profession and the engineering profession to the point where neither one seems to know much about the other? We have no

method of producing what could be called the "master builder" under our educational system.

WRIGHT: You put your finger on something very, very difficult but extremely simple too. Now Bob Moses and I are doing a sort of little public act as though we were not friends—we're very good friends. Bob took me down to a meeting of the engineers in New York City in September and they asked this question: "What's the difference, Mr. Wright, between an engineer and an architect?" Now I said: "Well boys I believe an engineer is only a rudimentary undeveloped architect." Now, I use an engineer the way that engineer uses his slide rule and that's his relation to the architect.

STUDENT: Wouldn't you say though that the trouble is with most architects is that they know so little about engineering that this immediately . . . ?

WRIGHT: They're not architects if they know so little about engineering. You can't call a man an architect who doesn't know the principles that are basic to engineering; that make a building stand up; and he can tell the engineer, I do, what the scheme of construction is. I have it all in my mind. All I want to know is the depth, the strength, the relationship, and the proper details for the connections.

STUDENT: You have the fundamental grasp for the engineering principles . . .

WRIGHT: An architect has to have. He's not an architect if he doesn't have.

STUDENT: Well, the ones they turn out today don't seem . . .

WRIGHT: Don't talk about . . . they don't turn out architects today! They just turn them under!

STUDENTS: (laughter)

STUDENT: Mr. Wright, could we go back to

your feeling on education? Are you against the whole process of university education as it applies to architects or is your discontent with that part dedicated to the teaching of architecture in the universities? My question being do you not feel that there is a certain amount of social awareness and information from the university that the university trained graduate in architecture obtains? Or, do you feel this is bad?

WRIGHT: I feel it is a frustration. I think it is a terrible imposition upon democracy, upon our freedom as a nation. I think we need the architect more than we need anything now, of course we do, and we're not going to get him. We aren't getting him now. See what I've done . . . it's all gone into a facade, gone into the old steel frame of the nineteenth century instead of blossoming, as I thought it would, into a whole new phase of life and that's what it could do if we had the proper training—if we had the proper sense of the thing.

What is architecture? There is no civilization without it as a basis; that's true and everybody will admit it but they won't go further and say that a civilization without a culture is like an individual without a soul. Now what is the culture of the civilization? It consists, first of all, of environment. Doesn't it? The quality of and beauty of environment—how you live—what you live in and how to get it and how to make it more beautiful—there's your architect.

STUDENT: There are many forces in society not necessarily concerned with beauty, social movements, political thinking, all on a broad scale of what we're involved in today and notably because of instantaneous communication. And how is it possible that under the shall we say the free use of the system that it is possible to orient these young men fully to integrate themselves into what is known as society?

WRIGHT: Of course, you know it isn't easy to do anything with a trampling of the herd. If you wanted to train a buffalo you wouldn't take him on a stampede would you? If you want to train a wild horse you wouldn't take him on a stampede of wild horses. You'd take him individually, wouldn't you? You'd have to deal with him on a basis that is not educational today. Here you have 18,000 students—the trampling of the herd. All your architectural departments in the country would probably run from 250 to 1,000 students. What are you going to do with them? What can you do with them in the trampling of the herd?

STUDENT: There aren't enough people like yourself . . .

WRIGHT: There are plenty of people like myself! The country is lousy with them but they won't work! They won't make the sacrifice. They won't say "yes I will" and they themselves are not sure and that's the trouble. Our architects today lack surety. The poor devils have all been made by comparison. When they want to learn they compare this, that, Wright with Corbusier, with Mies, with the other fellows, and the young fellow comes in, and well, let's compare him. You don't learn anything. If you analyze and say: "What is the *nature* of this, what is the *nature* of that, what made this what it is?" Take it apart, put it together again, does it fit better? Now that's what's lacking in the architectural training of today and, of course, lacking in the architect's mind. It's lacking in the educational system. That's what's the matter. We don't "play ball" we don't get down to the hard work and the hard things—we don't like to think!

With the Students of the Profession

STUDENT: Have we ever been any different? Is today different?

WRIGHT: Do you know why it is worse today? Because we had something, we had something of our own, we were on the way to something, and the first shock setback we got was the Chicago World's Fair. That did us in for fifty years. Then what came? We got going again. We gathered ourselves together and we were really producing something called *organic architecture*. And then came the closing of the Bauhaus and we got the imports over here and I helped bring them in too. And they all came over here thinking that this nation was Frank Lloyd Wright country and it didn't take them more than three years to find it was nothing of the kind and they might as well take over and they did. And that's where you are now. Now what they took over was my negation in the early end, Louis Sullivan's negations, it was the American negation of the old order and the old way of doing. Now they've still stayed with that negation.

Now Mies—I like Mies, he's a fine old German—he stayed with the negation but he got the light when he built the Barcelona Pavilion. Now that was straight "Frank Lloyd Wright." Now he says so, he used to write to me during that time. But he's gotten into it and has got the old German scientist idea of working with a steel post and beam, you see, which was a negation with me.

I used that steel post and beam with a left hand only for a little while and I used it and I threw it away. And today you've got your Mile-High Building over there which is from the inside out. You couldn't build a thing like that with framing. The highest thing you can do with framing is that church of lead down there in New York called the Empire State Building. Now that's rickety too—that's the outside/inside work.

Well now this wood is fine—this building is built the way you're building. First of all, as a youngster I went through the forest and I'd see trees flat with the roots just standing up vertically like a hand tipped over then I'd see certain trees bent a little bit but standing there and I found that those trees were tap root trees. That's where I got the tap root foundation— that's the Johnson Building; that's the Price Tower; that's the Mile-High—the tap root foundation. Now that's the only way you can build taller that building. As though you were to take a rapier or sword, the handle would be about the breadth of your hand and the blade would be utterly rigid—it would do this you see [*Editor's note*: Wright makes a motion with his hand.]—it would be a spine and you'd stick it into firm ground and go away and leave it— you wouldn't come back and find the wind had blown it over. It would be there and that's the Mile-High Building built that way. There wouldn't be any sway at the peak of that building at all. Another feature of it, of course, are these cantilever floors. The floors are like your arms extending from your body and the walls are just your fingers glued to the ends of your hands that's all—they hang—the whole outside of that building hangs from the inner spine at the corner so that shower of wire at the outside of the building—like this—suspending all of the floors from the central core. So it has an enormous stability by the way it's built you see. Then next is an interesting circumstance too . . .

STUDENT: Mr. Wright, I was down at Taliesin [Taliesin West] about three weeks ago and heard about the Frank Lloyd Wright Foundation.

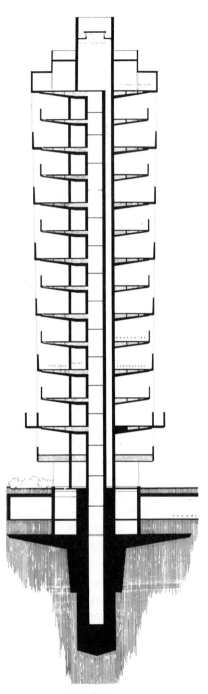

Section drawing of the Johnson Wax Research and Development Tower (1944) at Racine, Wisconsin showing the taproot foundation. Copyright © The Frank Lloyd Wright Foundation, 1957.

The Johnson Wax Research and Development Tower under construction at the Johnson Wax Administration Building grounds. Photograph courtesy of Johnson Wax.

I don't know if you want to comment any on that or not?

WRIGHT: Well I just hinted that right here now. My Foundation is only taking everything that I earn and building with these boys a place for architecture and for architects to grow up in. We have 4000-some odd acres in Wisconsin and five miles of river front—my old farmstead uncle's home—all brought together. We destroyed some fifty-seven buildings there now counting chicken houses and speakeasies and one thing or another. We're in bad with the neighborhood since we burnt up so many buildings. They think we're a fiend in destruction!

STUDENTS: (laughter)

WRIGHT: That we've done there and on the desert we've done the same thing because we work outside all the year around. Work is the essential condition of learning. How are you going to learn anything without doing? I don't understand. If I were to tell you even what I'm telling you now won't mean anything until you've tried it out and that's the way it is with these boys. Now I'm hoping, I don't know how many years I can love this thing and keep on having fun with it, but when I get through with it I want this thing to become a young *college.* Oh . . . that's a bad word!

STUDENTS: (laughter)

WRIGHT: In architecture a forum for young architects—I'm now using the word because I now want them to stay there—is a place where they can be refreshed, get direction, encouragement, and find out what it was that really was the soul of this thing we call *organic architecture.*

Now our enemies have discarded the word like

Exterior view from public street of the Johnson Wax Research and Development Tower (1944) and Johnson Wax Administration Building (1936) with linking pedestrian bridge on the left side of the photograph. Photograph courtesy of Johnson Wax.

dear old whiskers Russell Hitchcock. Russell says: "It's an awkward term, Mr. Wright, can't you think of something better?" Yes, I can think of something better as a word but nothing better in the meaning of the thing. Well he said: "It's something hanging in a butcher shop." I said: "Of course it is but that isn't all it is. So use something hanging in a butcher shop if you were to stop your heart action and hang it to a tree or something." But it's a living thing—the living sense of the living thing—it's missing in our great profession.

Our profession is no longer a great profession—it's a misnomer. I'm inclined to believe that being a profession is what the hell is the matter with us and I'm not sure that any form of professionalism today isn't a refined form of gangsterism. So far as I got with the architectural profession that's my feeling about it.

STUDENT: Mr. Wright, you've commented on several leaders of thought in architecture—van der Rohe, Corbu, etc. I'd be interested to know who, among our colleagues in the world, do you feel *do* produce "organic architecture"? If there is such a person or is a . . . ?

WRIGHT: You'll not like my answer and you'll not like me for it—there isn't any!

STUDENT: Outside of our profession, what about Bucky Fuller [R. Buckminster Fuller]?

WRIGHT: We like Bucky. I know Bucky Fuller well. He's been one of my fans from the beginning. We've had a little something between us but Bucky is a scientist; he's not an architect.

STUDENT: Mr. Wright, on the following question you have also had some pretty strong views on how an architect should be trained . . .

213

Price Company Tower for Harold Price, Sr. (1952) at Bartlesville, Oklahoma. Photograph by the editor.

With the Students of the Profession

I think important that how an architect could be brought into being, let us say . . .

WRIGHT: Brought into being?

STUDENT: . . . you say that there is no one who practices this architecture that you believe in . . .

WRIGHT: I don't say there is no one.

STUDENT: . . . well, that "you know" and certainly you know most of them.

WRIGHT: I see sporadic indications. I see something there that could be and I hope will be.

STUDENT: You've had a long time to teach and guide, Mr. Wright, does this not dismay you that your method of teaching . . .

WRIGHT: Oh, you're talking about the youngsters . . .

STUDENT: . . . does not produce?

WRIGHT: . . . they're not practicing yet.

STUDENT: But you've had . . .

WRIGHT: My "spawn," and I guess that's the word, will take at least another twenty years before you'll hear it from them. You know architecture isn't something that you can make in a new university course or make overnight. It requires building up by experience—testing here, testing there, and learning by failure.

STUDENT: In other words, there are spawn of yours, you hope, that will produce organic architecture?

WRIGHT: But you can give them direction. You can tell them that where it is and they can see the sun rising over there and not go toward the sun setting behind them. And that's about all you can do. You can't teach an architect architecture. You can't make an architect. But

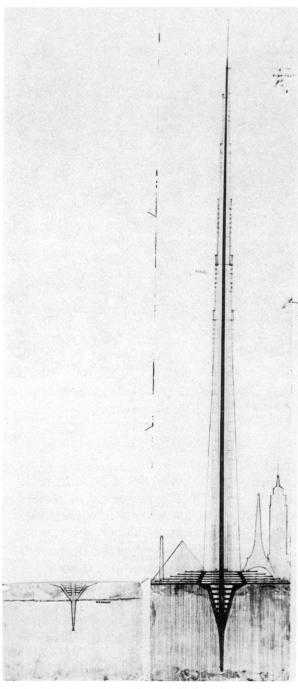

Section drawing of the Mile-High Illinois Skyscraper Project (1956), Chicago, showing its taproot foundation. Copyright © The Frank Lloyd Wright Foundation, 1957.

what you can do—bring him in and inspire him with a love of the thing and a respect for the nature of it and then open the doors and windows toward the light as you see it. And then wait. And you'll have to wait. You'll see your own reflection for a long time—you'll see them imitating you for a long time—some of the weaker ones. Some of the stronger ones you'll see emulating you. But it's going to take longer than I can live for the boys that have been with me to come into fruition—I hope—I don't think they will [sic].

For instance, myself, let me contrast the way we get our architects. First of all, my father was a preacher and his father was a preacher—my own grandfather—and way back they're all preachers. My mother's maternal grandfather was a preacher and a hatter in Wales. My mother came over here when she was ten years old and became a teacher and my aunts were teachers. A whole family of teachers and preachers. Now my mother wanted an architect for a son. I don't know why, but I suppose she was a teacher and she read these things. Really her home was way [in] advance of all the other homes around there in simplicity and beauty but she went to the Centennial and saw Froebel's—Friedrich Froebel's—kindergarten system. Montessori came out of it—there are lots of other things later on but Friedrich Froebel was the first kindergarten man and he believed that a child should not be allowed to draw from nature until he had mastered the forms that made the effects that he saw in nature. He was a pretty wise old man. Once she became undo to that idea she went to Philadelphia and took all the lessons and they had what they called "gifts" in those days. You know, there was this square in outline, there was a triangle in outline, there was a circle in outline—three fundamental

215

The R. Buckminster Fuller–designed Climatron (1960) geodesic dome in the Missouri Botanical Gardens at St. Louis. Photograph by the editor.

forms. Now you have them in cube (the square)—tetrahedron (the triangle)—sphere. In the corner there were little copper things that enabled you to hang them on a little gibbet you had and spoil them you see to make subordinate forms out of primary forms. Well, I give you my word all those things are in my hands today—the feeling for those maple [wood] forms—and the sight of those figures and forms. Then the table on which it was administered was a two and one-half by five feet rule on top—modular—modular system was Froebel. You have a book on it by Le Corbusier, I believe.

STUDENTS: (laughter)

WRIGHT: Well, anyway, this is what I started with. When my mother sat me down to that table and I looked at all these things and they had pieces and sticks to construct things with and then the color sense. In those days they had wonderful German glazed and matte papers and that was the game. Well I was six years old going seven when that hit me and when I got through with it I never wanted to draw from nature. It's a fact. I never made but one drawing from nature in my life but I wanted to design. I wanted to put these things together. It was fun. It was my play time—part

216   *With the Students of the Profession*

of it. I loved dancing and skating and all the rest of it but my real recreation was that until I could read the poet.

There is the modular system that has been back of every design I ever made. Even a small house is made on nothing but a modular system and the module is taken from experience by what I would think would be the best pattern or spacing that would work best with the materials chosen for that work. Now it's integral, it's something that I was never educated to. Was I? Or, was I? Is that education? I guess it is.

But then I studied engineering. My family, of course, my father being a preacher and teacher of music, we were desperately poor and so I had to go to the Madison university [University of Wisconsin at Madison] where they had no architectural course, or course. And my boss was Alan D. Conover the engineer—civil engineer and strong bull—a mechanical engineer. And that was my training and I was dissatisfied with it. I went through all this calculus, analytical geometry, all these mathematical things, descriptive geometry. I cast a shadow on an upright screw . . .

STUDENTS: (laughter)

WRIGHT: . . . I did (ha) all these monkey actions. Didn't understand any of it. I could put it all away and never wink except the distress of wondering what in the hell it was all about. Well, that's the education I received until I went to Louis Sullivan. Before I went to him I had a year with the best residence architect in Chicago, J. L. Silsbee. Silsbee was a genius—undisciplined—untrained. A great lag fellow with a long chain on a pair of gold eyeglasses. A real aristocrat. I used to stop drawing and

The architectural office of Conover and Porter, Architects in Room 23 of the Brown Block Building at 1 South Pinckney in Madison, Wisconsin (circa 1894). Allan Darst Conover was Frank Lloyd Wright's first employer in architecture while Wright attended the University of Wisconsin in Madison. Photograph courtesy of the State Historical Society of Wisconsin.

Frank Lloyd Wright with the Student Architect

watch him whenever he'd come into the drafting room. See him standing before a drawing and make some insulting remarks to the draftsman, turned his foot over sideways contemptuously, he had a way of rolling his foot (ha, ha), and going out.

STUDENT: Might sound a little impertinent. I wonder if you got any ideas from him? Do you admire him?

WRIGHT: Silsbee? Yes, I think I did because I got an idea of what to avoid anyhow.

STUDENTS: (laughter)

WRIGHT: He was a wonderful draftsman. I used to admire the way he drew. His touch was like a field of standing corn, big broad black strokes you know—oh, he could draw.

STUDENT: You just touched on the fact that you started reading, then, after your earlier work. Is there anybody among the writers today that you enjoy reading? You often . . .

WRIGHT: My boy, what a funny question!

STUDENTS: (laughter)

WRIGHT: But I enjoy reading. I have on my table, beside me, an original copy of Walt Whitman—a Boston copy and Walt's signature is in it.

STUDENT: What about anyone who writes today?

WRIGHT: No. Then there is also William Blake. Now you can get a Blake for a dollar and a half—a yellow copy of the paper-covered books—a wonderful edition. William Blake—there was a great inspiration, a great source. And, of course, there is a poet and you know Coleridge . . .

STUDENT: John Donne, do you ever care to read . . . ?

WRIGHT: . . . Coleridge was the man who first—well, Lao-tse, of course, was the man which proclaimed modern organic architecture and that was 500 years before Jesus—but Coleridge said: "Such as the life is, so is the form," that's Coleridge—*The Ancient Mariner.*

Poets are the ones you want to consort with if you're architects. Forget the other fellows. And music, Beethoven, all the real originals, Bach, too.

STUDENT: To put your form and ideas into reality it would be materials. It seems to me that you started using steel fifty years ago at the turn of the century. Are there any new materials since then that you can . . . ?

WRIGHT: Oh my, steel is new. Steel is still new. Steel is a strand. The buildings now that are organic can tell you that century buildings are these buildings, see, not these that are riveted together like this that's nineteenth century. From this century when continuity of steel pulls—when you can do that with a building—you've got twentieth-century buildings.

STUDENT: Would you care to comment on the relative merit of the steel and concrete aspect of prestressed concrete?

WRIGHT: Well, of course, I'm very partial. I love the natural materials for their beauty and their character and I use them continually but the structural materials in my category now are fully the steel strand. Steel strands on which you can pull, buried in concrete which is the flesh. Just the way you're made and the way God made you is the way I want to make a building.

STUDENT: Well, we do everything using a lot of so-called prestressed concrete actually using your idea here—pulling the steel against the concrete.

With the Students of the Profession

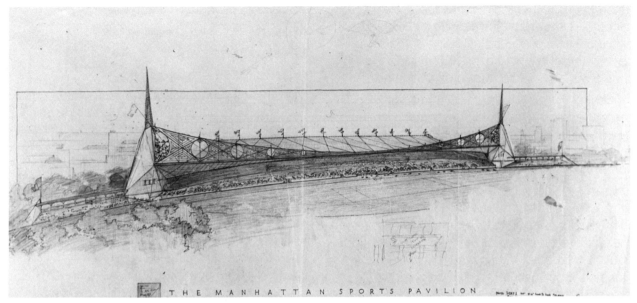

Manhattan Sports Pavilion Project (1956), Belmont, New York. The building consists of a massive slab with four levels reached by escalators and is covered by a translucent plastic roof suspended on a lacework of tensile steel cables. There are no pillars, thus, about 80,000 spectators are afforded total visibility, and there is parking space for 5,000 automobiles. Copyright © The Frank Lloyd Wright Foundation, 1957.

WRIGHT: That is something I've tried tentatively and hardly find it worthwhile in circular forms. When you can get a big ring then you can prestress or when you have a very long span you can do something with it but it's hardly worth the trouble.

You can do just as well with the natural tensile strength of the steel. I just designed, for Harry Guggenheim, a race track for Belmont [Long Island, New York], a beautiful old place, and that race track has a 400-foot span. Oh my God, wait a minute, nearly 900 feet with a tower on each side and between a hanging canopy suspended from the top. John Roebling had it when he did the bridge—he was the first prophet of steel in tension as far as we're concerned. Now in this design we can seat 80,000 people for $18,000 and in a beautiful thing without a thing in the way. The best they could do with their thing was 20,000 people for $19,000 using ordinary construction. Well that's quite a difference. A difference between a clumsy full of posts and girders and things and a thing that's as clean as a butterfly's wings.

STUDENT: Well, what covers would you use over the cables?

WRIGHT: Plastic—plastic—pale blue plastic so the whole light coming through the place is pale blue. The plastic is about less than an eighth of an inch thick in sheets four by eight and, of course, it's like an umbrella—it's a canopy—it's woven, almost, with steel strands and these laid over each other like shingles you see. All these things in architecture are extremely simple but take the form of organic character.

STUDENT: This is one of the few times you've mentioned cost in anything I ever read before or heard you speak about but aren't most of your buildings relatively expensive as far as the common man is concerned?

WRIGHT: I wouldn't say so although the profession has slapped me with that. I don't think that my buildings, wherever they stand, for the space they enclose and the accommodation you'll find in them, cost as much as those standing around them and I'm prepared to demonstrate.

STUDENT: I wish you would.

WRIGHT: Why? What for? I haven't time!

STUDENTS: (laughter)

STUDENT: Are you not avoiding it?

WRIGHT: Somebody else . . . No, I'm not avoiding it. Why am I avoiding it? For what? Why would I avoid it?

STUDENT: I've practically never seen a low-cost thing that you or any of your students have done.

WRIGHT: You haven't? Then you haven't seen the Millard House. You haven't seen the building there in Phoenix—the hotel [Arizona Biltmore Hotel]. You haven't seen the concrete block system I evolved. You haven't seen nothing!

STUDENT: I'll grant it. Perhaps it's lack of education on my part or lack of practice.

WRIGHT: I think it's lack of experience. You should go look!

STUDENTS: (laughter)

STUDENT: I was at Taliesin last year.

WRIGHT: Taliesin isn't expensive either.

STUDENT: It's a beautiful thing.

WRIGHT: I think Taliesin is the cheapest thing ever built but you work for it. I don't think that's the test. I'm not proud of it. I'm not anxious to do that thing that way. What I'm anxious to do is the best that can be done no matter what.

Now you don't sell houses, you don't sell buildings, you sell your services to help the man get the best thing that can be had according to his idea of the thing—you're working for him. I don't think I ever built a house for a client that I know of—they never come to me afterwards anyhow—that he isn't delighted with beyond his limits almost and wouldn't trade it or exchange it for any other house I ever built or anybody else ever built. He likes the houses that I build for other people, he admires in them. How does it happen they didn't get it beautiful unless he did? Now what's that? Is that anything to do with money? I don't think so. Now he's going to live in those houses. His children are going to live in that house. It's characterizing their whole experience here on earth as human beings. It has liberated them, given them new thoughts, new aspirations, new inspiration, a new meaning in life most always and they write these things. What is that cost feature? Ask them. Lots of them will say: "Well, it cost more, Mr. Wright, than we wanted it to cost but we're glad to get it." None of them are sorry. Now isn't that the real thing instead of having built something and being dissatisfied with it and it's being complete and they're unhappy with it? But I'll repeat what I said. I don't believe that one building that I've built

With the Students of the Profession

and in the location in which you find them, per square foot in accommodations, costs anymore than those standing around it and often times very much less. Now I'm telling this to the profession. I've never had the chance to tell it before.

STUDENTS: (laughter)

WRIGHT: But everywhere I go: "Oh yes you've got a nice house you two go hand in hand but God can you pay for it? Can you take it?" And then another thing: "He's an awfully hard old guy to work with." Well, he's only hard to work with when the thing is being ruined that they want for themselves. Don't let them ruin it. They don't mean to ruin it but they don't know and they hire you and employ you to tell them. And you're like a physician. If you let them tell you what to do you might as well, when you go to a doctor, say "I don't want that medicine give me another." Mr. Sullivan used to say—I heard him say once to a lady that came in—the door was open between our rooms and I sat here and he sat over there—and she wanted a Colonial house and he said to her "Madame you will take what we give you!"

STUDENTS: (laughter)

WRIGHT: And he came in to me and threw the thing on the table and I took the thing home and did it at home. He'd never touch a house. That was his idea . . . (Wright breaks into laughter)

STUDENT: I'd like to change the subject to bridges now. Several years ago there was a proposal to build a butterfly bridge across the Bay.

WRIGHT: Yes.

STUDENT: Since then there was another bridge proposed. Do you care to comment on those

Mrs. George Madison Millard "La Miniatura" Residence (1923), Pasadena, California illustrates economy of construction through an early use of modular concrete blocks. Photograph by the editor.

View of the front of the Arizona Biltmore Hotel (1927). Photograph used by permission of The Arizona Biltmore.

The Gold Room of the Arizona Biltmore Hotel (1927) under construction at Phoenix was designed by Frank Lloyd Wright and Albert Chase McArthur and utilizes economic modular concrete block construction. Photograph used by permission of The Arizona Biltmore.

two bridges? The proposed butterfly and the . . .

WRIGHT: Now that's the damndest bridge ever built.

STUDENTS: (laughter)

WRIGHT: Now tell me boys how could a thing like that happen to an intelligent community like . . . all of you fellows are here and that could happen to you? It happened to you! That didn't happen to the people. It happened to the architects of the region. Now if you were any .good, if your society is what it ought to be and your union was effective, could that thing happen? No. That's the kind of fault I find with you. I think it would be justified calling it a conspiracy and going in and blowing the damn thing up.

STUDENTS: (laughter)

WRIGHT: In behalf of humanity and the future a violation of nature like that, and engineers are capable of it all over the country, that's why I say they're rudimentary undeveloped architects and they've done a great harm. Look at New York—look at Pittsburgh—look at any of the great cities—they are murderers. I don't think they're thieves and yet I believe that's what thievery is about too.

STUDENT: What about the Golden Gate Bridge?

WRIGHT: It's a nineteenth-century bridge. It's not a modern bridge and it's not a beautiful bridge in my estimation.

STUDENT: What would your kind of bridge be if you could design that bridge all over again?

WRIGHT: Well, I would have a different type of suspension entirely. I would have a suspension coming this way across the Bay not this way you see. All these things are inherent in Mr. Froebel's little geometric forms. Now why is that

Mile-High Building a tripod? Why is it a tripod? Have any of you ever visited a tall building on a tripod? There isn't a tall building extant that is tripod. Why not? It's the most favored form in the world, isn't it? If you want to put a camera—you put it on a tripod don't you? The tripodial form is nature's substantial form. Don't you know a thing or two? Now any force exerted on that from any given direction meets the opposition of the two sides working with the one. You can't do this with it you see. It's absolutely static and absolutely force resistant from any angle, any side, all the way around. The plan is there, isn't it? (Wright looks around the room for a plan of the Mile-High Building)

STUDENT: No.

WRIGHT: No the plan isn't but there is the way nature builds tall—that way. And that's the way man can build tall with his steel and if he can build that high he can build two miles—there's no limit to the height he can build. If that is scientifically sound for a mile it can be just as sound with no limit to the height you can build. You can build according to nature.

STUDENT: Mr. Wright, if you're so against building the tall skyscrapers why . . . I was quite surprised when I heard that . . .

WRIGHT: I like tall buildings. I like to build tall but I don't like to build tall where it has no business to be. I only like to build tall where a tall building has freedom and an excuse for being there.

STUDENT: Another question—I think I heard some place that this building will hold 100,000 people?

WRIGHT: One hundred and thirty!

STUDENT: Wouldn't that be a problem in getting them in and out? I don't see how . . .

Frank Lloyd Wright's 1949 design sketch for a concrete bridge for the southern crossing of the San Francisco Bay at San Francisco, California. Copyright © The Frank Lloyd Wright Foundation, 1962.

WRIGHT: Sure it would, that's why there are four approaches—double each corner of the tripod is an avenue and you can double deck it if you want to making eight instead of four and the parking is at the base and the escalator goes up to the fifth floor.

The main floor of that building is the fifth floor. That's where your elevators start and your elevators in that building are a new system of elevators. When Mr. Otis invented the vertical street, you know, then you could go up and down just as well as you could run in circles. He gave the realtor, the Zeckendorfs, and the Greenwalds, and all the rest of them, a great break and he gave us a crucifixion. But it can be used—everything can be used to good advantage. Now how to get the elevator system working here as a vertical street—we couldn't use a cord to pull the thing up because the wire would probably weigh more by the time you got it a mile long . . . you can't handle it and it's awkward to handle it. So we invented a system that runs with a motor under the cars engaging a sprocket at the edge and runs right up here you see—a mile high. And then the cars

themselves are five stories high. You go up one notch, two, three, four, five with one hundred people at a time. You see all these things work out naturally in connection with a good idea and they all fall into place as they should. But you don't learn that the day before yesterday!

STUDENTS: (laughter)

STUDENT: You have said that one of the things that the profession has neglected is the city and this is a criticism . . .

WRIGHT: Yes, it is a Medieval plan—the city now. Try to do something in it cramming it with gadgetry. We've changed nothing in the thinking concerning it with a change in space for the human being. Thirty miles today is about what a block used to be. You, today in your car, what do you measure? What's your allotment today as compared with in the Middle Ages when you were forced to carry a rapier by your side hurrying down the street? What's the difference in the actual need of space today for you as compared with them? Would it be a hundred times? Certainly would be ten, fifty, I think a hundred. All right now, the city was

With the Students of the Profession

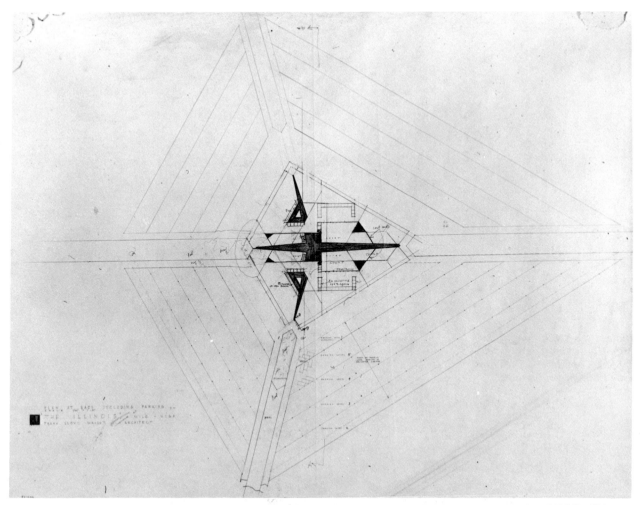

Plan at the base of the Mile-High Illinois Skyscraper Project (1956), Chicago. Copyright © The Frank Lloyd Wright Foundation, 1984.

planned for him. The city was planned when there were no other means of contact except by direct contact, by personal contact, you'd have no culture otherwise. You had no culture as a family of human beings until we got together.

Today what's this? I've gone to see people often times and been kept sitting there while they held this thing to their ears and kept me waiting. And there's the television, what about that? See anything anywhere through the walls and everything. Telephone, television, airplanes, what about my being able to cover this country in the course of a few days? Now how is that old city going to live? It isn't going to live. It's dying. It's jammed up now to the point where, if people weren't so susceptible to habituation, if they weren't so outrageously gregarious, the

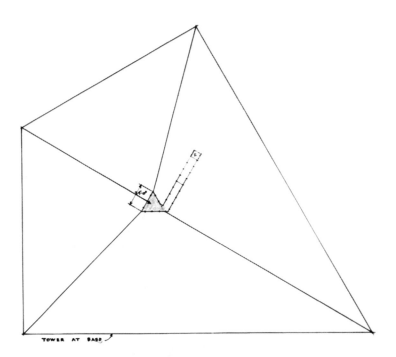

TOWER AT BASE

Plan at the 528th floor of the Mile-High Illinois Skyscraper Project. Copyright © The Frank Lloyd Wright Foundation, 1957.

city would have disappeared fifty years ago and you can say that if you look it square in the face and that's the job of you fellows. That's the job of the architect. Where is he? Is he doing anything about it? No, here is Mies van der Rohe doing hundred-story . . . what is it fifty-story skyscrapers right in the middle of the congestion? Here's Zeckendorf going into cities and buying them up and building bigger towered skyscrapers to get more rent while the getting lasts and fools buy and buy and see it and they don't know where they're going.

STUDENT: But you're promoting vetical density there yourself, sir.

WRIGHT: That is the only way out! You could build three of those—two of them in Central Park and destroy the rest of the city. That's one of the answers. I'm an architect that's doing something about it two ways.

STUDENTS: (laughter)

WRIGHT: Either inside or outside, take your choice. Well, architecture is the greatest of all human endeavor. There is nothing to compare with it. There is nothing that comprises the depth, the strength, the vision, and the persistent capacity that architecture requires and we ought to have the best materials possible in it and today do we get it? We don't.

With the Students of the Profession

The rewards are much greater in any other profession than they are in architecture. Good men—[I was] talking to Walter Benson, the star banker of our region, on Wednesday and Walter said: "I started to be an architect, Frank, but I had to make a living, I had to make a living— I had to make a living, I couldn't make it in architecture so I became a banker." And there you are

You aren't big enough, good enough, strong enough, enough in love—you've got to love this thing. It's got to be your life and you've got to exude it before you'll ever do whatever is needed now. And that's the truth.

Well, where's this helicopter? Isn't it about time I disappeared here?

STUDENTS: (laughter)

WRIGHT: Well, gentlemen, it's been a pleasure to beat you up!

STUDENTS: (laughter)

WRIGHT: And for God's sake stop comparing things! Stop learning against this man, against that man, and what this man is, and what that man is. Analyze them all—take them apart, put them together and find out what's in them. You won't find much.

STUDENTS: (laughter)

WRIGHT: But you will get something yourself. You'll begin to build up a surety—a strength— not only of conviction because lots of phonies have convictions.

STUDENT: How about listening to poets a little more? Maybe that will help.

WRIGHT: Cultivate the poet. You know that the poet is the unacknowledged legislator of this universe and the sooner we knock under to that the better. Get Emerson's essay on the American scholar and read it once a year. He delivered it at Harvard and he couldn't go back there for twenty-three years!

STUDENTS: (laughter)

WRIGHT: Those are the boys—Thoreau—read *Moby Dick* every once in a while. It's a great work of art. Read the big boys, the boys that really have the feeling of it—that have the thirst and hunger for it—for life. Life is something you can live and it isn't something to be educated in either. That's the stuff of poets.

STUDENT: Mr. Wright, what do you think of building codes in this country in general?

STUDENT: (laughter)

WRIGHT: The same thing that another man is asking me what I think about experts. I had the religious privilege of firing several when I built the Imperial Hotel.

STUDENTS: (laughter)

WRIGHT: An expert is a man who has stopped thinking because he knows and you can do nothing with him if *you* got a good idea. If you'll let him tell you where he got and how far he got and what he'd got that's all right but you'll stay right there. There will be no progress. There's no progress by way of experts. There's only progress by way of men with vision. Men who can see in not at or not only at. It's nice to see at but it's greater to see in and that's what's lacking.

The common man, you know, is a man who believes only in what he sees. He has no vision and he sees only what he can put his hand on. He has no vision. What he can put his hand on he sees. Now without the uncommon man the common man is merely a worm in hell—so hope, promised the opportune, will try and justify his place to the uncommon man and not go with the politicians who get their place and keep it by patting him on the back and make him think he is it. That's the weakness of our democratic system. You can gather in the trampling of the herd and put it behind your back and when you do there's no rules that are greater than the devil's. It's when the mediocrity—rising into high places—and that's where we are now. I dare say your government—mediocre; I dare say nearly every member of your legislature—mediocre. Your doctors—largely mediocre. Your architects, undoubtedly—mediocre.

STUDENTS: (laughter)

WRIGHT: Everything is mediocre and everything being made safe for mediocrity and profitable.

And that makes it quantity instead of quality? Depreciate quality, exaggerate quantity, and democracy has gone to hell. Yes. Now that's your fight—that's our fight—that's my fight in the profession.

I did this building here—that's why I did it. And it's amazing what effect that had on the world not on the United States. Telephone calls from Sydney, Australia; telephone calls from London too; telephone calls from France, Germany, Italy, all over the world. Why? I didn't think so much of it when I did it. I just thought well hell if these boys—they're going to stay in the city and they're going to fool around when they might as well—why don't they do it?

STUDENTS: (laughter and applause)

With the Students of the Profession

13

Frank Lloyd Wright with the Student Architect of the University of Arkansas– Fayetteville

Now what we need in this nation is a University of Architecture—well, in this case, a College of Architecture— pure and simple. You don't want it mixed in with all the other things that are considered wise or expedient to learn about because until we get this thing on straight, until we know why a building is good, until we know why a plan for a city is organic *in character, until we know the meaning of the word* organic, *we are not educated. I don't think we can call ourselves enlightened.*

One year after Frank Lloyd Wright appeared before the students of architecture of the University of California–Berkeley and one year before his death, Mr. Wright appeared on April 15, 1958 before a similar audience at the University of Arkansas at Fayetteville. The event was not as lengthy as the University of California–Berkeley lecture and seminar but his rapport with the students of architecture at Arkansas was just as great. Mr. Wright's appearance consisted of a lecture followed by a question and answer period. Dr. John T. Caldwell, the president of the University of Arkansas, introduced Mr. Wright and later solicited written questions from the audience of students for Mr. Wright to answer.

Courtesy of John G. Williams, Professor of Architecture, School of Architecture of the University of Arkansas. Text of the lecture and questions copyright © 1984 Frank Lloyd Wright Foundation.

The Lecture and Questions

PART ONE

The Lecture

CALDWELL: This evening we are going to hear the greatest architect of our time. What makes him great is not that everybody likes what he creates, for not everyone does, and he would shudder to think that he had been so commonplace. What makes Frank Lloyd Wright one of the greatest men of our day are his extraordinary qualities of spirit and intellect which have influenced men's lives through architecture. A creative genius of uncompromising integrity, Frank Lloyd Wright possesses also the courage and the daring which have set his course toward tomorrow and never toward yesterday. Those qualities have separated him from what Toynbee [historian Arnold Joseph Toynbee] calls "the ordinary lump of humanity." This wonderful man, that I like to think of as being in the mature years of his own youth, speaks to the young in heart, in every age.

I have the signal honor to present to you Mr. Frank Lloyd Wright—Architect. Mr. Wright.

STUDENTS: (applause)

WRIGHT: Thank you very much, ladies and gentlemen. There are so many of you here tonight, I wonder if you can hear what I have to say? Am I heard all through the house? Can you hear me back there? Well, no one is objecting, I guess they do.

I suppose I am to talk about architecture, the blind spot of the nation, you know. We would have a culture by now, had we had architects.

STUDENTS: (laughter)

WRIGHT: And I suppose to consider any institution of learning as adequate, or even thinkable, without a splendid strong foundation of what constitutes a good building is more or less ridiculous, but we don't seem to think that way about it. We have neglected the architect and may I add that the architect has neglected us. I have frequently said, and I believe, that the architect is really all that is the matter with

Frank Lloyd Wright circa 1950s. Photograph by C. A. Thompson, courtesy of The Capital Times, *Madison, Wisconsin.*

230

architecture today. He has been educated, he was overeducated by way of what has been, and has never looked at what might be; and so by way of his Beaux-Arts education and by way of his education that we have patterned upon it, he has been, more or less, you know, just one of those things. We haven't heard from him. You can see by looking at the ugliness of America, the need for him. Where has he been all of this time? Why is this nation so ugly that Henry Mencken and men like him have said that "Americans seem to have a lust for ugliness"? And they do.

Now, of course, a building is just a building. Unfortunately, a building is property—we own buildings, somebody owns it, and it's good only for a short time as they are built now. It has been a negligible element in our culture but no great culture has existed in the course of time, among those now lying in ruin down the ages, without the basic cornerstone of its culture as its architecture.

Now if we are ever going to have a culture of our own, we are going to have to have an architecture of our own. Now an architecture of our own won't be based upon a culture that goes back through the Middle Ages. It won't be anything except something in line with that new idea of ours which we proclaimed to the world—the sovereignty of the individual. That will be the architecture that we will enjoy and that will really mark us as having something really worthy of that great Declaration of Independence. Don't you know that we represent something new in this world? What is it that we stand for, that never occurred in the world before, that no government was framed to support, to promote and interpret? That was the sovereignty of the individual—the free man.

Now, of course, what kind of architecture for a free man?—a free architecture. What would a free architecture be? It would be an architecture according to the rules and laws of nature. It would be according to the very nature of materials; the nature of man; the nature of the freedom of the opportunity; of the beauty of the life we live—which, as it stands now, of course, it seems a little ridiculous to be standing here talking about it even. But I have been talking about it a great long time now and gradually doing what I could to build it—to make it a living circumstance—for my people and my country; and I didn't begin it all alone, but at times I have thought that it was practically left to me. Now, of course, I know better. Now we have made some progress but not in education.

Education today, where you find architecture, will probably be in the basement or in the building that was used for military purposes, left over somewhere—it's just a department. Now what we need in this nation is a University of Architecture—well, in this case, a College of Architecture—pure and simple. You don't want it mixed in with all the other things that are considered wise or expedient to learn about because until we get this thing on straight, until we know why a building is good, until we know why a plan for a city is *organic* in character, until we know the meaning of the word *organic*, we are not educated. I don't think we can call ourselves enlightened.

An education today consists more in conditioning you than it does in enlightening you. What should a boy go to college to learn about anyway? What should be the thing that he would go to find out about? First of all, wouldn't it be himself? Who he is. What he is. What makes him what he is. What can unmake him. What that thing is within him that is of great value and that he should cherish rather than get it from various references that are of no account—can't be of much account. When this time is going to come I don't know but we are making progress.

Throughout the country today we have probably about one-tenth of one-millionth percent of the buildings we might have, and ought to have, in order to be really a culture. The buildings that really count are the *organic* buildings and they are very rare. We don't have many of them and when we do have them they shine out and appear to the conservative as something really not quite legitimate. And why is that? Why are they so set against the truth of anything, whatsoever, wherever you find it, and especially if it's a piece of property? And a building is a piece of property, unfortunately.

Now we are trying to take architecture into the realm of the spirit—into the realm of the human spirit—in order that we may have ourselves a culture of our own with an integrity that never existed in the world before, because in the world before, the individual has not been free. We haven't had this opportunity in history for individuals to develop and to grow into something fine and splendid on their own, even by themselves or for themselves. An individual home today can be an individual home. It doesn't have to have columns and gables and do the manner of doing that our forefathers brought over here. No, it's too bad they didn't have an architect among them. It's too bad America never got in the early days an architect who could have perceived the great opportunity and great beliefs that were his by coming into this country absolutely free with nothing established for or against.

But what we got from our forefathers was the old London dormitory town. Now, how many of you have ever seen the old London dormitory town? You've seen it here in our country in almost every town that we have—houses side by side, neighbors standing on each others' feet, elbows at each others' ribs, rows on rows. That's the old London dormitory town— predigested, conditioned, redigested—to be further congested.

So, we have the realtor. We have everything in the line of the realtor that they ought to have and I think now that perhaps we're going to gather him together and take him out and maybe shoot him at sunrise or something of that kind. We've got to do it to save ourselves. Of course our cities are in the same fix. Where do our cities come from? Who has made any plans for a city in the land of freedom and democracy? Have we done a city plan of our own anywhere? We haven't! And we don't know how to make one either. You see, the old city had its excuse for being what it was. It was necessary—the thing to do—and the crowding of human beings in the early days was the only way they could get culture from one another. They didn't have all these amazing new advantages that we have. They didn't have television, radio coming through the walls; they didn't have flight; didn't have the car; didn't have space; they didn't have the new scale. It's now a time scale. It's no longer a scale of feet and inches. So the whole system under which we live has been so completely changed that it's just ridiculous to see the plans or think of the plans of the old feudal cities. But it's all we've got!

Now, why hasn't some kind of thinking been going on? Why haven't we seen from the ranks

With the Students of the Profession

of our architects the proper way in which to proceed to decentralize these old cities? When I was in Russia some years ago, I think it was 1939, the Russians were blowing those old churches down and putting those high buildings up into the air to clean up the center of the town to open it up wide. You could build high buildings then, but you had to go out to build them; and the higher they were the further you had to go. They were the first ones to see that decentralization was inevitable and that the old centralized city was done for. Now, why don't we see it? Have we seen it? Look at New York, at Philadelphia! All proceeding, stampeding virtually along the old, old lines that were dead practically when this country was discovered.

Now what is the matter with education? What is the matter with business? What is the matter with this whole set-up? We have so closely interlocked corporations of incorporations until our whole nation is becoming an incorporation of corporations. Something is pinching and crushing the very spirit that should be ours by way of our own form of government and our privilege in it.

But, first of all, we need a sense of what we are, who we are, what it is we want, what it is we represent. I dare say today we haven't a friend in this world who is not suspicious of us and believing that we don't believe at all in what we have declared and what we represented—afraid of us and so afraid of us that we are afraid of them. When you scare anybody it isn't well to be scared yourself because you scare the other fellow; but we are—we're scared! We are scared all down the line, especially in this matter of architecture; and I suppose it's because architecture costs a lot of money and it's there for a long time; and you

have to be very careful about it, or you ought to be, and you are! It astounds me, and I am continually flabbergasted, to see the commissions given to the incompetent, to the inexperienced. Buildings that will last for hundreds of years, maybe thousands, are turned out, turned over, turned inside-out or upside-down by young minds that really don't know what it is about anyway or even by old minds that can't do any better.

But it's time and I am here merely to urge, at the top of my bent, that architecture, with a capital A, get its place in society, get its place in education, of course, as it must first of all, because it can't stand this tide of conformity that enters into education now. Look at you, all here in this *mass!* What would conformity mean to you all? How many, in you and among you, would have this spirit of independence, this spirit of a desire for something finer, something better, and fight for it? Now that is not undemocratic, that is democratic. That is not selfish. There is a difference between selfish and selfhood. Have you ever figured that out? Do you know the difference between selfish and selfhood, or sentiment and sentimentality? They are not the same. Well, sentiment is a fine thing. Sentimentality is a bad thing—it's a thing gone to seed, so it is the other way with what we need in architecture now. We have got to wake up, and we have got, sooner or later, to acknowledge that this civilization—that which we are planning and promoting by way of taste—is based upon an idiosyncrasy and not upon the solid ground of principle.

Now, of course, I would say and anyone like me would say, that unless you do know the difference between the curious and the beautiful, you are not educated. I wouldn't say that one of these big boys, who has gone out into the world and made a great pile and brought it back, has the great power to change things in his own town or in his own country. What's the matter with him? What happens to him when he gets power? Everything seems to close up, shut down, become inhibited; he becomes conservative when he gets his. He may be very progressive up to that point, but you know, not even then. But that's the death of architecture, that's the death of the human spirit, which is expressed by great buildings, by great architecture. Architecture is essentially human, it is the human spirit manifesting itself. You can say architecture presents man—now literature tells about him—but only architecture presents him, because when man builds, there you've got him. He can't hide. You know what, who, and how that man is.

So, where are we now, with our young architects? And this, of course, is for the young; architecture, I am afraid now, is for the young. If our teenagers don't get architecture—if they are not inspired—fifteen years from now we won't have the architecture that we ought to have, and that we must have, if this country is going to be beautiful. What cheers me up, and has for the last ten years (maybe not so long, I'd say seven) is that from all over this country—Maine, California, north to south, these youngsters write in: "Dear Mr. Wright—Will you kindly give us some helpful material? We have chosen for our thesis 'Organic Architecture.'" Some say "your architecture," but anyway architecture. Now we know that they want us to help them write their thesis, and that's natural enough; but at the same time, why architecture? Why this new architecture? They speak of it very often as the new architecture. Why is that interest in the

young today? And it is a great hope. It is the greatest hope I have of the great future architecture for America because I know it isn't coming from the successful. I know it isn't coming from business. I know it isn't coming from education—my apologies, Mr. President [Dr. John T. Caldwell, President of the University of Arkansas]. He can't help it!

STUDENTS: (laughter)

WRIGHT: So, where is architecture today? Where do you see it? Fay Jones has built a little house over here with some of it in it. Go and look at it, and there are other little houses, there is a feeling coming. Join it, get wise to what the substance is in it because it is not merely a matter of taste. It is not something that you can choose because you like the taste of this or that. It is something that you have to know about. You have to know why it is good—know why a building is bad. And, of course, it all begins back there with a study of nature—the study of nature.

We use the word "nature" in a very careless way. Nature to us is the cows in the fields and the winds and the bees and the trees, unfortunately. But the theory of nature goes deep into the character of whatever it is. What is the nature of this thumb of mine—or anything you want to take to investigate—what is the nature of it? There lies the very essence of its character; the very essence of that thing, which by study, you come to know; and then you are a safe person where culture is concerned but only so because you are not a safe person when you are only activated by what you call your "taste." It was the old lady who said when she kissed the cow that "it was only a matter of taste, anyway."

With the Students of the Profession

STUDENTS: (laughter)

WRIGHT: Well, that's about all it is in our country. We are a taste-built culture—idiosyncratic. I could say idiotic and be perfectly correct nine times out of ten. So this is something that is missing. This is something that has been left out because it didn't come over with our forefathers. They had no interest in it particularly because Old England was beautiful. But we never got any of that beauty of Old England, we just got that congested town—made it into suburbs—made it into cities—made it into what we've got. Now who is going to change it? How is it going to change? That's the problem for education.

And, of course, education, in other ways, needs bringing to book. Here in the qualification of the vote is another thought along this line. Thomas Jefferson wouldn't allow the vote to be qualified—that was his quarrel with Alexander Hamilton. Hamilton said if you don't, you are going to have mediocrity rising into high places, and pretty soon what we desire and what we have all hoped to bring about will be ruined by mediocrity. What was Jefferson's answer? Do you remember? He said no. Education—we will educate the masses! The masses? The masses—we will educate them. Have we? Have we educated the masses to know; to make them voters—independent according to their own principle of life and their own true feelings? They can't until they know what a good building is. They can't until they know the difference between the curious, the merely curious, and the beautiful.

Now science is helpless to do anything for us in this connection. Why? Science will get the same reaction—I'm speaking of a scientist as a scientist now—will get the same reactions from the curious that a scientist will get from the beautiful. Now you see, the beautiful leaves his realm. He is incorporated. He is factual. He is body. This other thing of which I am speaking is of the spirit. The spirit of the man. The thing that can make things live that have never lived before, not that just takes things apart and can never put them together again, but can learn certain things by taking the thing apart—that's science. Now we are overscientized. We are over the brink by way of science and we have all our gadgetry in old feudal city and we can't do anything with it pretty soon. We are going rapidly into a blind alley. Now the architects of this nation should be the ones who see the way out, who see what's happening, who have a remedy for us, who can help us, who can help us save ourselves from this infernal eternal destruction of our civilization. Where are they all now? Where will we be pretty soon? We have never got hold of anything that could enable us to persevere, to continue, to go up instead of getting closer and closer to destruction and going down.

And that's all education—for education—and maybe if it weren't for the regents of these universities who are successful businessmen and who are supposed to get the money to keep the universities going. If it weren't for them we might do something with education. But as things are—not much hope.

So what to do? I think I shall bring you a question here tonight. I think I have posed it for you. Where are we going now if there is not enough of the spirit alive among us as a people, to see the way toward the light, instead of taking the opportunities that are expedient in the direction of destruction? Is that too big for you? If it is, I will modify it and make it a little smaller. But that is the real question. That is really where education in America is today—to stop this easy conformity to conformity, this drift toward mediocrity, that is so easy and is safe and is conservative; and to whip up, if necessary, but anyhow to spark, to inspire, this desire for the things that are more excellent, that are what you would call *beautiful.*

Thank you very much.

STUDENTS: (applause)

PART TWO

The Questions

CALDWELL: Mr. Wright has invited questions. Mr. Williams, will you collect a few?

WRIGHT: At MIT three weeks ago there were twenty-seven questions that I had to answer. That was a very keen young architectural audience. How many architects are there here tonight?

CALDWELL: We'll have them stand up. Would you like to see them?

WRIGHT: Yes, I would like to see them.

CALDWELL: Mr. Wright, would you like for the architects in the audience to stand, please.

WRIGHT: Yes, let's see what they look like. My goodness! Well, boys, there are enough of us here to save the nation. Let's go at it!

STUDENTS: (applause)

CALDWELL: Shall I read the questions?

WRIGHT: Yes, please. And if it isn't sensible, I won't answer it!

CALDWELL: "Do you still have faith in man that would lead him toward building Broadacre City as you see it?"

WRIGHT: Absolutely. I see it that way and we are now working on the revision of the book written in 1931 called *Broadacre City,* because the only city is the Broadacre City. We have been unhappily switched from what our gift as a nation was. We were intended to be a great agronomy—agrinomical as well as industrial. But following the pattern of Old England on the cinder strip of the North and the East we wiped out agronomy and day by day we are rendering the agriculture less emendation [*sic*] so far as society is concerned. Do you hear of any farmer playing golf with the President? Not yet.

STUDENTS: (laughter)

CALDWELL: There is one word here I can't read but the first part of the question will be complete in itself, I think, and the word in here is Wright, spelled W–R–I–G–H–T and it should be. I am just explaining the question. "What happens to the young mind exposed to extreme Wright influence . . . ?" And that next word I can't read.

WRIGHT: It doesn't matter.

STUDENTS: (laughter)

CALDWELL: You have the question, sir.

WRIGHT: You see, the more extreme to the WRIGHT you go the safer you are. Somebody asked me once if I weren't making a lot of little Frank Lloyd Wrights? And I said, I can't, maybe, but I don't believe there is any such thing as a little Frank Lloyd Wright!

STUDENTS: (laughter and applause)

CALDWELL: "Several years ago, you designed a home for some people in the Southwest—

Oberan, I believe. Why did you tear down their redwood fence?"

WRIGHT: I don't know where this questioner has been. I was never there. I don't know anything about that episode. But I would tear down any fence—redwood or anything else.

CALDWELL: "Mr. Wright, what is the point of the steeples on some of your buildings?"

WRIGHT: Television, as a rule.

STUDENTS: (laughter and applause)

CALDWELL: "Mr. Wright, do you see the end of the big city or a drastic change in it?"

WRIGHT: It's impossible to see a change in it. You can see a change overcoming it, and you can see a change dispersing it, but can't see a change in it. There is no cure for the changing face of the city. Give up your car. Give up all the other things you've got and keep the city. Or, give up the city and keep the other things. Now which? It's one or the other. There is no having both.

CALDWELL: "Won't your proposed Mile-High Building add to centralized city congestion?"

WRIGHT: On the contrary, it would abolish congestion because it is the city . . .

STUDENTS: (laughter)

WRIGHT: . . . 130,000 people each. All you would have to do would be to sweep New York into the Hudson and build two of them in Central Park and that would be the city.

CALDWELL: Mr. John Williams is screening these questions, Mr. Wright. "Can you create an 'organic architecture' on the basis of the philosophy of the sovereignty of the individual?"

WRIGHT: You can't create it on any other basis. It is the natural basis for that creation. Because for me, our Declaration of Independence was

organic and natural to humanity—the only basic structure—governmental according to the spirit of man. Now the only architecture that would be valid, in my estimation, would be one according to the spirit of man and therefore naturally in line with the sovereignty of the individual. You can take that apart if you want to.

CALDWELL: "What examples of architecture do you consider to be good architecture other than your own?"

STUDENTS: (laughter)

WRIGHT: Is that a fair question? Why do you want to know? Why, aren't you satisfied? Why look a gift horse in the mouth? But there are plenty if you want to look. This has gone very far. They are building in Italy, today, one of the most beautiful of tall buildings according to the principle of the Mile-High—according to the principle of the Price Tower. It's taken root in Italy but not in America. So you see it's coming. And good houses are nearly everywhere and in the U.S. I think we could count on 100,000, maybe 250,000 houses, which, of course, is only one-tenth of one percent of the houses built. I think that only one tenth of one percent have architects anyway—of the houses built—of the buildings built. The architect is an undiscovered country which is perhaps just as well so far as he's got. But now I think he ought to be discovered.

CALDWELL: Mr. Wright, we have a very philosophical question here now. "Sometime ago, you stated that your conception of God was *nature* with a capital N. What, in your opinion, is man's relationship to the capital N?"

WRIGHT: I am glad to answer that. It happened to get on television and a Methodist minister wrote me five closely written pages trying to save my soul from hell fire. [*Editor's note:* See Chapter 17—The Mike Wallace Interviews.]

STUDENTS: (laughter)

WRIGHT: Now apparently the thought somehow got to him that I had substituted Nature for God. Not at all. All the more because I study Nature do I revere God because Nature is all the body of God we will ever know. Did you ever think that? That's why I put a capital N on it—out of reverence and respect—because who knows about God who does not know the laws, the rules, the principles of Nature that made him what he is? That gives him all he can know about life and leaves him nothing but a feeling for something, somewhere, somehow. Is that understood? If I have done nothing more for you than that, it would have been worth coming down here tonight.

STUDENTS: (applause)

CALDWELL: "Mr. Wright, what do you consider your greatest work?"

WRIGHT: Oh, I would make no such consideration. How would I know? I only feel that the one I am going to do next is the greatest and those that I have done are all very well.

STUDENTS: (laughter)

CALDWELL: "Do you see a decline in contemporary architecture in the International Style?"

WRIGHT: I don't think it ever was a style or even international. But such as the case may be, if you want to call it a style, everyone is so darn sick of it, that I don't think any of them want to see it any more themselves. I see them now searching for something new, a little better, a little richer, a little warmer; something more in accord with the human spirit—all of them. And,

of course, the ones chiefly responsible for it were very bad painters who were trying to be architects and they didn't succeed.

CALDWELL: "Technology is now such a vital part of architecture. Has our great dependence upon technology been a false one? Is technology too dogmatic a force to allow architecture to be free?"

WRIGHT: It could be, and for many reasons is, but technology should be a help, not a hindrance to architecture. After all, do you know what the word "architect" means? Now, an architect uses technology and uses the engineer the way the engineer uses his slide rule. But an "architect" (the word is Greek), "arch" meaning high, top—the archbishop—the "arch" this—the "arch" that—the "arch"—now what? "Tech," technology—the "tech." There you have the top of technology—the master of the know-how. Now that is the definition of the word "architect" and there isn't an educational institution that I have ever been able to get that out of. The architects themselves don't know it.

CALDWELL: "Which do you consider the most abstract of the arts?"

WRIGHT: Architecture and, next, music. Architecture and music are like this—architecture is sublimated . . . let's see now, music is sublimated mathematics and the architecture is also. That's why music and architecture are so close to each other, why they are practically one feeling. Beethoven was probably the greatest architect who ever lived—Beethoven. My father taught me to see a symphony as an edifice of sound and I never listen to a symphony now that I don't see a building—see how it was built—see them proceed to lay the foundation, to make the edifice out of the sound. Those are the two consistent and great arts—music and architecture. And don't ever take it that

With the Students of the Profession

architecture is frozen music. It isn't. If it were frozen, it wouldn't be architecture. It is only as it is living—the rhythm and expression of the human soul and the spirit that is architecture.

Good Lord, look at that thing down there, I've got to get out of here! [*Editor's note:* Mr. Wright was commenting on the large collection of written questions that were being sent forward from the student audience.]

STUDENTS: (laughter)

CALDWELL: I'm not going to stop asking questions until you stop answering questions, Mr. Wright. "Is an 'organic' building automatically beautiful?"

WRIGHT: Not automatically—naturally.

STUDENTS: (laughter and applause)

WRIGHT: Can't we get away from that word "automatic" somehow?

CALDWELL: "How do you propose that the streets and sidewalks of Manhattan be eliminated, as you recently stated?"

WRIGHT: By planting grass in place of the streets. Yes, I think what Manhattan needs is a good many acres of grass planted.

STUDENTS: (laughter)

WRIGHT: I am going to destroy Manhattan if it takes a whole year!

STUDENTS: (laughter and applause)

CALDWELL: Don't let us tire you, Mr. Wright. Will you take a few more questions?

WRIGHT: Oh yes, go ahead. They are good questions.

CALDWELL: "In an early work you stated that you had to choose between honest arrogance and hypocritical humility. Do you think your work would have been different if you could have chosen honest humility?"

Frank Lloyd Wright (right) and architect E. Fay Jones a few minutes after Mr. Wright's lecture at the School of Architecture of the University of Arkansas in Fayetteville on April 15, 1958. Photograph courtesy of E. Fay Jones, FAIA.

WRIGHT: I don't think there would have been any.

STUDENTS: (laughter and applause)

WRIGHT: But let's have a word about this matter of arrogance. You know it is too bad that the word isn't better understood. When I used the crack (which it was) that I had chosen honest arrogance, I meant that there could be no such thing as arrogance that is honest. You can't have honest arrogance. Arrogance is pretentious, arrogance assumes, arrogance is phony, arrogance is not true. [*Editor's note:* See the Hugh Downs conversation in Chapter 2.] But I made the best of it and did as well as I could with it. But I am telling you now the truth. No man who believes in himself and who is not pretentious, who is not trying to swindle you out of your eyeteeth pretending that he is something that he isn't, no such man, if he is sincere, is arrogant. We have come to mistake this thing we call arrogance, mistake the sureness of one's self, the faith in one's self which rejects the inferior, which will not countenance interference or destruction. Now make of it what you please but there is the thing that most people call arrogance. It is not arrogance. I am not an arrogant person and I never was. But I am a person who believes in what I believe in, and I am always willing to fight for what I believe in, and I am never willing to take less than what, to me, is the best. Now is that arrogance? [*Editor's note:* Mr. Wright walks away from the lectern into the shadows off stage.]

STUDENTS: (applause which continues for some time)

CALDWELL: May I read to you a letter which Mr. Wright handed to me this evening and this will close our evening in this auditorium? This is from the Academy of Fine Arts in Venice, addressed to Mr. Frank Lloyd Wright, Architect—Taliesin West, Scottsdale, Arizona: "Dear Mr. Wright"—and this comes from probably the oldest existing institution in the world—

"Dear Mr. Wright: I have the great pleasure and honor to communicate to you that the assembly of the College of the Academicians of Venice, an institute founded in 1750 and recently renewed, has acclaimed you, in its general meeting held on March 27, 1958, Honorary Member of the Venice Academy. I do know that your creative genius does not need any formal recognition, as it is universally admired and respected. I am sure, however, that you will be so kind to accept this nomination as a sign of the devotion of humanistic Italy, as represented by one of the oldest and most glorious cultural institutions. Venice and Italy express to you their love.

"Sincerely yours,
"Bruno Zevi
"Professor of Architecture
"Director of the Architectural Class in the College of Academicians"

You are excused.

STUDENTS: (applause)

The Friendly Titans

Frank Lloyd Wright and Carl Sandburg

The First Meeting
of the Titans

Frank Lloyd Wright and
Carl Sandburg

*. . . I tried to bring Carl up at an early age but he was too
far gone on along the lines of Lincoln he was writing. I
couldn't do much with him. Here he is. He has done fairly
well. Look at him. I think Carl is all right—but he is Carl,
I wouldn't have any one of my friends improved. It would
be just too bad. I like them as they are. And I like Carl as
he is.*

Frank Lloyd Wright and poet–historian Carl Sandburg had been good
friends for almost fifty years since Wright's architectural practice in Oak
Park, Illinois. Carl Sandburg had visited Frank Lloyd Wright at Taliesin near
Spring Green, Wisconsin twice during Taliesin's early years. The first visit
was with Lloyd Lewis (editor of *The Chicago Daily News* and later client
of Wright's) during the mid- to late 1920s. Frank Lloyd Wright jokingly
reflected on Sandburg's first visit to Taliesin in his *An Autobiography* (New
York: Horizon Press, 1977, p. 512):

*. . . I have on raw linen. Loose wide-sleeved jacket buttoned at the wrist, wide
baggy trousers tied close around the ankles. Carl (Sandburg) once visited me
while working on his* Lincoln. *I dressed him up in a spare velveteen suit in
similar style. Lloyd Lewis there got a good "shot" of us in this artistic, semi-
elegant négligée . For years Carl has been trying to buy that picture from
Lloyd for the fear someone will see it!*

Frank Lloyd Wright with the "loose wide-sleeved jacket buttoned at the wrist, wide baggy trousers tied close around the ankles" and Carl Sandburg with the same velveteen suit minus the jacket at Taliesin circa mid- to late-1920s. Photograph courtesy of the State Historical Society of Wisconsin.

Frank Lloyd Wright and Carl Sandburg together again in 1957 after about twenty years. Photograph by Arthur Siegel used by permission of Mrs. Arthur Siegel.

The Friendly Titans

Sandburg's second visit to Taliesin was around 1937, perhaps early in 1937, during a time when Wright was very ill with pneumonia. Sandburg briefly recalled this second visit with Wright in a letter to Wright dated June 28, 1947 (in Herbert Mitgang's *The Letters of Carl Sandburg*, New York: Harcourt, Brace and World, 1968, pp. 446–447):

... there had been time for you to take me thru that little theatre where your students had put on plays from the Rootabaga Stories, then that winter night at the [Ken] Holdens when you dropped in to hear a reading of The People, Yes in manuscript ... I hope—and have a premonition that way—our ways will cross sometime this coming year.

Their ways did not cross in 1947.

Frank Lloyd Wright and Carl Sandburg had not met in twenty years and, finally, in April 1957, both men were in New York at the same time. *Newsday* had discovered this and arranged for a conversation between the two to take place at Wright's Plaza Hotel suite. Alicia Patterson, the editor and publisher of *Newsday*, moderated the conversation and provided the questions. The text of this historic meeting of these two titans follows.

The Conversation

PATTERSON: Which will live longer in time, architecture or literature?

WRIGHT: Architecture has and always will, of course. Architecture is the nature of form and it is the best of everything, even music—especially music. And so long as literature has music and has form it will be indebted to architecture. You see, literature tells about man—that's what Carl does, you know. He's a story teller. He tells about man. But architecture presents man as he is.

SANDBURG: Well, I look at Egypt. I look at Egypt and I say, let 5,000 years pass and nobody knows what either the architecture or the literature means.

WRIGHT: I didn't suppose a literary man would ever know anything about architecture.

SANDBURG: I was made an honorary member of the American Institute of Architects because they said, it is debatable, of course, that there was an architecture to my writing.

WRIGHT: It is the architecture to your writings that is the poetry in them to me.

SANDBURG: I gave the Western North Carolina Council of Architects ...

WRIGHT: I hope you gave them hell.

SANDBURG: I opened with telling them about my friendship with you across the years and about a handy man around your place in Wisconsin. Some truck driver comes in delivering something and he says to this handy man: "Who's this bird? I hear about him. What is he?" And the answer came from the handy man: "He's the biggest archy-tect of them all . . ."

WRIGHT: Yes, and he would add: "He's got an h'eye like an h'eagle. One look he's got it all."

PATTERSON: Which is Mr. Wright's favorite among his buildings?

WRIGHT: A man who has favorite work is never a real creator. What is most interesting to him is the next one he is going to do. That's my favorite building; nothing that I have done. Does that sound theatrical?

SANDBURG: No, no. It just sounds like you. You can talk in paradoxes. They persuade people and they repeat them.

WRIGHT: Do you think people would be persuaded by anything but a paradox?

SANDBURG: Maybe not.

WRIGHT: Those charming little fantasies of yours that I love so much—that you call the *Rootabaga [Stories]* fairy tales—wouldn't they be paradoxes?

SANDBURG: Yes. That's right.

WRIGHT: We're even. There was the story of Henry Hagglyhoagly who played the guitar with his mittens on; the skyscrapers that wanted to have a child; but the loveliest of them all, Carl, was the White Horse Girl and the Blue Wind Boy. Ah, that was a poem.

SANDBURG: I could shake your hand on that.

WRIGHT: You know, I had been reading [Irish poet–playwright] Lord Dunsany before I got that and I thought, the *Rootabaga Stories* ought to go to him and show him truly what poetry can be.

SANDBURG: About time we were meeting up again.

WRIGHT: I used to put bloomer pants on you Carl, tied around the ankle. And a short velveteen jacket, and we would sit by the fire and talk about art—but you didn't know much about art in those days. You didn't care either. You stayed with me once for a week when you were writing your Lincoln—you remember, Carl—you were writing the first chapters. When you were going away, "Frank" you said, "we have had a glorious time riding around in that Cadillac of yours with that leather boot top and a chauffeur and everything. I enjoyed it thoroughly but when you put those pants on me and we sat down before the fire and talked about art—you made me sick."

SANDBURG: I doubt that. I may have filed some mild demurrer but I was *not* insolent.

PATTERSON: Which is Mr. Sandburg's favorite among his writings?

SANDBURG: Well it's a standoff. Maybe that one volume that is a distillation of the six-volume Lincoln—that six volumes ran a million and a half words—the final distillation, 430,000 words. It was a mean job doing that.

WRIGHT: How wrong he is. I knew he would be wrong. He takes the biggest, the hardest work he did but it is not the best he ever did. The easiest, the quickest is the best.

SANDBURG: I have a competitor for the one-volume Lincoln. When I'm asked what poem I did of all of them in my book *Complete Poems* —there are 816 poems for $7.50—less than a cent a poem— "The People Yes," is the one.

WRIGHT: Do you remember when you read that to me the night I was going to Michigan and stopped to see you down on the sand dunes? I was in a hurry to get where I was going and you came out with the poem—it hadn't been published yet—and said "Frank, I want to read this to you."

SANDBURG: Forced feeding.

WRIGHT: Then you started reading it and read and read. I wanted to get going but I didn't want to be impolite to Carl. But he has a trick, a real Sandburg trick. When he saw me lapsing he would shout out loud—Garump harump—and then I would come back again. It was a long night and a nice one. That was a night. I think it was one of your great things, if you want to ask me—"The People Yes." I think it was great.

SANDBURG: Did you see what we did with a letter out of your autobiography about *Rootabaga Stories?*

WRIGHT: Well I wrote you the prettiest posy a man ever had. You could put it in your hat band.

SANDBURG: And then I waited ten years to answer it. It was such a dandy letter that a reply had to have something. Then I wrote an inscription in the *Rootabaga Stories* for the Unitarian Church at Madison—that's a poem of a building.

PATTERSON: Which is Mr. Sandburg's favorite among Mr. Wright's buildings?

SANDBURG: There are two in Oak Park, Illinois that I have seen more often than any two others of his works. I would get off at the Wisconsin Avenue station of the elevated and walk north—to the house where you lived in Oak Park. Well, there was something about that house that intrigued me. I would go out of my way to see it and then circle around to the Des Plaines River on into Maywood where I was living at the time.

WRIGHT: That's just what I would think of a poet—he knows nothing about architecture. That house is the most inferior desecration I ever performed.

SANDBURG: And then there was the Unitarian Church, Unity Temple in Oak Park.

WRIGHT: Ah now—there is a building.

SANDBURG: Those two were on a par.

WRIGHT: No they weren't. They didn't have anything to do with each other. The Church was creative, the little house—they used to ask me whether it was seaside or colonial. And I didn't know.

SANDBURG: The first time I met you was when I saw these buildings in Oak Park and didn't know you designed them.

WRIGHT: That was a proper introduction. Unity Temple today is a great building, stating the principle that has made me what I am today, whatever that is. The interior space is the reality of the building—the space in which we live and not the walls and the roof. Now that's Lao-tse the ancient Chinese philosopher I found out afterward—and when I found it out I was like a sail coming down. I thought I had originated something and I found out the idea was 500 years older than Jesus. I was deflated. Then I began to think of being Welsh and naturally an eagle and I thought—but he didn't build it. I built it. And I began to come up again and I have been up ever since.

PATTERSON: What makes a genius?

SANDBURG: When certain factors are understood more basically we may possibly know what is genius. About him always is the quality of the unexpected—like Frank's mile-high Chicago building. He would want a mile-high building on the Lake Shore at Chicago. If I

Exterior detail view of the rostrum of the Unitarian Church (1947) at Shorewood Hills, Wisconsin. Photograph by the editor.

had the $90,000,000 I would build it. I would like to see it go up. I would do a poem about it. I may yet do a poem about the one that ought to be.

WRIGHT: That would be better yet. Well, here is the definition of a genius. It came straight down from King Arthur's Round Table. You will find it in the Welsh Triads, a collection of three wise sayings on great subjects. It says this and I think it is the best definition I have ever heard: "A genius is a man with an eye to see nature and a genius is a man with a heart to feel nature and with boldness to follow nature."

SANDBURG: Now all you need is a definition of *nature.*

WRIGHT: *Nature* with a capital N is all the body of God that we will ever see. How is that?

SANDBURG: That ain't so bad. That's kind of a poem. We will have to be remade in several different ways across the ages.

WRIGHT: You can put it any way. Write that poem—that who would see the lineaments of God—see nature. I can say it several ways more myself.

SANDBURG: Jesus was a genius in his earliest miracle. It is my favorite miracle of Jesus. It is told in the Apocrypha, it is probably not established or they would have had it in the New Testament. There had been rain and the soil of Nazareth was just right for molding and shaping and a gang of boys was working on it making pigeons. Some of them came to little Jesus, the smallest boy in the gang, and said "That doesn't look much like a pigeon—that's the worst looking pigeon in the gang." And Jesus said nothing—passed his hands over that hunk of mud and said something under his breath and no one knew just what he had said,

Frank Lloyd Wright Residence (1889), Oak Park, Illinois. Photograph by the editor.

Frank Lloyd Wright Studio (1895), Oak Park, Illinois. Photograph by the editor.

Exterior view of Unity Temple (1905), Oak Park, Illinois. Photograph by the editor.

and the mud began to move and slowly rose from the ground and took shape and had wings and then scrolls and spirals it disappeared in the blue yonder. Now that is genius.

WRIGHT: Yes—because why—because of what I have just said.

PATTERSON: Is any genius developing in the new generation?

SANDBURG: At the present time in all the American landscape? Well I would say, for instance, Thomas Hornsby Farril—Tom Farril—in Denver, Colorado—is a major poet who has not had recognition. I could read pieces of his, poetry and prose, that would establish him as a figure, and he is not.

PATTERSON: What about T.S. Eliot, Frye, or Ezra Pound?

SANDBURG: Do I have to give my analysis of Pound?

WRIGHT: Don't analyze—just pontificate.

The Friendly Titans

SANDBURG: That's a good line. No, Pound will puzzle me as long as I live.

WRIGHT: Pound is a genius but a crude, brittle one.

SANDBURG: Well he is anti-democracy. He is anti-United States and he was pro-Mussolini, much more deeply and genuinely than he would admit at the present time. He would claim now that he had Mussolini on the way to conversion to Thomas Jefferson.

WRIGHT: I don't think he ever had democracy on straight. That's the trouble with Pound and I am not sure that we have, but I think we are nearer than Pound. I wanted to tell you what I feel about democracy. I would like to get it on the record. True democracy is the highest form of true aristocracy that this world has ever seen. And it is aristocracy innate, out of the nature of the man who now being free and having been freed by the Declaration of Independence to be himself, now has the sovereignty of the individual. Today aristocracy consists in the expression and the perfecting of the power and creative nature of the individual. That is your aristocrat today. But we are drifting toward conformity so fast that the common man—H.I. Phillips said that the uncommon man is already unconstitutional. Pretty soon he's going to sue for a pardon. The democratic expression so-called, which is only mobocratic not democratic is: "What's the guy got that we haven't got?" "Why he just got the breaks—that's all Maria." That's the democracy of today. It is all twisted and all wrong. And Thomas Jefferson said as much, don't you know. Don't you know that Thomas Jefferson said that the aristocracy would arrive after a man was free. Don't you know that he made a little mistake as to time that's all. He will, but not now, not with mediocrity rising into high places. No. No, the common man is going to ruin the dream if we don't look out.

PATTERSON: How can this be prevented?

WRIGHT: By qualifying the vote somehow and making education do its job which it hasn't done at all well. Education is now a conditioning of the mind, not an enlightening of the mind, and Thomas Jefferson thought it would enlighten the mind. How are you going to do that? You have got to do that before we can have a democracy, before we will have anything resembling it—anything above the lowest form of socialism this world has ever seen now. Education is to blame. Education, bring it in here. Bring in these teachers, line them up, let Carl take the hide off them. He can do it.

SANDBURG: A while back I was going to Chicago for a couple of days and I was told I could meet a friend of mine out there at the convention of Educational Broadcasters. The Educational Broadcasters! Education! It haunts me as one of the ugliest words in the language today. Alfred North Whitehead tells Lucien Price—and it's a pretty good book—Dialogues of Alfred North Whitehead—

WRIGHT: I think so. Probably the best man we have had is Alfred North Whitehead.

SANDBURG: He says at one point—there's a possibility of an evolution downward. It is a fearful thing to think of. There have been evolutions of species downward. Who knows but what the human beings might become ants. As I pass and go along certain city blocks I wonder . . .

PATTERSON: What is the answer to a whole man?

WRIGHT: Cultivation; culture and education are not on speaking terms today. What is culture? It is what we are doing at Taliesin for one thing. There is a little garden flower called larkspur; beautiful pattern, lovely design. Here comes the wise Dutch. They see this beautiful little flower in the garden and they love it and they dig it up and they study it carefully to see what it liked best, what made it more and more the thing that it was and they gave it to it. Then they took the best ones and they planted these. They knew more by this time, what the thing was, what conditions made it. So finally out of it came the queen of the garden—the delphinium. That's the little larkspur, by the Dutch. They cultured it; they cultivated it; and how did they do it? By giving it more of that thing which it was in itself and needed to grow. Now education is just the reverse. Education would look at that thing and give it a curriculum, a run around; do this and that and the other to it. See? Not with it, but on it. There you have the best definition I can give you.

SANDBURG: I couldn't do better.

WRIGHT: Well listen to that. The old troubador is modest.

SANDBURG: In dialectics one of the best things I have ever heard was a couple of comedians that I used to see whenever they were in town. Moss and Fry. Moss was short and dapper and dandy and Fry was tall, a beanpole, six feet two or three. And Moss would say, "If you plant something and nothing comes up, what is it?" And then Fry, supposedly the stupid one, would say "Well if nothing comes up what did you want to plant it for?"

PATTERSON: What do you want from life that you haven't gotten?

SANDBURG: Well, at the present moment I would like to walk up any flight of stairs as spry as I did 30 years ago.

WRIGHT: You know, I don't believe there's anything in life that I haven't got and if there isn't it is my own fault. I sincerely believe that.

PATTERSON: What about regrets?

WRIGHT: I don't think regrets are [sic] the proper word. I could wish that I might have acted differently and I might not have done this and I might have done that but I am not cast down by it.

SANDBURG: Regrets? I got a million regrets. I have got a million small regrets, maybe two or three large ones.

WRIGHT: Well, if you have them, Carl, they are standing in your way. Get rid of them. They are the worst things you can cultivate.

SANDBURG: I regret that at a certain point in my life—I had the friendship of a man and we were in the same town, community and everything, and he was great in mathematics and I could have done something in mathematics—*at that time*. Since then I have lost interest. I think I would go in for it now but I haven't got the time to spare from work I am doing.

WRIGHT: I don't know about that. I think you are wasting your time on that.

PATTERSON: How do you account for the fact that both of you are productive at your age?

WRIGHT: Being young is something you can't do anything about. You are not responsible for how many years you have lived. But youth is a spirit and once you get it you never lose it and they will put it into the box with you and it will be your immortality. The spirit of youth. Now, Carl has it.

The Friendly Titans

SANDBURG: I approximated saying something like that in a broadcast on my birthday. I mentioned that you have done some of your best work in your eighties. And I expect to move on into the 80's and do some of my best work.

WRIGHT: What's the matter with ninety?

PATTERSON: What about Corbusier and Mies van der Rohe as architects?

WRIGHT: I think they are two very pretty men in the wrong place. I think that Corbusier should have been a painter. He was a bad one but he should have kept on painting. No painter can ever understand architecture. And as for Mies— he is a very honest man and a very nice one but he has a heavy scientific list to starboard and he has never gone sufficiently far left. He is still in the nineteenth century doing the old steel frame that was the great contribution of the nineteenth-century engineers to building; he is trying to make the old box frame beautiful. He has come as near to it as anybody, but it can't be done.

SANDBURG: I am glad that is in the record. Wasn't it some kinsman of yours, some elder who told you about two kinds of humility?

WRIGHT: Yes . . . humility. You know that's been greatly overdone by the common man and in behalf of the·common man. You know I suspect the humble. And I prefer the honest. Now the honest are not necessarily humble and the humble are not necessarily honest. Somebody asked me the other day what the secret was—

I suppose I am a spry old man at my age and I am still functioning and alert—and I said well, I love my work, that's the well spring of activity; I love my wife, that's another; and I tell the truth. And those three things, I think, will stand you well and see you through. It is quite enough. And that combination is not common.

PATTERSON: What do you think of each other?

WRIGHT: Carl, dear old troubador! Well, I tried to bring Carl up at an early age but he was too far gone on along the lines of Lincoln he was writing. I couldn't do much with him. Here he is. He has done fairly well. Look at him. I think Carl is all right—but he is Carl, I wouldn't have him changed. I wouldn't have any one of my friends improved. It would be just too bad. I like them as they are. And I like Carl as he is.

SANDBURG: I think that someday I will get a poem. I have tried two or three but they don't quite come off. But sometime why I think I will get a Frank Lloyd Wright poem and it will have music and it will have dimensions in it.

WRIGHT: Third dimensions?

SANDBURG: I will even suggest a fourth one.

WRIGHT: The fourth dimension is derived from the third. When you look at the third as thickness you are lost. You have but three dimensions. But you look at the third dimension for depth, it is a quality, and out of that quality comes your fourth dimension. See. Now that's the best thing I can give you, too, boy. Isn't it good?

The Second Meeting
of the Titans

Frank Lloyd Wright and
Carl Sandburg

We're supposed to give to the American people poetry,
beauty and a sense of it in forms they've never seen before
and that belong to them, that come out of their own lives.

On October 29, 1957 Frank Lloyd Wright and Carl Sandburg appeared on
a television program in Chicago produced by WTTW-Chicago Channel 11
called *Chicago Dynamic* with moderator Alistair Cooke. This program was
a part of what was called "Chicago Dynamic," a series of events
designed to dramatize Chicago's architectural heritage and focus attention
on its architectural potential in the so-called coming building renaissance.
The entire program of events was initiated by the United States Steel
Corporation and was sponsored and assisted by an impressive list of local
Chicago corporations and associations including the Chicago chapter of
the American Institute of Architects. The *Chicago Dynamic* television
program began at 9:30 PM and was to run only one-half hour but the
conversation extended to forty minutes, which was past the regular
signoff time of WTTW television.

The following day, October 30, Wright continued his participation in the
"Chicago Dynamic" series by appearing on a panel shared by city
planners and businessmen. Alistair Cooke also moderated this panel
discussion and recounted this, his last meeting with Frank Lloyd Wright,
for the April 16, 1959 issue of *The Manchester Guardian Weekly* following
Wright's death:

The last time I saw him, a year ago, was to "moderate" a debate in Chicago
on the present condition of our cities. The panel consisted of real estate men,

254

a housing commissioner, a young professor of architecture and Wright. It was sponsored by a steel company that legitimately hoped to popularize "the steel curtain" which is now the first constituent of most of the skyscrapers going up.

Wright outraged his sponsors and almost broke up the forum, first by professing boredom over the arguments of the builders and real estate men and consequently walking out to take a nap; and later by indicating a diorama advertising the steel curtain and saying: "These steel frames are just the old log cabin; they are all built from the outside in, first a steel frame, then they bring in the paper hanger, and what have you got?—a box with steel for horizontals instead of lumber."

Driving back along the lake front he had done most to glorify, he ridiculed the glinting skyscrapers and the whizzing autos ("rectangles on wheels"), but he could work up no steam or bile. His only genuine sigh was for the universal misuse of steel, "this beautiful material that spins like a spider and produces a tension so perfect that you can balance a monolith on a pin point."

I felt that this lament for the city he secretly adored was a little recitation for Buncombe. In his 90th year he could afford to be agreeable to everybody, though he tried valiantly to resist the inclination. After all it had been 58 years since he had pioneered the sweeping horizontals of the first "prairie house" (which would pass creditably anywhere as a distinguished "contemporary" house), 51 years since he built the first air-conditioned building, 54 years since the first metal-bound plate-glass door, 48 years since the cantilevered floor, poured concrete, and all the other explosive solecisms that are now the grammar of the modern architect.*

The following is the complete text of the conversation of the second meeting of the titans—Frank Lloyd Wright and Carl Sandburg with Alistair Cooke—from the October 29, 1957 television program *Chicago Dynamic*.

The text of this heretofore unpublished conversation between Frank Lloyd Wright, Carl Sandburg, and Alistair Cooke is published by permission of WTTW-Chicago Channel 11; The Frank Lloyd Wright Foundation; The Sandburg Family Trust, Frank M. Parker and Maurice C. Greenbaum, Trustees; and Alistair Cooke.

*Reprinted here with the kind permission of Mr. Alistair Cooke.

The Conversation

COOKE: Ladies and gentlemen, my role in this evening's performance has been grossly exaggerated already and any suggestion that I will get even one sharp remark—this is probably the last speech I'll be allowed to make so I'm going to make the most of it. Now the idea of having an Englishman—even an ex-Englishman—introduce Carl Sandburg and Frank Lloyd Wright to a Chicago audience strikes me as rather like importing a Russian peasant to explain Bing Crosby to Bob Hope.

SANDBURG: The most humble Englishman that ever came to Chicago.

COOKE: There have been many.

SANDBURG: (laughter)

WRIGHT: Is Alistair really speaking English?

COOKE: I just want to say . . . you see how it's going to be. I just want to say that they are both great men whom all Americans revere who honor individualism in the arts and they are both sons of Chicago. Now aside from that I know that they're both very formidable monologists and I'm told that my function is to guide them into the more restrained form of social intercourse known as a "conversation." I say no more—Mr. Wright—Mr. Sandburg—converse.

WRIGHT: How do you do Mr. Sandburg?

SANDBURG: We are good monologists . . .

WRIGHT: (laughter)

SANDBURG: . . . he is afraid we will not be dialogists tonight.

WRIGHT: Well, I'm afraid we won't be. Can you think of anything to talk about?

SANDBURG: I can think of the humility of this Englishman. We're not accustomed to having one so modest as you are.

WRIGHT: Aren't you aware of the fact that the English have always made a profession of humility?

COOKE: Thereby . . .

WRIGHT: That's how they got to where they are today.

SANDBURG: (laughter)

COOKE: Mr. Sandburg what do you think? What does "Chicago Dynamic" mean to you? I mean besides it's being the title of this forum and this week that's coming up?

SANDBURG: The present Chicago dynamic move—move is one of a series—the town has had them, it began when Chicago was being built on a mud hole of a swamp. And, I wouldn't say with every generation but at regular intervals, a good historian who did his research properly could chart a series of Chicago dynamic movements. One of the most illustrative periods, of course, was the World's Columbian Exposition which had a nightmare of architecture. Nevertheless, nevertheless had its influence on America and the world.

COOKE: How was the folk singing at the Columbian Exposition Mr. Wright?

WRIGHT: How was what?

COOKE: The folk singing? Mr. Sandburg has already taken care of the architecture; he said it was a monster.

SANDBURG: (laughter)

COOKE: Do you have any dynamic ideas about the Columbian Exposition?

The Friendly Titans

WRIGHT: I thought you meant some ideas of what is "dynamic"—a "dynamic idea."

COOKE: Yes, yes.

WRIGHT: Well, I guess the skyscraper has gone into the dynamics of civilization hasn't it? Don't they judge now the degree of the success you've attained as a civilized organism or a society by the tallness of the skyscrapers you can build?

COOKE: Do you approve of that Mr. Wright?

WRIGHT: I don't approve of it—no.

COOKE: You don't think there is anything essentially dynamic about a skyscraper?

WRIGHT: No, I think not: I think, of course, there's something in the human spirit that loves something tall and the idea of a tall building is very beautiful and a tall building can be beautiful. But I think it's degenerated to a mere exaggeration of the box. What are these things around us here that we see? These frames—steel frames—steel lumber—steel rolled into lumber and framed into these tall edifices and then they bring in the paper hanger and hang a facade on them. I don't think you could call that really architecture because it's not permanent. None of them are permanent but they are spectacular.

COOKE: How do you feel about the dynamism of the skyscraper Mr. Sandburg?

SANDBURG: Well it's reached the point where one architect, on a twenty-two–foot length [of paper], outlined a mile-high building.

COOKE: Do you find them much the same all around the place? Do you find skyscrapers much the same wherever they are? Do you think that Chicago has a style all its own?

SANDBURG: Well there's some that I go out of

Frank Lloyd Wright as he appeared on the WTTW-Chicago television program Chicago Dynamic *on October 29, 1957. Photograph used by permission of WTTW-Chicago Channel 11.*

Carl Sandburg as he appeared on the WTTW-Chicago television program Chicago Dynamic *on October 29, 1957. Photograph used by permission of WTTW-Chicago Channel 11.*

Alistair Cooke as he appeared on the WTTW-Chicago television program Chicago Dynamic *on October 29, 1957. Photograph used by permission of WTTW-Chicago Channel 11.*

my way to see and there's some skyscrapers I pass. They are neither salt nor pepper. They a . . . well, like I heard a fellow say one time: "I could write bitter about that fellow with my left hand thinking about something else." Yes, the Tower of Babel . . . did something like that happen?

WRIGHT: Nothing like that Carl. The Tower of Babel, I imagine, was a ziggurat. It was a ramp winding and winding up like this. You could walk clear to the top . . .

SANDBURG: . . . like the Guggenheim Building in a . . .

WRIGHT: . . . well like they do on any ramp.

SANDBURG: . . . and then it failed of completion of structure because all of a sudden the languages changed?

WRIGHT: I never knew much concerning the details of the Tower of Babylon. Are they on record anywhere?

SANDBURG: Not that I know, not that I know of.

WRIGHT: Well, maybe we could call some of these modern things "Towers of Babylon."

COOKE: Why do you think they came about Mr. Wright? I mean here they are and the whole world imitates them and feels grand in having them.

WRIGHT: Well originally, of course, they were a grand economy and I guess they're a great economy now but to build them in cities at this time is pushing the city to its end and stating its doom a little too early perhaps. They have no business in the city and never did have. They belong out in the country where they can cast their shadow on their own ground. They are in themselves, of course now, a cliché. They're all

very much alike. They're made in the same way. They're all built from the outside in. The steel framing you see outside and they hang a curtain on it of some kind that they devise— some pattern or other. I don't think they're wrong, so far as the facades they make are concerned for the city, but I don't like to see them called architecture.

COOKE: Well Mr. . . .

WRIGHT: I doubt if they are and I doubt if they're ever going to be considered so in the future.

COOKE: If you could take over the future of Chicago, by which I mean you might be able to destroy it and start again or go from where it is today, suppose you were given absolute power and money and the blessings of the state Legislature, what would you do with it?

WRIGHT: Well I think I would do what the people themselves would dearly love to do if they could—decentralize the entire affair and send the people back to greenery where they belong—most of them—and maybe build a Mile-High or two for those brain workers who have to get together no matter what nor whatever the situations might be. Build them a Mile-High or two or three and then let them live in the country. Perhaps create a commodity belt around the tall buildings about a mile or so.

COOKE: But you'd still have tall buildings in the country?

WRIGHT: I'd have tall buildings in the country because the tall building is in itself essentially a poetic beautiful thing—can be—but not in the city. Not while they're eating each other up, competing with each other, casting their shadows down on the less fortunate neighbor who can't build a skyscraper—they eat up his

The Friendly Titans

ground—they've taken on themselves an unethical privilege.

And if you look at New York when you come in from the harbor you see a great series of fingers threatening the sky all there for one single purpose—rent—all competing with each other for one soul benefit—rent—none of it planned, it has no organization, no thought, no feeling. It has been a negation of all the human attributes that should make buildings beautiful because the buildings are not humanly expressive beautiful. And if they don't mean that when you see them if they look cruel—rat traps—man traps—just a sign advertising something or other—soap—or whiskey—or what have you then I think we shouldn't call them architecture.

COOKE: Mr. Wright, thank you for that. I'm going to ask Mr. Sandburg if Mr. Wright is correct and [if] all the human attributes have been obliterated by these great cities how come that you're still at it, Mr. Sandburg, writing poetry? What do you find that is worth celebrating in the human individual who lives in cities?

SANDBURG: Well I've lived with skyscrapers so long that I've come to accept them just like some people.

COOKE: But you don't find that men are crushed into ants or unrecognizable?

SANDBURG: Oh, the Northwestern Railway Station of the morning and of the evening is something hideous to look at. They're like cattle, for all that is said of the suburbs and life in the suburbs, the way they herd themselves into the suburban trains. There's a pathos about it. There's something animalistic that ain't so good to look at.

COOKE: Well that's a fit subject for poetry though isn't it, the pathos of man?

SANDBURG: Yes, yes the fate of man. And they ride, of course, in the elevators in the thirty/forty story building and what you can see from the top—it's worth the time.

COOKE: It's worth going up you think?

SANDBURG: Yes particularly in the Board of Trade Building where they showed me. Two or three railroad stations are going to be

Frank Lloyd Wright in front of his rendering for the Mile-High Illinois Skyscraper in 1956. Photograph courtesy of The Capital Times, *Madison, Wisconsin.*

discombobulated; they're going to move into disuse except for suburban traffic and there will be a Union Station that a . . . that will be a . . . well, it'll be a help in a city where more trains start and stop every day than any other city in the world.

WRIGHT: (laughter)

SANDBURG: That's one of Chicago's records that is good—it stands. New York would have a hard time with that.

COOKE: I sense that Mr. Wright is not very impressed with that statistic but I'm interested to know how you as a poet . . .

WRIGHT: No, I'm not at all impressed.

COOKE: . . . how you as a poet keep your equanimity and your interest in human beings and your good nature through all of this terrible thing that Mr. Wright's been telling us we've been going through?

SANDBURG: I'm aware of it. I know what he's talking about. I'm an old Socialist (laughter). I had my dreams and I still have them but I don't allow them to dominate me. I improve the present layout of living.

COOKE: Now what would that entail? What would that entail? Suppose we dream a while.

SANDBURG: Well, I'm not sure but what aren't there cities in . . . what are the cities in Europe that regulate the height of the skyscrapers?

WRIGHT: Oh well, they all do

SANDBURG: They all do and we don't?

WRIGHT: Paris is the most beautiful city in the world just because it has space. It's resisted these tall buildings that [are] dumping thousands down into the street.

SANDBURG: Well, I'd like to hear more about

that and see movements toward that end in this country but . . .

COOKE: Now is Washington a good example because there's a city with compulsory space? At least in the beginning, wasn't it?

WRIGHT: It would be, among other things being equal, a very beautiful modern city but of course it's only a museum piece as it stands now. They're all reminiscent of old-fashioned buildings not at all representing our ideas of sovereignty of the individual . . .

COOKE: But if they are . . .

WRIGHT: Not a building there I think expresses it. Certainly not the Capitol.

COOKE: But they were built by Americans. If Americans want to look like Greek wedding cakes that's . . .

WRIGHT: You see Americans cannot claim a culture of their own. The difficulty with America is that when it came over here it had too much of English on it as it came. It didn't have anything of its own culture and it has very little, if anything, of its own now.

COOKE: Are you going to let that pass Mr. Sandburg?

SANDBURG: Well I'm going to ask what about Walt Whitman? What about George Ade out of Chicago here?

WRIGHT: Oh well, you're talking about the English influences that our ancestors came over with—the lace at their wrists—the buckles on their shoe. The culture that they had is all we had to go on except various other cultures which came in and made the situation a little more hybrid but not all.

COOKE: Don't you think the hybrid situation is the American situation?

WRIGHT: Well it's an American characteristic—yes. But I hope to see America evolve perhaps the noblest greatest culture of its own that any nation ever had just because we have such great facilities. Because we can do these skyscrapers.

COOKE: Mr. Sandburg.

SANDBURG: What was it that Walt Whitman said?—"the American dream"?—"the American dream" and it's not English.

WRIGHT: That's not English, no.

COOKE: Not a bit, not a bit. But how close do you think we've come to it Mr. Sandburg?

SANDBURG: Oh we could well have had something [of] the English dream during this period of time in which physicists, scientists, were under a vigilance that ran into suspicion of everyone resulting in . . . Sputnik—I told you we would!

WRIGHT: (laughter)

COOKE: Now these two have been plotting. Now this is completely unrehearsed on my part.

WRIGHT: I've been totally unable to get excited about Sputnik because I'd like to see something of the human spirit and soul, characteristically a beautiful expression of human nature, rather than this triumph of the scientist. I think scientists have pushed us to the edge to go over the brink so far as scientists are concerned. But we have no religion of our own any more. We have no art of our own particularly. And the little start we made in architecture has gone around the world and it has amounted to something but it is now going off in a cliché again and the first thing you know this sort of thing you see around you here is going to be "Classic."

SANDBURG: Well in this time when abstractions are so enjoyed by this so-called . . .

WRIGHT: Isn't civilization an abstraction in itself? (laughter)

COOKE: You mean there never was a civilization?

SANDBURG: I was going to ask you what you think of Sputnik as a form?

WRIGHT: I don't know the form of the Sputnik myself.

COOKE: It's a football isn't it?

SANDBURG: (laughter)

COOKE: We were going to send a baseball and they sent a football.

SANDBURG: A football with a long spike through it.

WRIGHT: I've been totally unable to get very excited over Sputnik. I'd like to see a "puttnik" that came out from the human spirit rather than from scientific formula.

SANDBURG: Well there are some pretty good philosophers who make the point that Sputnik, entirely aside from all international relations and complications of any kind or dangers of war or whatnot, entirely aside from that, Sputnik is a testimony that man, whether he's Russian or American, wants to know and he's going to penetrate. He wants to know about the spaces beyond the earth—beyond the atmosphere that surrounds the earth and he's going to keep it up until he journeys to the moon. And there are theorists like J. B. Haldane who hold that if it becomes necessary, if earth is going to chill and an ice age come, mankind will detect that in advance and it will move to the planet Venus or some other one.

WRIGHT: Well there's no question that the . . .

COOKE: And in comes the skyscraper again.

WRIGHT: . . . fellow who has the curiosity . . .

COOKE: How?

WRIGHT: He's curious about everything . . .

COOKE: Well, isn't that a good . . .

WRIGHT: . . . but he himself will degenerate into a curiosity if he isn't careful by way of all these "puttniks" and advantages science has given to him that he can't interpret. He doesn't know what they mean to the human spirit. He doesn't know this great . . . these great gifts. Even the motorcar he doesn't know how to use that properly; he doesn't know how to make one properly.

COOKE: Now Mr. Wright . . .

WRIGHT: All these great advantages are being twisted.

COOKE: . . . would you tell us how to make an automobile properly and use it?

WRIGHT: Well I should think at least . . .

COOKE: I would like to know.

WRIGHT: . . . have something about it that you should think was mobile except the name. The only thing mobile about the automobile today is the name and perhaps the engine. It's a ferryboat coming down the street gnashing its teeth at you. It's not at all mobile. Mobility is something like this you know—it's like a school of fish, isn't it? They all work together. Well now if the corners of the fish were stuck out . . .

COOKE: It's the rectangle again.

WRIGHT: . . . and they were made rectangular and you were to put lights on points on the corners and you were to put guards on the lights how many fish do you think would be living very long?

COOKE: Now there's . . .

WRIGHT: They'd all be floating on the surface. So mobility is something that has in itself—if you study nature—it has form; it has a shape and the automobile denies it all and it's oversized. I don't know, somebody said that these great big cars were characteristic and favorites with Americans because they themselves, having a tendency toward impotence, found when they got their hands on the wheel of a great big ferryboat and a thing like that that they were somebody.

COOKE: Do you think there's anything . . .

WRIGHT: It made up for their deficiencies.

SANDBURG: We were going to keep off of sex.

WRIGHT AND SANDBURG: (laughter)

COOKE: This whole thing has been plotted I swear! If Mr. Sandburg . . .

SANDBURG: (laughter)

WRIGHT: If the automobile, excuse me for continuing this thought . . .

COOKE: Excuse me!

WRIGHT: . . . for a moment, if the automobile is an indication of what production and the big boys who run it is going to do to the consumer when production really controls consumption I think we might as well sign off right now and call it a day.

SANDBURG: Frank, could I ask you have you done any meditating peddling your mind about those scientists in Russia who produced Sputnik and who produced atomic power, the hydrogen bomb, and intercontinental ballistic missiles? They, the testimonies of them, when they meet other scientists is that they have nice houses, good cars, and servants and that they live well.

WRIGHT: Oh ya.

SANDBURG: But do they have the traditional freedom of mind and desire for freedom of inquiry, independence of spirit that has gone in past ages with all the great scientists?

WRIGHT: No, I don't think I like a scientist. I'm an artist. I believe in the human spirit and the wonders and splendor of the spirit. And I'm not so excited over these things of the intellect. I'm not so excited about powers that can take things apart and analyze them as I am about powers that can put things together and make them live with a life never known before and I don't think "puttnik" lives . . .

SANDBURG: Would you rather have been . . .

WRIGHT: . . . and I think science does.

SANDBURG: Of the two which would you rather have been, Picasso or Einstein? There's a good one isn't it?

COOKE: Oh that's . . .

WRIGHT: Neither one.

SANDBURG: (laughter)

WRIGHT: I think that Einstein would make a good Picasso and I think that Picasso would make a good Einstein.

SANDBURG AND COOKE: (laughter)

SANDBURG: I find myself wondering about those scientists enclosed there . . .

WRIGHT: And you're a poet my dear boy . . .

SANDBURG: . . . they are confined.

WRIGHT: . . . and I'll love you for your poetry and I'm sure that you're not talking out of your own heart when you talk about the scientist the way you do.

COOKE: Well he's concerned about the imprisonment . . .

WRIGHT: We're supposed to give to the American people poetry, beauty, and a sense of it in forms they've never seen before and that belong to them; that come out of their own lives. Now science has given us a great chance to use a great many things to do that thing and we haven't had a chance to do it, have we?

COOKE: Had the chance?

WRIGHT: Not to any very great extent.

COOKE: We've more leisure than any large population has ever had.

WRIGHT: Well, I don't know, we grew too large a population too soon and we haven't grown that way on our own. We're a lot of tidbits of various times and conditions and peoples trying to amalgamate. Who was it that called us the "melting pot"? We don't seem to melt very well. We seem to mix and not melt. What we want is something that will bring about that melting and nothing could do it except a culture of our own from in here not up here.

SANDBURG: You've got some fixed and frozen mold for this thing—scientists on the one hand and artists on the other. What about Ben Franklin?

WRIGHT: Ben Franklin was no artist!

SANDBURG: He wasn't an artist?

WRIGHT: Not a sense. He was a pragmatic old guy and he never wrote poetry.

SANDBURG: (laughter)

COOKE: Didn't he write pretty good prose?

WRIGHT: He wouldn't be interested in the Rootabaga Tales. [*Editor's Note*: Sandburg's *Rootabaga Stories*.] No he wouldn't . . .

SANDBURG: (laughter) He cornered me there just like a lawyer see—he brings that up.

WRIGHT AND SANDBURG: (laughter)

WRIGHT: No, don't give me Ben Franklin!

COOKE: Well let's give him somebody else Mr. Sandburg.

WRIGHT: Give me Thomas Jefferson!

SANDBURG: Well, I was just going to say Thomas Jefferson.

WRIGHT: Give me some of the fellows that really had this idea of freedom of the individual at heart. And if man was free the best and bravest among him would come up and do what ruling there was to be done and the less of it that was done the better. Didn't he say that government is best government that governs . . .

SANDBURG: . . . least.

WRIGHT: That was the ideal we started with. Where is it now? What do you see of it now in existence?

SANDBURG: Well I'll offer you Jefferson as a combination—as a blend of the artist and the scientist. He was an artist in terms of quality of song . . .

WRIGHT: No.

SANDBURG: . . . in nearly all his sentences yet the science of agriculture fascinated him to his last days.

WRIGHT: Well it fascinates me.

COOKE: He was a very bad farmer wasn't he Mr. Sandburg?

WRIGHT: I'm a very bad farmer too.

COOKE: When they discovered his books didn't . . . wasn't he losing three thousand a year?

WRIGHT: Yes but Thomas Jefferson was as near the aristocrat that we need and that we should produce of any figure that I can imagine.

COOKE: Well now how are you going to have an aristocrat in a democratic society? Do you have a special use . . .

WRIGHT: You can't have anything else my dear Alistair. You haven't got a democrat until you have an aristocrat. But not by privilege—not something given to you—but it's something you are and work out from within yourself because you're free.

SANDBURG: Of course drama is one of the arts.

WRIGHT: What is?

SANDBURG: Drama. Drama is one of the arts . . .

WRIGHT: Yes, drama is.

SANDBURG: . . . and it was great drama when man was able to take the atom which is present in all matter and smash it to such fine flinders suddenly. Suddenly there was energy that could be harnessed and controlled. A kind never known before. I should think you'd have some curiosity as to what's going to be the result or effect on architecture?

WRIGHT: Now, now, now, now, now, now Carl you're getting off your own beat! Who was the greatest poet who ever lived? Who was the master poet of the world? Who was the greatest student of *nature* who ever lived?

SANDBURG: You've got something locked in your mind there, let's have it.

COOKE: It's a tribe called . . .

WRIGHT: No. I think . . .

COOKE: I'm avoiding Shakespeare.

WRIGHT: . . . the man was Jesus of Nazareth. I think he was the greatest of all *nature* students and the master of human nature.

SANDBURG: Do you think he is documented?

WRIGHT: I don't think he was documented. He didn't want documents, nor organizations, nor churches, nor anything.

SANDBURG: (laughter)

The Friendly Titans

WRIGHT: What he wanted was in here and he knew the great depth and value of it if it could be brought to bear upon human conduct.

SANDBURG: Do you believe he performed miracles?

WRIGHT: I believe that everything he said and did was miraculous in the sense that it was natural.

SANDBURG: Well, you could have preached the Sermon on the Mount.

WRIGHT: I think everything he ever said, all of the parables he used, everything he said and did, was that of a great artist and a great poet. Now what made him a great artist and a great poet was because he was the greatest deepest student of *nature* who ever lived. Human nature and that's what made him so valuable to us and what made him a shining light throughout the world today was the fact that he was a master poet of *nature*—man's nature—human nature. And there is all phases of *nature* but no man is valuable to his kind, where a culture is concerned, until he's a deep devoted student of *nature* with a capital N.

SANDBURG: Wasn't there a great preacher lost in him?

WRIGHT: Yes.

COOKE: Yes indeed.

WRIGHT: Lost?

SANDBURG AND WRIGHT: (laughter)

WRIGHT: Well I don't think that's preaching. I think that's just good sense.

Frank Lloyd Wright as he appeared on the WTTW-Chicago television program Chicago Dynamic *on October 29, 1957. Photograph used by permission of WTTW-Chicago Channel 11.*

SANDBURG: Well it's interpretation, it's interpretation.

COOKE: Mr. Wright, I've often wanted to ask you and since one of the great living authorities on Lincoln is here, may I ask you now do you think that the Lincoln Memorial is a fitting memorial to him?

SANDBURG: (outburst of laughter)

COOKE: What do you think?

WRIGHT: Ask him, do you hear that laugh? That expresses it. It's a laugh.

SANDBURG: (continues laughing)

COOKE: What do you say Mr. Sandburg?

SANDBURG: Well I used to think it was a monstrosity but I have met so many people that are just smitten by it.

COOKE: So moved.

SANDBURG: It's become something to me out of what people regarded, people who would have followed Lincoln's cause and people who . . .

WRIGHT: Are you speaking of the masses?

SANDBURG: How? (laughter)

WRIGHT: The masses?

SANDBURG: I hate to be a magazine—the masses. He transforms them into the masses. The Lincoln Memorial lighted at night . . .

WRIGHT: It's one of the most ridiculous, most asinine, miscarriages of building material that ever happened.

SANDBURG: You talk just like Gutzon Borglum.

WRIGHT: (laughter) Gutzon made his mistakes too just as I have I suppose.

SANDBURG: You would take one of God's finest mountains and improve on it with human faces?

WRIGHT: Well now I never agreed with it.

SANDBURG: Faces that are on all the postage stamps and you'd know what the men of the past looked like. If you're a quarter mile high you can see their whiskers in stone (breaks into laughter).

WRIGHT: He wasn't a great artist you know.

COOKE: If you had to devise a memorial, if you can conceive such a thing, for Lincoln, what kind of a thing would it be?

WRIGHT: You know I don't agree with Carl on Lincoln myself.

COOKE: On the Lincoln Memorial or Lincoln at all?

WRIGHT: On Lincoln himself I don't agree with Carl.

COOKE: Oh dear.

WRIGHT: I think he was a great individual and a tremendous fanatic and I think he destroyed a culture that we should have preserved and might have been preserved but for the fact that he didn't know any other way than the way he took. And now . . .

COOKE: Mr. Sandburg.

SANDBURG: And Jefferson . . .

WRIGHT: Jefferson . . .

SANDBURG: . . . the opposite.

WRIGHT: I think he would have been all right. I think he would have worked it out because we should have been a great agronomy. We never should have followed the pattern of England and become a great industrialist nation.

SANDBURG: What do you think of the Jefferson Memorial? I think an argument can be made for the Lincoln Memorial but the Jefferson . . .

WRIGHT: Now isn't that poetic or unpoetic

Carl Sandburg: "What do you think of the Jefferson Memorial?" Carl Sandburg as he appeared on the WTTW-Chicago television program Chicago Dynamic *on October 29, 1957. Photograph used by permission of WTTW-Chicago Channel 11.*

American lapse of justice to build a public comfort station to Thomas Jefferson?

SANDBURG: (loud laughter)

WRIGHT: And a great . . .

COOKE: In the classical mode though.

WRIGHT: Yes, in the classical mode and why not? It can be done in the classical mode. [*Editor's note*: At this point, 10:00 p.m. and thirty minutes into the program, the program was scheduled to end but instead the program began to run past the signoff time of WTTW television and continued on for about ten more minutes.]

SANDBURG: And then halfway that immense obelisk out of Egypt who George Washington of Virginia . . .

COOKE: Now what's that signify?

WRIGHT: You know we're not in to build an obelisk. There's the Washington Monument for instance, have you ever looked at the point of it? You know it's stone and the great beauty of it is that it's a shaft of solid stone. Now when they got to the top instead of doing what the Egyptians did, giving it a low point like this you see, they had to improve upon it and make it sharper and steeper like the point on a lead pencil and destroy the power of the stone. There is a conspicuous imperishable evidence of our inability to see the *nature* of anything from within. The Washington Monument is positively the act of an ignoramus unaware of the dignity and beauty of the shaft that he was finishing when he made it pointed instead of strong and low like that. Well this is getting off the track here . . . let's get back.

COOKE: Let's get back to what?

SANDBURG: (breaks into laughter)

COOKE: Does the Washington Monument . . .

WRIGHT: Let's get back to the a . . .

The 555-foot-tall Washington Monument at Washington, D.C. designed by Robert Mills in 1833 began construction in 1848 and was completed in 1884. T. L. Casey, who was an army engineer, sharpened the pitch of the monument's pyramidon and then crowned it with aluminum. Photograph by the editor.

COOKE: Mr. Sandburg, I've never noticed this—I can see the point now in my humble fashion.

WRIGHT: You see it whittles away nobility and character of the material.

COOKE: Actually to go across the grain of the material do you mean?

WRIGHT: Well it doesn't add to the shape. Shapes have expression—they're plus, they're minus, they're negative, they're positive—they're stone, they're wood. You wouldn't put the same shape in wood that you would in stone.

SANDBURG: No but at the same time it was . . .

WRIGHT: You wouldn't have the same shape in flesh that you would in tin or metal. And according to the *nature* of materials comes the form.

SANDBURG: At the same time they built that obelisk it went higher than anything that the hand of man created here in this century.

WRIGHT: Is that anything?

SANDBURG: (breaks into laughter) I make a nice American and brag!

WRIGHT: Here this use of steel—that's a misuse of steel. You know when they got steel first,

The Friendly Titans

these great steel masters we have now, all we had to build with was lumber wasn't it? Lumber—and what did they do with steel? They made lumber out of it. They rolled it into beams and posts and began to tie it together the way they tied wood together; they're still doing it. Why?

COOKE: Well what could you do with steel?

WRIGHT: Why steel is the spider spinning. Steel is the strongest and most economic when a strand and when you shred it and pull it into these strands and use it for the pull that is in it then you are using steel. And when you use it the way you use wood in beams you're wasting the steel.

SANDBURG: You make yourself clear.

WRIGHT: No doubt the men who sell steel are willing to waste it.

COOKE: Are you going to have a Frank Lloyd Wright building that looks like a . . .

WRIGHT: No but you have already a building that I built that looks like the way it's built—from the inside out not outside in. And I don't know why they consider themselves steel framers and paper hangers decorating a facade after they make a steel frame and they hang paper wallpaper on it you know—I don't know why they consider that modern; that's nineteenth century. It's all nineteenth century.

COOKE: Mr. Sandburg I'm just wondering if you have to live in Chicago more than Mr. Wright does because I never expected one Chicagoan to intimidate another? I thought you were going to get up and sock him at some point; you're taking all this. Is it because you're such good old friends?

WRIGHT: I think Carl is trying to be nice to me.

SANDBURG: All true Chicagoans long ago got themselves accommodated to thinking about Frank Lloyd Wright.

COOKE: Well now how about the passion of Carl Sandburg? Is there nothing you want to take off on Mr. Wright because he's a very, as you know, strong man and he can take an awful lot. His talk about Lincoln doesn't matter?

SANDBURG: I believe he had dressed me in velveteen jacket like an artist.

WRIGHT AND COOKE: (break into laughter)

WRIGHT: Remember, I used to put one on you Carl?

SANDBURG: Yes, yes I have photographs.

WRIGHT: Bloomers with all the rest. We'd sit before the fire and talk about art and we rode around the countryside and had a nice time together. Carl wrote the first two chapters of his *Lincoln* at Taliesin. Didn't you?

SANDBURG: Ya, ya.

WRIGHT: And we had a good time and I enjoyed myself in front of the fireplace when we were talking about art. And then said Carl to me when we went away "Frank" he said "you've been an ideal companion we've had a fine time together when we'd go out in the countryside and ride around. I said you're an ideal companion but when you put those damn clothes on me and put me before the fire and talked about art, God I said, you made me sick."

SANDBURG: (breaks into loud laughter) I don't remember saying that!

COOKE: Well Mr. Sandburg I think has mellowed. He definitely doesn't convey any of that emotion at all tonight. Maybe because . . .

WRIGHT: Those were great times we had a lot of . . . two or three . . . one precious boy that isn't with us anymore is Lloyd Lewis . . .

SANDBURG: One of the great Chicago news . . .

WRIGHT: We both loved him. He was a great Chicagoan and a great individual.

SANDBURG: Lloyd Lewis . . .

WRIGHT: Lloyd.

SANDBURG: . . . he wrote a great biography. Sherman fighting . . .

COOKE: Mr. Sandburg if you were young today would you be as excited by Chicago as it is today as you were when you first saw it?

SANDBURG: That's a psychological question.

COOKE: Well you're a psychological man.

WRIGHT: Come on you old sentimentalist— come on.

SANDBURG: Well I'm one of the American poets that's got a young heart; there aren't many. I'm as naive about moving around some parts of Chicago now as I was many years back. I will never tire—I will never tire of the lake—I'll never tire of Michigan Avenue.

WRIGHT: Say something interesting about the lake.

SANDBURG: (laughter) I've walked with Englishmen, Frenchmen during the First World War who commented on Michigan Avenue as one of the most beautiful streets in the whole world. They'd been in all of the world cities and this was one of the best.

WRIGHT: Who said that?

SANDBURG: Streets. [*sic*]

WRIGHT: Who said that? Who said that Michigan Avenue was the most beautiful street in the world?

SANDBURG: John . . . oh he wrote for . . .

COOKE: We're not going to identify him for you Mr. Wright because you have your gun ready again. I had hoped that we were, ladies and gentlemen, achieving a dying close there; a quiet friendly agreement that Chicago, at least Michigan Avenue, was one of the most beautiful . . . in the world but Mr. Wright had a glint in his eye again and I'm afraid he's going to go on and you are not going to be privileged to hear. You realize that two men are hopelessly intimidated by the indestructible Frank Lloyd Wright. Need I say that . . .

SANDBURG: He's going to macerate me (laughter)!

COOKE: He will do that when we go off the air.

WRIGHT: Oh no Carl!

COOKE: Ladies and gentlemen you've been hearing what is called a "conversation" between Carl Sandburg and Frank Lloyd Wright.

[*Editor's note:* The television picture faded and WTTW went off the air at 10:10 p.m. However, a microphone was left open by accident and caught Frank Lloyd Wright saying to Carl Sandburg: "I think we'd better get out of here, Carl, before somebody gets up and tells the truth!"]

PART SIX

Social Critic
of the Twentieth Century

16 The Social Critic in Conversation with Jinx Falkenburg

My tragedy in architecture is that I like so much the fellows that do such bad things that I don't like. I don't like the things they do and then I meet them and I like them.

On April 24, 1952 Frank Lloyd Wright participated in a one-hour interview on the NBC radio program *Tex and Jinx* originating from New York City. The two commentators of the *Tex and Jinx* radio program were the husband and wife team of John Reagan (Tex) McCrary and Eugenia Lincoln (Jinx) Falkenburg. Wright was interviewed, during this program, by Jinx Falkenburg. The interview that appears as a part of this collection was the second of two Falkenburg interviews of Wright—the first of which occurred on the preceding day on the same radio program. During the course of the second interview, Wright refused to talk about architecture at any length and stated: "I don't know why I should be interested in it to talk about it. I build it. Why should I talk about it?" However, Wright did talk about his ideas, as a social critic, on politicians, women's rights, and the rearing of children.

Transcription of this conversation furnished to the editor courtesy of Professor George R. Collins and the Avery Architectural Library of Columbia University at New York. Reproduced by permission of Jinx Falkenburg.

273

The Conversation

FALKENBURG: I'm reading here from *Current Biography* about our guest this morning: "Frank Lloyd Wright is regarded by many as the greatest architect of the twentieth century and is conceded, even by skeptics, to have one of the most restless and imaginative minds the art of architecture has ever known. Countries as remote as Holland and Japan count him a major force in the development of their contemporary styles. Thirty-one states in this country contain his work and there is no state which doesn't have buildings dominated by his influence. At seventy-one Frank Lloyd Wright is a living old master." Well, Mr. Wright, that's what it said about you at seventy-one—today you're eighty-two.

WRIGHT: I think it's partly true. But I don't know how far I should subscribe to all those beautiful statements. What would you say?

FALKENBURG: Well, I wanted to find out from you at eighty-two, eleven years later, if it's all the same.

WRIGHT: I wonder if it's eleven years later or eleven years earlier. Who knows? Nobody yet.

FALKENBURG: Do you know that you look better and younger than you did five years ago when we did an interview?

WRIGHT: You mustn't compliment me too much or I'll get silly—say something foolish myself. I don't know, this matter of age, you see in the provinces is one of the things that's quite the matter with our culture. They think a chicken has so many eggs to lay, at a certain age a horse so much more work to do, and they begin to put human beings in the category of the animals, which has put us in the position of really making old age a disqualification when it should be a qualification. If any damning count can be brought out against civilization, our culture is just that—that old age is a disqualification.

FALKENBURG: It certainly hasn't stopped you or slowed you up one bit because you've just returned from Europe where you visited many many countries and you came back with lots of rewards and gold medals, didn't you?

WRIGHT: Yes, they were very nice to me indeed, and decorated me and I came home. And I think they have a feeling that freedom—our profession, isn't it, freedom—and we as a democracy—we profess ourselves to be a democracy—should have a culture of our own. They don't consider that our success and our high standard of living and all the money that we possess is a good enough accounting. So when they see a culture, an architecture, see a work which astonishes them with its precedence, newness, and its vitality, why they are pleased as well as astonished. And I think they regard me as a living proof of the fact that freedom works and it has got into architecture. So they want to say their nice little compliments in the way they say them—medals and citations and all that—I suppose that accounts for the collection.

FALKENBURG: Mr. Wright, have you done buildings abroad?

WRIGHT: The Japanese Imperial Hotel, of course.

FALKENBURG: That, of course, I know.

WRIGHT: I have been asked to do many others but I have refused because I have been so busy

274   *Social Critic of the Twentieth Century*

Frank Lloyd Wright circa 1950s. Photograph by Cameron Macauley, courtesy of the State Historical Society of Wisconsin.

at home. I think I should stay at home and build. I don't think I should build for foreign nations.

FALKENBURG: You built the Imperial Hotel in Tokyo in 1916, didn't you?

WRIGHT: That's because I was getting a worm's eye view of society at the time, and so when the Mikado sent a commission around the world to find an architect for his new hotel, they went around by way of Germany. From the Germans they heard of me and they came straight to Oak Park to see me and see my work and they liked it, employed me to come to Tokyo right away, and I came and we did the building. But I think if they had gone to America to ask about me, they probably never would have found me, because I doubt if very many people in America could have told them where to go. But in Germany they knew. So I think we owe a great deal or at least—I said we: it's editorial—I owe a great deal to our friends across the water, because we as Americans look over there for culture, don't we? And when I began to come back to my own people from Germany, France, Italy, and England, they began to take notice, thought there must be something in it.

FALKENBURG: You weren't appreciated by America until you went away.

WRIGHT: By a certain few. Let's call it the upper third—the upper one-third. I think they appreciated me always and my clients. Rich people have never come to me much. Rich people want a fashionable thing. My work, fortunately so far, has never been fashionable. I'm deathly afraid now it's going to be fashionable, in which case it will be headed for the gutter before very long.

FALKENBURG: Meaning that you were about thirty or forty years ahead of your time?

Aerial view of the side elevation of the main entrance lobby wing of the Imperial Hotel (1915) as reconstructed at the Museum Meiji Mura near Nagoya, Japan (1976). Photograph by Juro Kikuchi.

WRIGHT: I wouldn't know as to the number of years and I don't know that it was particularly ahead of the time, but I wasn't in it and of it too much, except in spirit. I think I had more of the spirit of my time than most of the people around me, and I don't think I have lost out to it as most of them did. You see, the time we live in is exceedingly engrossing and in a sense fascinating but confusing. The truth is very hard to come by in our time, in our day. I really don't know what's become of it. It's hard to find it in almost anything, isn't it? You know we have so many of these rams in the ram pasture stamping and shaking their horns, trying to scare the sheep and huddle them, and they do. The sheep will huddle. And out of that huddle a politician gets what he wants to get. And I think that's where we are right now. Nobody knows the truth about anything. It's about the last thing that the times can stand—the truth.

FALKENBURG: You mean you were comparing sheep and rams to a politician?

WRIGHT: The rams are the politicians at Washington. Isn't that the ram pasture? And the

Social Critic of the Twentieth Century

sheep are the people, of course, all through the U.S., and they huddle and it has scared them. And the politician knows this. He can get anything they've got. They'll give and give over when they're scared. That's the American psyche, because they are not certain of anything particularly. They are extremely sensitive to suggestions that have something to do with fear. They are very likely to be afraid, especially if they have a lot of money.

FALKENBURG: What do you think the solution to all this is?

WRIGHT: You know, Walt Whitman said a good thing. Somebody asked him what he felt about the evils of democracy and he said he thought the cure for the evils of democracy was more democracy. And I think what we need is more democracy, more freedom, more realization of where freedom comes from. Freedom doesn't come from government. Freedom is something you work out for yourself under your own vest. And you work at it all your life and you never stop working at it. Now we don't know that as a people, do we?

FALKENBURG: You think we have fear instead of freedom?

WRIGHT: We think that Harry Truman can give us freedom. We think that Ike Eisenhower can give us freedom. They can't. They can protect us while we struggle for it, and that's all a President in a democracy can do.

And I don't think a democracy can afford heroes either. You know there was a very wise civilization that preceded ours by a great many years—the Mayan civilization. You know they had a lot of marvelously well-thought-out customs. One of them was when they went to war they came home, of course, with heroes.

You can't go to war without coming home with heroes. Now they regarded heroes preferably. They would give the hero everything he wanted—wealth, women, song, prestige—for a year, one year only. At the end of that year they appointed a fête day, had a great celebration, and took him out and executed him. Why? To safeguard the future. So that the hero couldn't run away with the show that civilization was putting on. Otherwise they would be pretty badly off. You see, now that's where we are.

FALKENBURG: I think it's the people's fault if they make heroes.

WRIGHT: The people, of course, are faulty. But a democracy cannot afford a hero. One of the things a democracy should beware of, as the Mayans were wary of it, is worshiping a hero.

FALKENBURG: I don't know of any hero at this moment, do you?

WRIGHT: Well Ike Eisenhower, isn't he a hero?

FALKENBURG: He's asked that he not be called a hero. He asked that when he first came back from Europe.

WRIGHT: Whether you call him a hero or not doesn't matter. It's what the people want him to be. Don't you think that if the women really wanted peace we'd have it? They don't want peace; they want a hero too.

FALKENBURG: No they don't, they want peace.

WRIGHT: They want their husbands to be heroes. They want to marry a hero. They want their children to be heroes. They want a hero for a son. Oh yes, they do!

FALKENBURG: That's only if there's a war on, I think, they feel they must go in and so on.

WRIGHT: War or no war, you see, woman has been behind the man, walking along quite submissively. Now she's out in front and she wants to stay there and she can only stay there by giving birth to heroes or marrying one.

FALKENBURG: Mr. Wright, what do you mean that the woman is out in front? I hadn't heard that!

WRIGHT: Hadn't you? Oh yes she is!

FALKENBURG: What woman?

WRIGHT: Very much out in front; well, the American woman. That's why the Europeans don't want to marry one unless she has very . . . has got lots of money.

FALKENBURG: Well, these are Frank Lloyd Wright's ideas. They seem almost revolutionary, don't they? Maybe he is thirty or forty years ahead of his time. He's fascinating, and we've got lots more stories from him in just a few minutes.

[*Editor's note:* A commercial for Savarin Coffee, one of the sponsors of the *Tex and Jinx* show, followed.] But right now, Mr. Frank Lloyd Wright, it's time for our Savarin Bouquet, and it goes to you today. Along with it, a case of Savarin Coffee, which we'll send out to Taliesin for you and your many, many young architects who work around you and with you, very much with you, a part of you, to enjoy.

Now let's meet again the great exponent of natural architecture and the greatest influence on contemporary architecture all over the world, Mr. Frank Lloyd Wright, who's been said to have one of the most restless and imaginative minds the art of architecture has ever known. Mr. Frank Lloyd Wright, I think you told me the last time you were here on this program that you had eight children of your own and quite a lot of grandchildren, but since then I've discovered that one of your family is a movie star—Anne Baxter. What relation is she to you?

WRIGHT: She's my granddaughter.

FALKENBURG: Anne Baxter is Frank Lloyd Wright's granddaughter?

WRIGHT: That's right. She's my daughter Catherine's daughter.

FALKENBURG: Aren't you proud of her?

WRIGHT: Well, very much. Anne's a nice girl. Trouble is they're trying to glamorize her and make a glamour girl out of her when really she's a good actress. They're wasting a good actress to make a, well, a fairly nice glamour girl.

FALKENBURG: Has Anne ever visited you at Taliesin?

WRIGHT: Oh yes, often. I saw her at Taliesin about two months ago with her baby. She has a baby now. She brought the little baby along and was altogether too solicitous concerning it. thought she ought to throw it away or throw it to one side and let it cry, but she said no. She fussed over it a lot.

FALKENBURG: Is that the way you brought up your children?

WRIGHT: Yes, more or less so. I used to teach them to swim by taking them down to Lake Michigan on the high part by the piles where the water was thirty feet deep, pick them up by the scruff of the neck and throw them in and let them holler and swim.

FALKENBURG: Oh, you didn't!

WRIGHT: I did!

FALKENBURG: Did they all learn to swim?

WRIGHT: I think that's the way to teach a boy to swim. I think the way to teach a baby to grow up is to neglect it; neglect it all you can.

Social Critic of the Twentieth Century

You know how hard it is to kill a baby? The hardest thing in the world. You know, they're the toughest little objects that ever happened.

FALKENBURG: But how about their insides and their feelings?

WRIGHT: Oh, their feelings don't develop very soon. They have only one feeling at first and that is for food.

FALKENBURG: Some don't want it at all.

WRIGHT: Food? Oh, well, they would if you let them alone for a while. The trouble is they try to give them too much too often, implore them, you know. I think if you let the baby alone he'd grow up a great deal better than with all the attention he's getting now.

FALKENBURG: Do you also feel, Mr. Wright, that you shouldn't give him affection?

WRIGHT: Well, affection, yes, of course.

FALKENBURG: But, I know, but . . .

WRIGHT: But not coddling.

FALKENBURG: . . . you talk about throwing them in the river?

WRIGHT: Not coddling. Affection is one thing; coddling is another.

FALKENBURG: Not cuddling [*sic*]?

WRIGHT: Not coddling. I don't think he should be softened up too much. He ought to be let develop on his own legs as soon as possible. You know, they activate patients now in hospitals very soon after an operation. I think the kid should be activated just about as soon as he's born. I don't believe he ought to be swathed in cotton batting and babied too much.

FALKENBURG: Is that the way you were brought up, Mr. Wright?

WRIGHT: I dare say I was, although, of course, I can't remember.

FALKENBURG: That was eighty-two years ago.

WRIGHT: My mother was a teacher, and she had ideas about architecture. She wanted an architect for a son. And I think she cut my curls at the age of eleven, sent me out to the farm, and I was tossed in then as I tossed my children in to sink or swim; and I think that's the thing to do with the children—toss them in to sink or swim.

FALKENBURG: But long before eleven, you think?

WRIGHT: I think the earlier the better. I think just as soon as possible.

FALKENBURG: You have some amazing ideas about life. I wonder . . .

WRIGHT: Are they amazing? I don't know why they should be.

FALKENBURG: Well, I don't know.

WRIGHT: I came by them honestly enough. I came by them by living them, you know, myself. It's very little that I've got from books. I wouldn't say that, though, because I've been an omnivorous reader in my youth, and I have come by an education chiefly by way of reading and experience. The two must go together. You can't get experience out of reading, but you can get reading out of experience, and that's the best kind of reading, isn't it? We don't have much of that kind of reading today.

FALKENBURG: Aren't you going to talk about architecture at all?

WRIGHT: Why should I? I'm an architect. I see that every day.

FALKENBURG: But here I am . . .

WRIGHT: I don't know why I should be interested in it to talk about it. I build it! Why should I talk about it?

FALKENBURG: But you're the most distinguished and you're the greatest architect of the twentieth century, Mr. Frank Lloyd Wright, and I've got questions to ask you about architecture.

WRIGHT: If that were so, I wouldn't need to talk about it.

FALKENBURG: Well, aren't you? *Time* magazine, in its cover story about you, said that. It's just taken for granted. Everybody . . .

WRIGHT: Well, you see, I'm supposed to be very arrogant. But I, at least, would not be able to verify that statement myself. Very early in life, of course, being very sure of my ground and very sure of my star too, I had to choose between honest arrogance and hypocritical humility. Well, I chose honest arrogance, and I'm still at it.

FALKENBURG: I like that—honest arrogance or hypocritical humility.

WRIGHT: Humility—well now, if you're sure of yourself, if you're sure of your ground and you're sure of your star, you're not going to go about with a humility. Are you professing humility? No. Why? Can't do it, honestly. And it's a very healthy thing for the spirit to be ·honest.

FALKENBURG: Let me ask you a question about some of your buildings. The Imperial Hotel in Tokyo survived the great earthquake there.

WRIGHT: Yes, it did.

FALKENBURG: I understand . . .

WRIGHT: And it was built to do it. It was thought-built to stand against an earthquake.

That was the thought from beginning to end, and when the earthquake came it got up against that thought, and sneaked off.

FALKENBURG: Was it the only building in Tokyo to stay standing?

WRIGHT: The only building, practically, that's ever been built on that principle of flexibility. Like putting your hands together this way, you see, and locking them and rocking them. Instead of taking things this way which might let go, you see. It is welded together on the principle of flexibility and that was new in the building world where earthquakes were concerned. Instead of fighting the quake, outwitting the quake, going with it and coming back.

FALKENBURG: I like the way you demonstrated that by putting your fingers . . .

WRIGHT: Well, you see, there is the new architecture.

FALKENBURG: . . . together.

WRIGHT: There you have the principle of *organic architecture* as against the old architecture of post and beam. You see, the old architecture was this, something on a post and the beam, and then the old architecture was the butt and the cut and the slash. Whereas the new architecture, if it is *organic,* is again this locking of the fingers and making it all as one, you see, one thing. The wall going into the floor and the column spreading out into the ceiling and so on.

FALKENBURG: I wish our audience could try that. Lock your fingers together and move them from side to side and you get a very good picture of what kind of architecture Mr. Frank Lloyd Wright is talking about.

FALKENBURG: Part two in the story of a man who has more to do with the roof over your head than anybody else in America, Frank Lloyd Wright, eighty-two years young, father of American architecture, brilliant and always controversial. His flashing wit produces more quotations than any man since George Bernard Shaw. This morning his targets range from airports to Italian fashions, and atom bombs, and slums, and children; and there's a little dynamite in everything he has to say. Here's just a sample.

WRIGHT: One thing, I think, women should do now if we want peace. I think they should stop having children. I think they should refuse to have a child until there is a basis of peace before that birth and which would assure them that they were not providing cannon fodder for experiences like Korea.

FALKENBURG: Mr. Frank Lloyd Wright's prescription for peace.

WRIGHT: I think the whole Korean experience should convince the women of America.

FALKENBURG: That was Frank Lloyd Wright's prescription for peace. We may not agree with it, but we can't help but listen to it. And our office reports, at the RCA Building yesterday, that we had more phone calls about Mr. Wright than we've ever had about any guest in our six years on the air. I think the same thing will happen after this morning.

Do you remember, by any chance, yesterday morning, Mr. Wright talking about his granddaughter, one of his many, many grandchildren, Anne Baxter, the movie star who was in *All About Eve?* And he said the trouble with Anne is that Hollywood is trying to glamorize her. They forget that she's a good actress. Well, Anne's picture is in the paper this morning dressed as Cleopatra. She wants to be glamorous in her next movie so I think she and Mr. Wright have to get together on that.

You remember yesterday Frank Lloyd Wright also talked about the United Nations Building and the Lever House on Park Avenue. Little did I know that I'd be in the Lever House today posing for some pictures for *Town and Country* magazine. I have a date there at one o'clock. I hope they let me in. After all, it was Mr. Wright who said those things, I just asked the questions.

Now let's meet again eighty-two-year-old or young Frank Lloyd Wright, a man who has left his fingerprints on blueprints of buildings around the earth. He's the pioneering father of American architecture; and he's even more famous in Tokyo than in New York. His ideas have influenced millions of homes. And now let's find out what kind of a home he has built for himself. The name of his home is Taliesin and he built it in Spring Green, Wisconsin. Mr. Wright, it's hard to tell, even from the best pictures, what it's really like. Do you think you could describe it for us?

WRIGHT: Well, I've been describing it to you, when I put my hands together this way and made the thing *of* the thing instead of *on* it.

FALKENBURG: But how about the colors, the wonderful colors and open spaces that you have everywhere?

WRIGHT: More or less the quality of space and *organic architecture* believes that in the interior

The Social Critic in Conversation with Jinx Falkenburg

space we live in is the reality of that building. Just like this little cup here of water, you see. If I hold this up to you, what would you say was the reality of that cup? What is the real cup?

FALKENBURG: I don't know.

WRIGHT: Yes you do. Try again.

FALKENBURG: Just a cup of water?

WRIGHT: No, what is the reality of the cup itself? Not the water.

FALKENBURG: I don't know what you mean?

WRIGHT: Well, I mean the reality is *what* in this object? Is it the thing the potter did to it, making the cup? Is it in the physical property of the cup? Or is it in the idea of the cup, which is the space within it to put something in? You see, that's the reality of the cup.

FALKENBURG: Yes, oh, I see.

WRIGHT: Well, now that's modern architecture's—that's the *organic architecture.* The reality of that building is that space within which you live, you see. It's very simple.

FALKENBURG: Do you think Taliesin . . .

WRIGHT: But to do it isn't so simple.

FALKENBURG: Well, do you think that it's the most beautiful place that you've ever seen?

WRIGHT: I don't know about that. I've seen more beautiful places that I'm going to build than that one.

FALKENBURG: Taliesin has burned down twice, hasn't it?

WRIGHT: I've seen them but they're not built.

Taliesin has burned down twice. We're living in the third building. And with that went a lot of suffering, of course, and still all that went into the building that came next probably purified it and made it even more beautiful than it could

have been without the destruction and the suffering, don't you think so? It might be. And I guess life is like that. Hasn't yours been like that? For every experience which has brought you suffering, hasn't it brought you some wisdom and some beauty in life you wouldn't have had otherwise? I think so.

FALKENBURG: Sure. Much later though.

WRIGHT: Oh, well, it doesn't matter how much later; we live a long time anyway.

FALKENBURG: Look, I have a question.

WRIGHT: Someday, I guess, we're going to live longer. I don't think eighty-two years is very long to have lived. Do you?

FALKENBURG: I do. I certainly do.

WRIGHT: I don't see why.

FALKENBURG: You and Bernard Baruch are eighty-two years old.

WRIGHT: Is he?

FALKENBURG: Yes, or should I say eighty-two years young?

WRIGHT: He's what you'd call a financial success.

FALKENBURG: I don't know. I think he's more spiritual.

WRIGHT: You think he is?

FALKENBURG: Uh-huh.

WRIGHT: That's good. I hadn't thought so. I hadn't thought any of our great successful capitalists were very spiritual. If they were I don't think they would have been successful capitalistically, perhaps.

FALKENBURG: Aren't you successful financially?

WRIGHT: I'm not capitalistic.

FALKENBURG: But financially?

WRIGHT: I wouldn't say so. No, because money

Aerial view of Taliesin (1925ff), Spring Green, Wisconsin. Photograph courtesy of the State Historical Society of Wisconsin.

means to me only something to be spent. I would never dream of accumulating the stuff.

FALKENBURG: What do you do with it?

WRIGHT: Spend it. Build with it. Make more spacious and more beautiful the place I live in. I don't give much of it away because I don't believe in that either. But I'd spend it on a friend; I'd spend it on anything I did for him. Money is to be spent and as long as we can keep the spenders spending we're going to be successful. As long as they start—as soon as they start hoarding we're going to lose out.

FALKENBURG: You have lots of children and grandchildren, haven't you?

WRIGHT: Lots of them. Let's see, I have had seven of my own and an adopted one—very charming one—and lost her. That makes eight. That's too many!

FALKENBURG: Did you give your children a lot?

WRIGHT: I don't know. I don't think I did. Ask them. See what they say. They had a lot. They lived in a beautiful atmosphere. They lived in the expression of these ideas we've been talking about. They've all imbibed them to a certain extent. They're all going institutions and they're all successful.

FALKENBURG: The children?

WRIGHT: The children. Like the little granddaughter Anne Baxter. Some of them are architects. They're all doing well. I didn't have much to do with it. I was only their father, that's all. And I don't think a father does much for his children as a rule.

FALKENBURG: You think the mother does?

WRIGHT: I think she does. I think she is the cup which has been fashioned by nature into which the future has been put. And I think she is the grand conservative element in nature. Mother is the conservative and father goes out and tries to bring in the bacon, puts it on the doorstep and mother prods him once in a while to do better than he's doing and he does. But mother is the element which really nature depends upon for her future.

FALKENBURG: Well, I'm glad you've said something nice about women, finally, having started out by . . .

WRIGHT: Oh, I've said a lot of nice things about women.

FALKENBURG: Well, you said that women were leading men now, ahead of them, and that wasn't good.

WRIGHT: Was that bad? I think that's where she ought to be.

FALKENBURG: Oh, you do?

WRIGHT: Out in front. Sure. That's where she ought to be. I think that man's leadership has proved a great failure and I think now the women ought to try.

FALKENBURG: Do you think there should be a woman President?

WRIGHT: But the trouble is when they were given the vote did it change anything? They just voted the way their husbands voted. That was all. Do you vote the way your husband votes?

FALKENBURG: Yes.

WRIGHT: That's it. So does every woman. Well, what was the use of giving them the vote?

FALKENBURG: Well, I think you marry because you respect the man.

WRIGHT: Now, that's what I mean by getting out in front and voting for herself.

FALKENBURG: Well, I like the person my husband votes for.

WRIGHT: All right. If it's legitimate but then I don't see why, if women are like that universally, we should give them the vote. It's wasting a lot of time and effort and money.

FALKENBURG: Well, it's only because a woman marries a man because she likes him, she respects his ideas in every way, you see. So naturally she would follow along—not naturally, but she might follow along in that way of thinking.

WRIGHT: You're saying something that I guess is true; that it is her nature to complement her man. And that is good if the man is worthy of it. But she isn't always a good judge of human nature and she doesn't always marry a man who's worth that emulation on her part. And when he isn't she ought to get out in front and she does, as a rule, nowadays doesn't she? I'll bet she does.

FALKENBURG: Do you think a woman will ever be President of the United States?

WRIGHT: I think so. And I think the day isn't very far distant unless we improve the Presidents we've been having.

Social Critic of the Twentieth Century

FALKENBURG: Do you see any woman in the horizon or in the country . . . do you know of any one woman or women that you think . . . ?

WRIGHT: Sure, I think my wife would be an excellent President of the United States.

FALKENBURG: You mean that?

WRIGHT: I bet you that if you were to ask Tex he would say that Jinx would make a good President.

FALKENBURG: Well no, that's not right, if husbands just think their wives are . . .

WRIGHT: Oh, they should anyway. I think a husband should put his wife as high as he knows how—put her and hold her there and the same thing with a husband—the same thing with a wife and her husband. But a husband doesn't often get it in America. No, sir. He gets behind the lighthouse. And the lighthouse is not on. Am I saying something here that's rather traitorous to my social system?

FALKENBURG: No, I'm just very interested in what you're saying, in everything you're saying.

WRIGHT: There's one thing, I think, women should do now if we want peace. I think they should stop having children. I think they should refuse to have a child until there is a basis of peace for that birth and which would assure them that they were not providing cannon fodder for experiences like Korea, see? I think the whole Korean experience should convince the women of America that they should strike. Now, why don't you all strike? Why keep on having cannon fodder to be sent to Korea? My God, it's obvious enough. And yet women never do anything about it. They keep having children. The birth rate is increasing with every war. The more wars we have the more cannon fodder is provided. Well, isn't that the woman's fault? Of course it is.

FALKENBURG: Do you feel that the women could do a great deal about having a peace? You said before that . . .

WRIGHT: I think that peace is largely a matter for women to determine and when the women make up their minds that there's to be peace in the world I think we're going to have it.

FALKENBURG: Aside from not having any more children, how else can we do it?

WRIGHT: Well, that's fundamental and short-cut quick. Now, I don't know. I haven't thought of any better scheme than that for the time being. But I think there could be a lot of other ways that women could come to the front and assure the peace of the world. And I think they would probably have to be differently educated and perhaps differently situated. I think we've got to look to them for a good deal we never had from them. I don't think they've lived up to their privileges, the women, as a rule of course, there are an enormous number of exceptions. But woman, by and large—you see her smoking a cigarette in a nightclub, you see her anywhere she goes now—she isn't a reassuring picture for the future, I should say.

FALKENBURG: Would you like to see her out on the farm plowing?

WRIGHT: Oh, I'd love to see her on the farm. I'd love to see her in occupations that were really productive rather than in pastimes which were more or less disgraceful.

FALKENBURG: Do you think it's wrong for me to be interviewing you on the radio?

WRIGHT: Well, I think that's all right, Jinx. Yes, I think you're not going to be blamed for that too much. I think that probably you're doing a good job. I wish there'd be more women at it. I remember Mary Margaret McBride. She's done a good service to humanity by getting a little out of people here and there, now and then, hasn't she?

FALKENBURG: She certainly has. Oh, I'm glad to hear you say that.

WRIGHT: And you've done the same thing, haven't you?

FALKENBURG: Well, do you know that's the nicest compliment I've ever had that someone called me a junior Mary Margaret McBride?

WRIGHT: Well, that's very nice of you to feel that way. I think you women are little by little getting out where you're useful, where you're not just something you know in passing.

FALKENBURG: Well, that's the most encouraging thing Frank Lloyd Wright has said—where we're not "just something you know in passing." Mr. Frank Lloyd Wright, we're going to take time out here for our audience to sit back and maybe think about some of these ideas you've thrown at them this morning. They're fantastic. And I know you have lots more and they're all very definite and very clear-cut and we'll be back in just a few minutes for more stories and ideas from the mind of Frank Lloyd Wright, eighty-two-year-old father of American architecture.

Now, let's start some more arguments. Back to our guest, father of American architecture, eighty-two-year-old Frank Lloyd Wright, and his next subject—American cities versus airports. Mr. Wright, while you were in Europe this winter war broke out right here in New York between suburbanites and the airports. There were several tragic crashes in Elizabeth and one in Queens, with the result that Newark Airport was closed by the demand of irate citizens. Now, as an architect and planner, Mr. Wright, what do you think is the solution to the problem? Do you think that the airports should be moved away from the houses? Or the houses away from the airports?

WRIGHT: Well, of course, the airport and everything connected with it is in the nature of an experiment still. It's in a very crude state, but it's going to be a very valuable feature of our civilization. And everybody is working on it the best they know how. And I think some compromise should be effected where the airport should respect the rights of the citizens who got there first and if anybody is going to move I think it ought to be the airport. And I don't think there's any good reason why the airport should become a threat to the people who live below. There's many ways they could be managed while they're growing up.

The airplane now is very far from being the thing it's going to be in ten years from now. Of course, they're trying to standardize it. The whole effort of the manufacturer is to render his product static and then he would like to think of the airplane as finished. Then they could go into production on a grand scale, but, as a matter of fact, the airplane is only a gadget and flying is even today pretty much a stunt.

FALKENBURG: You think that the airports should be further away from the cities, then?

WRIGHT: Yes, I think the airport and the air route should be so laid out and designed that they are no threat to the living community as they pass. Certainly I think if I were President of the United States that that would be one of the things that I would see emphatically established.

FALKENBURG: I'm sure the residents of Elizabeth, New Jersey and Queens think you should be President with a thought like that.

WRIGHT: Oh, I don't know about that, but I'm sure that every resident in the United States of

America would feel the same way about the airplane. Why should our life on earth be threatened by a means of locomotion? The automobile is bad enough. My God, even today to go out into the street—what is that old crack about the only way to cross the street in New York is to be born on the other side? That's pretty nearly true that all of our advantages—so-called advantages—are becoming disadvantageous by way of this centralization that it's quite impossible to consider them advantages. I've been in New York City when to start walking on the tops of the taxicabs would get me to the place infinitely sooner than trying to ride there in one.

FALKENBURG: Have you tried that?

WRIGHT: I haven't tried it yet. I've been tempted to often.

FALKENBURG: Tell me, when you're in New York City, as you are at this moment, living at the old Plaza Hotel, why do you pick an old-fashioned hotel like that rather than a brand new one?

WRIGHT: I don't know of any brand new ones in New York.

FALKENBURG: Well, the Waldorf—it's under the same management.

WRIGHT: Waldorf brand new? It's practically the same vintage as the Plaza, only the Plaza is genuine. I should call the Waldorf an imitation of the Plaza. The Plaza was built by Henry Hardenberg, a master of German Renaissance architecture. He was imported here by the great Fifth Avenue set, you know, the "Four Hundred," to do that hotel. And he made of it an exceedingly thrilling fine thing for its time. Now, as a modern architect, I believe that what was good in its time should be preserved. And I

think they should preserve the Plaza as the initial performance which has been imitated by all the hotels that have been in New York since.

FALKENBURG: That's very interesting because you hear people in New York refer to it as the old Plaza. The Savoy-Plaza is new. The Pierre is new. The Sherry-Netherland is new.

WRIGHT: Well, the Savoy-Plaza may have some new wrinkles but substantially, architecturally speaking, all those hotels are imitations of the old Plaza—Henry Hardenberg's Plaza. Henry Hardenberg was a great distinguished German architect and the Fifth Avenue set, I guess they used to call them the "Four Hundred," brought him over here to do this work. And they all profited by it and they haven't had the sense to preserve it. They got a lot of little boys who are doing the French racket, which we think is the aesthetic thing to do, come in and destroy most of it. They had a few rooms there they hadn't touched which I went to plead for like the dining room and the men's room. Most of the rest of it has been destroyed. And lately they took the beautiful room done by Joe Urban and had Henry Dreyfuss, who's a nice fellow, come in and do something that destroyed it utterly.

FALKENBURG: What did he do?

WRIGHT: Well, he did a railway train thing there, you know. He wiped out all that beautiful romance and put in the kind of thing that he puts on the Twentieth-Century dining car. You can like it or not as you please.

FALKENBURG: You think Henry Dreyfuss is a nice fellow but you don't like what he does?

WRIGHT: My tragedy in architecture is that I like so much the fellows that do such bad things that I don't like. I don't like the things they do and then I meet them and I like them. What are you going to do about that?

FALKENBURG: What do they think about you saying things like that about them?

WRIGHT: Well, you ask them. I don't know.

FALKENBURG: Mr. Frank Lloyd Wright, time out again for just sixty seconds and then we'll be back with about five more questions for you. Have you ever heard anyone answer them as Mr. Wright does? Pulls no punches!

Now, back to Mr. Frank Lloyd Wright, eighty-two-year-old father of American modern architecture. Mr. Wright, since you've just come back from Europe you must have seen some of the new housing projects that are under way in Italy where whole towns had been wiped out in the war. Do you think that we could take a lesson from the Italians in small home architecture?

WRIGHT: Italy is still the beating heart of the creative art world just as it always has been. Italy today is doing the best work, I think, being done on the continent of Europe. She is coming along every line with all sorts of good things and she's taking the fashion center away from Paris.

FALKENBURG: How about . . .

WRIGHT: The Italian things today—Italian dresses—Italian goods—Italian everything—are getting the go sign.

FALKENBURG: What about Italian architecture? Have the architects there learned anything about how to build new apartments and new homes to survive?

WRIGHT: They have. Yes, they have. The railway station in Florence is one of the best pieces of modern architecture I've ever seen.

FALKENBURG: Oh, and how about the railway station in Rome?

WRIGHT: Well, that was troubled by Mussolini's yen for grandomania. That still is troubled with the old pandemonia of the Renaissance. Otherwise it wouldn't be so bad. But it's still all out of human scale, you see. The Florence station is in human scale. Then you get to the Mussolini station in Rome and it's, say, out of human scale again—too exaggerated. Mussolini did better in his stadium—too many statues but the stadium isn't so bad. But the railway station, no.

FALKENBURG: Mr. Wright, in Europe I think the fear of war during the past many years and centuries has crowded cities inside walls as you can see when you fly over Italy. On some of those mountaintops you can see a city that's surrounded by a wall. Do you think that the fear of the atom bomb in America will have any influence on architecture here?

WRIGHT: Well, the wall will do no good, of course, I think against the bomb and the developments that are sure to come. Because the bomb is only an initial one, the bomb is still a primitive beginning of what's to come in the way of destructive implements. Pretty soon it will be easy to press a button, perhaps, and put all the world out of commission. So I think nothing much you would do would have any salutary effect except to decentralize. Centralization has gone so far now that it is just becoming a curse. I think you should call centralization now murder because eventually it will be.

To decentralize and take the city and blend it with the country, make the two one, is entirely feasible because of our modern improvements—the telephone—the automobile—electricity— all that will enable us to do away with these cities. But, there again, you have the human habitation like the cigarette, like the liquor, like anything else they have and do. They're confirmed so easily in an unquiet, uncomfortable situation. It's hard to do anything about it. They get habituated and they like it. They can't think of anything else and imagination ceases to operate and the whole thinking apparatus of the man is turned inward. Well, that's happened to us too soon, happened to us as a people.

FALKENBURG: Have you anything, Mr. Wright, to suggest for redesigning homes or apartment houses so that people who live just six inches apart from the neighbor can feel more like a neighbor?

WRIGHT: You have a striking instance in New York City of what the insurance companies do with the people's money. To be sure to be able to pay it back they invest it in the "new slum," I call it. You see the old slum has become a sanitary slum. Did you ever hear of a sanitary slum? Well, that's it. The insurance companies of New York City are building sanitary slums and these great horrid prisonlike looking towers that you see made of brick, you know? You've seen great clusters of them around?

FALKENBURG: Yes.

WRIGHT: Well, that's the sanitary slum. Now, in ten years from now when decentralization has gone more on its way, to give that as an address is going to be quite as unfavorable as it would be to give the slum that smells so bad now as an address.

FALKENBURG: What do you mean in ten years? Why? What will have happened?

WRIGHT: It will have happened that we've grown beyond it, that the city will have disappeared to the point where it leaves those things standing up here for people to live in and nobody will want to acknowledge that that is a residence as an address.

FALKENBURG: What do you mean, the city will have disappeared?

WRIGHT: Well, I think centralization is going out whether we like it or not. I think people are going afield. I think the country is coming up. I think the city is coming down. In a survey made not so long ago by Dr. Van Morgan of Antioch every city in the United States was discovered to be a vampire. It couldn't live on its own birth rate for three years if the population is over 100,000. It has to be replenished continually from the villages, from the farms, and that's the truth about the city. And another little item that might be added to that is that there isn't a city in the United States of over 250,000 that isn't bankrupt. New York City is one of them.

FALKENBURG: Mr. Frank Lloyd Wright, do you suggest that we all move west?

WRIGHT: I suggest that the more we move out whether it is west, south, north or east, the better; provided you don't move into the Atlantic Ocean.

FALKENBURG: Thank you very much, Mr. Wright.

WRIGHT: Well, you're entirely welcome. It's been great fun as usual. This is the second time, isn't it, Jinx?

FALKENBURG: Yes, it is. And you're leaving the mike and I know you're going out of the door but thank you again. And I know that . . . well, we'll forward all the mail to you.

WRIGHT: Having just come from France where everything is "au revoir," who knows? Au revoir!

FALKENBURG: And with that Mr. Frank Lloyd Wright got up from the chair, picked up his cane and his hat and a package that he had, and disappeared out of the door and out of the studio. And back to Taliesin, Wisconsin where he'll be working for the future. We will hope to see him again and hear his ideas again because they are . . . they're fantastic, aren't they? They make you think and wonder, are they right or are they wrong? But at least they make you think a great deal about them.

The Mike Wallace Interviews

I've been accused of saying I was the greatest architect in the world, and if I had said so, I don't think it would be very arrogant, because I don't believe there are many, if any. For 500 years what we call architecture has been phony.

Frank Lloyd Wright was interviewed twice by Mike Wallace on Wallace's *The Mike Wallace Interview* television program in September 1957. These interviews appeared as a two-part program broadcast several weeks apart by the American Broadcasting Company television network. The two-part program was rebroadcast on February 29 and March 1, 1960; the text was transcribed from these broadcasts.

The Interviews

PART ONE
The First Interview

WALLACE: This is Mike Wallace with another television portrait in our gallery of colorful people. In 1957, two years before his death,

Frank Lloyd Wright honored us with two television interviews. They were so memorable that we're going to replay them tonight and tomorrow night.

Frank Lloyd Wright, at the age of eighty-eight, in

a two-part testament reaffirming his faith in the individual, in the independent mind, and in freedom. And we'll hear the first part of Mr. Wright's testament in just one minute.

And now to our story. Admirers of Frank Lloyd Wright hail him as a man one hundred years ahead of his time. Now eighty-eight years old, he's still designing homes and buildings which are revolutionary, including plans for a mile-high skyscraper for which he's had no buyers yet. But just as radical as Frank Lloyd Wright the architect is Frank Lloyd Wright the social critic. Mr. Wright, before we go any further, I'd like to chart your attitudes specifically by getting your capsule opinions, as an architect or social critic, of the following: first of all, organized Christianity?

WRIGHT: Why organize it? Christianity doesn't need organizing, according to the master of it. The great master poet of all time didn't want it organized, did he? Didn't Jesus say that "Where a few are gathered together in my name, there is my church"?

WALLACE: Therefore you would just as soon see your religion unorganized?

WRIGHT: Well, that may be why I'm building a synagogue in Philadelphia, a Unitarian church in Madison, a Greek Orthodox church in Milwaukee, and a Christian Science church in California.

WALLACE: Are you a religious man yourself?

WRIGHT: I've always considered myself deeply religious.

WALLACE: Do you go to any specific church?

WRIGHT: Yes, I go occasionally, to this one and then sometimes to that one, but my church— put a capital N on *Nature,* and go there.

WALLACE: All right, sir, what do you think . . . ?

WRIGHT: You spell God with a G, don't you?

WALLACE: I spell God with a G, you will spell it . . . ?

WRIGHT: I spell *Nature* with an N—capital.

WALLACE: What do you think of the American Legion, Mr. Wright?

WRIGHT: I never think of it if I can help it.

Frank Lloyd Wright working at his desk at Taliesin in Spring Green in August 1957 about one month before his appearance on The Mike Wallace Interview. *Photograph by Richard Vesey, courtesy of the State Historical Society of Wisconsin.*

Beth Sholom Synagogue (1954), Elkins Park, Pennsylvania. Photograph courtesy of the Beth Sholom Archives.

Annunciation Greek Orthodox Church (1956), Wauwatosa, Wisconsin. Photograph by the editor.

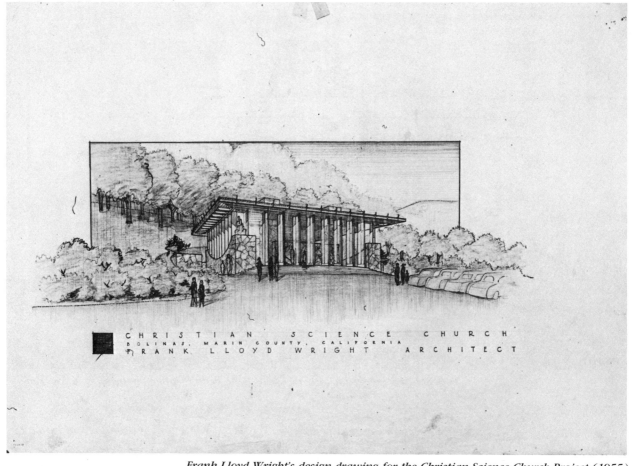

Frank Lloyd Wright's design drawing for the Christian Science Church Project (1955), Bolinas, California. Copyright © The Frank Lloyd Wright Foundation, 1957.

WALLACE: What do you mean by that?

WRIGHT: They're professional warriors, aren't they? I'm against war—always have been, always will be. And anything connected with it is anathema to me. I've never considered it necessary, and I think one war only breeds another, and I think I've been borne out by a reading of history, haven't I? One war always has in it, in its intestines, another—and another has another. So why be for war? And if you're not for war, why are you for warriors?

WALLACE: Mr. Wright, we will come back both to organized religion and the American Legion. I am trying, right now, just to get capsule opinions, as a sort of chart against which to play the rest of the interview. The third capsule opinion I'd like from you—and then we'll go on to other things: mercy killing. What do you think of them?

Social Critic of the Twentieth Century

WRIGHT: I think if it's mercy killing, I'm for it.

WALLACE: When you say "If it's mercy killing," you mean . . . ?

WRIGHT: Well, I think if killing is merciful, why not kill?

WALLACE: With those three opinions as background, let me ask you this, if I may. You obviously hold some fairly unconventional, even unpopular ideas, Mr. Wright. What do you think . . . ?

WRIGHT: I'm unaware of it, if so.

WALLACE: What do you think of the average man in the United States who has little use for your ideas in architecture, in politics, in religion?

WRIGHT: Are you speaking of the "common man"?

WALLACE: The average man, the common man—I think that you have sometimes called him "part of the mobocracy"; part of the mob.

WRIGHT: Well, he's a daisy sitter. I think the common man is responsible for the drift toward conformity now, that it's going to ruin our democracy, and is not according to our democratic faith. I believe our democracy was Thomas Jefferson's idea—I mean, I think Thomas Jefferson's idea was the right idea— that we were headed for a genuine aristocracy. An aristocracy that was innate, on the man not of him, not his by privilege, but his by virtue of his own virtue, his own conscience, his own quality—and that by that we were going to have rule by the brightest and the best. Well, now that the common is becoming a little jealous of the uncommon man, and as H. I. Phillips wrote the other day, he's going to the point where he says, "Well, what's the punk got we ain't got?"—"He's just got the breaks, that's all."

Now, that's going to ruin the common man, because the uncommon man is his vision. And I believe what you call the common man is what I call the common man, a man who believes in nothing he can't see, and he can't see anything he can't put his hand on.

WALLACE: Would you agree with me . . .

WRIGHT: He's a block to progress.

WALLACE: . . . he's a block to progress—would you agree with me that a pretty fair share of our audience tonight either can't or doesn't want to understand modern art, like the paintings of Picasso, or modern music, let's say by Stravinsky? Possibly they don't even know, do not even want to, or cannot understand you. What do you think of these people who either don't understand or don't care?

WRIGHT: I don't think they matter, as far as I'm concerned. I don't think they're for me; why should I be for them?

WALLACE: What do you personally think of Picasso? Some modern . . . no, let's not say Picasso, what do you think of modern paintings that some people say . . . ?

WRIGHT: Why not say Picasso? He's a good instance.

WALLACE: Well, he's a very good instance, but what . . . rather than go specific here, I'd like to talk about modern paintings. Some people say that they look like scrambled eggs. Some people say that modern music sounds like a bad night in a boiler factory. I would like to know *your* opinion?

WRIGHT: I've heard all those reactions, and don't you think we all see as we are? And our reactions will be that reaction which is most characteristic of us ourselves. And every time we express a reaction of the sort, we give ourselves away.

Somebody said the museum out here on Fifth Avenue looked like a washing machine.

WALLACE: This one that you're building?

WRIGHT: That's one of my buildings. Well, I've heard a lot of that type of reaction. I've always discounted it as worthless, and I think it is.

WALLACE: What do you think of Salvador Dali?

WRIGHT: I think Salvador Dali's an immensely clever individual. He's artistic, somewhat of an artist, not a great artist. I think Picasso *is* a great artist.

WALLACE: Is Salvador Dali a great public relations specialist?

WRIGHT: Probably.

WALLACE: Are you?

WRIGHT: I don't think so, because I never have cared very much which way the public was going or what was the matter with it.

WALLACE: You said many years ago that you would someday be the greatest architect of the twentieth century. Have you reached your goal?

WRIGHT: Well, now I think I never said it.

WALLACE: Well, I've done a considerable amount of reading . . .

WRIGHT: I know (laughter).

WALLACE: . . . by you and about you, this week, and I don't think there's a good deal of doubt about the fact that over the years you have said it, not once, but many times. Maybe not in that specific form.

WRIGHT: You know I may not have said it, Mike, but I may have felt it.

WALLACE: You do feel it?

WRIGHT: But it's so unbecoming to say it that I should have been careful about it. I'm not as crude as I'm generally reported to be, I believe—like this matter of arrogance. Now, what is arrogance?

WALLACE: What is arrogance?

WRIGHT: Arrogance is something a man possesses on the surface to define the fact that he hasn't got the thing that he pretends to have. A bluff, in other words.

WALLACE: Arrogance can sometimes be a shell to protect the inner man, too, can it not, even though that inner man has a good deal?

WRIGHT: Well, it's a pretty brittle shell.

WALLACE: Didn't you, in effect, suggest that about the teacher whom you loved best of all, Louis Sullivan? Did you not say that "he was a shell with considerable substance, but that he had this arrogant shell to protect himself"?

WRIGHT: No, that's another one of those things (laughter). I never said it and I don't think he had it. I think he had just plain great faith in himself. It would pass for arrogance. And I think any man who really has faith in himself will be dubbed arrogant by this fellows. I think that's what happened to me.

WALLACE: In other words, this article, for instance, from which I will quote now—*Philadelphia Enquirer*, Magazine Section, October 18, 1953, said as follows: "Some quarters have denounced Wright as an impractical visionary and a pompous windbag." How . . . how do you feel about that criticism, Mr. Wright?

WRIGHT: It doesn't affect me particularly.

WALLACE: Doesn't bother you?

WRIGHT: Not a bit. You always have to consider the source from which these things come. Now, if somebody I deeply respected had

Exterior view of the museum portion of the Solomon R. Guggenheim Museum (1956) at New York looking northeast from Fifth Avenue at 88 Street showing the flare of the overhang (bottom) above the sunken garden. Photograph by Robert E. Mates, courtesy of the Solomon R. Guggenheim Museum, New York.

said such a thing, I would be worried, I would have felt . . . I would have felt hurt. But as a piece in a newspaper, blowing into the gutters of the streets the next day, I don't think it counts much.

WALLACE: You say, if somebody you deeply respected said that. Is it unfair of me to ask you specifically whom you do deeply respect who is on the current scene?

WRIGHT: I respect any man or woman who respects himself sufficiently to tell the truth, no matter what or who it might hurt.

WALLACE: And . . . is it wrong of me to ask you specifically whom you, Frank Lloyd Wright, admire, respect?

WRIGHT: There are so many of those people.

WALLACE: Name some.

WRIGHT: Where would I begin?

WALLACE: I don't know, that's up to you sir. Or if you prefer . . .

WRIGHT: I admired and respected my old master, Louis Sullivan, in spite of his faults. I think if you're going to admire and respect anybody, you have to put up with a few faults, won't you?

WALLACE: I imagine.

WRIGHT: I think there's no unremitting consecration of opinion to any individual, because we all have something to apologize for, don't you think?

WALLACE: All of us, yes. I understand last week . . .

WRIGHT: What's that thing you have in your mouth now?

WALLACE: This cigarette?

WRIGHT: Is that something you feel like apologizing for?

WALLACE: Not at all, I enjoy it. Can I offer you one?

WRIGHT: That's just the point.

WALLACE: May I offer you one?

WRIGHT: No, thank you. I wouldn't know how to smoke it.

WALLACE: Have you never smoked, sir?

WRIGHT: Yes, I've smoked about six months. Well, I won't go through the story. This isn't cricket.

WALLACE: Oh, it's perfectly all right. Some do, some don't. I happen . . .

WRIGHT: Let's leave the cigarette smoker his solace.

WALLACE: Oh, all right, sir. I understand that last week in all seriousness you said, "If I had another fifteen years to work, I could rebuild this entire country. I could change the nation."

WRIGHT: I did say that. And it's true. Having had now the experience going with the building of 769 buildings, it's quite easy for me to shake them out of my sleeve, and it's amazing what I could do for this country. And some magazine has offered me the whole magazine if I'd design a new capitol for the country. It ought to be done.

WALLACE: Of course, you don't really believe that you could succeed in imposing your ideas on what you call the mob, do you, Mr. Wright?

WRIGHT: No. I don't think the mob knows anything of architecture—cares anything about it. I think it's going to be many, many years before the mob will ever get near architecture. I don't think architecture is for the mob. It certainly isn't for education. Education knows nothing of it and very few architects in the world know anything about it.

I've been accused of saying I was the greatest architect in the world, and if I had said so, I don't think it would be very arrogant, because I don't believe there are many, if any. For 500 years what we call architecture has been phony.

WALLACE: Phony in what sense?

WRIGHT: In the sense that it was not innate, it wasn't *organic*, it didn't have the character of *nature*.

WALLACE: Well, what in the world, if I may make so bold, is innate or part of our fiber here in America as a mile-high skyscraper? Now I'm told that you have had on your drawing board for some months now a mile-high skyscraper for which you have no buyers up to now.

WRIGHT: It passed the drawing board some time ago.

WALLACE: Passed the drawing board . . .

WRIGHT: And there it is.

WALLACE: Why in the world did you want to build it?

WRIGHT: Because they came to me and wanted me to do the highest . . . the highest television tower in the world supported by wire. And that was a silly thing, I thought. So, being able to build a mile-high building, I said: "Why not build it?"

WALLACE: Well, for what reason? You obviously would not want to build it just as a stunt, would you?

WRIGHT: No. The television tower would be at the top, and here would be a great useful structure which would make all these silly boxes they're trying to make look tall, foolish. You'd only have to build two of them in Central Park to take the whole of New York in, and you could destroy all the rest of it and plant green, plant grass there. Think what you'd have in the way of a beautiful city—with two mile-high skyscrapers in Central Park. Wouldn't it end the agony?

WALLACE: And what would happen, sir, in the case of an atomic attack?

WRIGHT: Nothing, because an atomic attack would probably do less damage to the mile-high than to anything around the town now.

WALLACE: Are you talking scientifically, or is it just your hunch?

Frank Lloyd Wright as he appeared on ABC's The Mike Wallace Interview *television program in September 1957. Photograph used by permission of Mike Wallace and the American Broadcasting Company.*

WRIGHT: No sir, scientifically. I never talked otherwise.

WALLACE: How do you square such a mile-high skyscraper with your theories on decentralization, Mr. Wright? You're for an end to cities, an end to congestion.

WRIGHT: Not an end to cities, but an end to congestion, yes.

WALLACE: All right, all right.

WRIGHT: And this would help end congestion tremendously. And that was one of the ideas I had in planning one, and then having a great belt of commodity built around it by all the trucks and trucking and commercialization of mankind that would take place, say, a mile away, where everybody would have room, peace, comfort. And every establishment would be appropriate to every man. This is an ideal that I think goes with democracy, isn't it?

WALLACE: Mr. Wright, you don't have much faith in the mob, and yet I'm told that you have a good deal of faith in the nation's youth.

WRIGHT: I do.

WALLACE: How do you square one with the other?

WRIGHT: Why? Is the nation's youth a mob?

WALLACE: Is it not?

WRIGHT: No. I believe the teenager is a teenager and I think with him lies the hope of the future. Now, architecture with us is a matter of the future. We don't have it now. We haven't had it, yet, to any very great extent. But we've had letters from teenagers all over this nation, for five, six, seven years, from Maine to Seattle, all over, and they want to know if . . . they say they've chosen this architecture I represent for their thesis, will I kindly send them some helpful material? So we're getting out a little pamphlet now. We can't answer all these letters. And we're sending the pamphlet to them. Of course, they want us to help them write their thesis. But why have they chosen this architecture?

WALLACE: Well, let me ask you this . . .

WRIGHT: Now, when they're a few years from now, fifteen, who are going to build the buildings of the country?

WALLACE: The mob.

WRIGHT: The teenagers, they're not the mob.

WALLACE: What is your reaction when I tell you that the nation's teenagers bought 11 million Elvis Presley records last year? Which group of youth do you think will inherit this country fifteen years from now—the Elvis Presley fans or the Frank Lloyd Wright fans?

WRIGHT: The Frank Lloyd Wright fans. Undoubtedly. Why? Because they're on the side of *nature*, and the other fans are on the side of an artificiality that's doomed. Do you believe it? I do.

WALLACE: *Time* magazine published an article back on November 5, 1951, Mr. Wright, that had been echoed by social critics ever since. *Time* said at that time: "The most startling fact about the younger generation today is its silence . . ."

WRIGHT: Its what?

WALLACE: "Silence."

WRIGHT: Silence.

WALLACE: "By comparison with the flaming youth of their fathers and mothers, today's younger generation is still a small flame. It does not issue manifestoes, make speeches, or carry posters."

WRIGHT: Who's writing?

WALLACE: That's *Time* magazine's statement and has been echoed by a good many social critics.

WRIGHT: I don't think it's true.

WALLACE: I'll come to some more specifics with you, sir, if I may in just a minute or two. Incidentally, a good deal of the research for tonight, and I'm sure that by no means a good share of it is going to be made evident, came from your new book, *A Testament* by Frank Lloyd Wright.

WRIGHT: Is that my new book? I haven't seen it.

WALLACE: You haven't seen the *A* . . .

WRIGHT: How did you get it?

WALLACE: I got it from your publisher here.

WRIGHT: Oh, well, well let me see it.

WALLACE: And from *Look Magazine,* which is going to be out on the stands this week, and has a fascinating article. Now, then, we only have about three minutes left, Mr. Wright. I'd like your opinion of Charlie Chaplin the comedian and Charlie Chaplin the man.

WRIGHT: Not knowing Charlie Chaplin the man, and only knowing Charlie Chaplin the comedian, I would say that he has given me more pleasant laughs and hours than any other individual living, so far as I've gone with him.

WALLACE: You've heard about Charlie Chaplin's anti-Americanism?

WRIGHT: Ah . . . briefly, perhaps, and vaguely . . . I don't . . . what do you mean by anti-Americanism?

WALLACE: Sir, if I were to start now answering that question, and inasmuch as we only have three minutes left, chances are we could talk just about that for three minutes.

WRIGHT: All right.

WALLACE: When you say what do I mean by . . .

WRIGHT: . . . anti-Americanism?

WALLACE: Well, for one thing, the fact that though he made his living here . . .

WRIGHT: . . . is there anything more anti-American than McCarthyism?

WALLACE: Is there anything more . . .

WRIGHT: . . . anti-American than McCarthyism?

WALLACE: Well, let's talk about Mr. Chaplin for just a moment. He lived here in this country for a good many years, made his living here, and yet refused to . . .

WRIGHT: Why did he go away?

WALLACE: . . . become a citizen.

WRIGHT: Was he abused or something?

WALLACE: Would you say that he was abused?

WRIGHT: I don't know the details, so I wouldn't be able to say.

WALLACE: What do you think of General Douglas . . .

WRIGHT: I always wondered why he left the country.

WALLACE: What do you think of General Douglas MacArthur?

WRIGHT: I think he's a heroic soldier.

WALLACE: A hero ex-soldier?

WRIGHT: A heroic soldier, not a hero ex-soldier.

WALLACE: An heroic soldier, I see.

WRIGHT: Well, that hero ex-soldier might do.

WALLACE: That is all you want to say about the general?

WRIGHT: I don't know the general.

WALLACE: All right, let me ask you this. As an intellectual yourself, Mr. Wright, what do you think of President . . .

WRIGHT: I deny the allegation and refuse to marry that girl!

WALLACE: (laughter) What do you think of . . .

WRIGHT: I don't like intellectuals.

WALLACE: You don't like intellectuals? Why not?

WRIGHT: Because they're superficial. They're up top. They're from the top down, not from the ground up, and I've always flattered myself that what I represented was from the ground up. Does that mean anything?

WALLACE: I'm trying to figure it out.

WRIGHT: (laughter)

WALLACE: What do you think of President Eisenhower as an intellect?

WRIGHT: Well, now, don't ask me "as an intellect" because how would I know? But he's a hell of a nice fellow. And one of the nice things I know about him is that my wife voted for him, and I voted for Adlai Stevenson.

WALLACE: Why did you vote for Stevenson, as opposed to Eisenhower?

WRIGHT: It was against my conscience, but I thought he was too good for the job. And I was glad he wasn't elected.

WALLACE: But you voted for him nonetheless.

WRIGHT: I voted for him because I thought he would make a good President, but against my conscience because I thought that he was too good for the job.

WALLACE: I understand that you may soon design a dream home for Marilyn Monroe and her husband Arthur Miller.

WRIGHT: Why a dream home?

WALLACE: That is the word we got from . . .

WRIGHT: A dream home?

WALLACE: Yes.

WRIGHT: Well, Mr. Arthur Miller has asked me if I'd be interested in designing a house for him, which would mean Mr. and Mrs. Miller, I imagine, and for Mrs. Miller and Mr. Arthur Miller I'd be very happy to design a house. But they haven't asked me in so many words yet.

Wright: "[Are] you going to give me this book?" Frank Lloyd Wright as he appeared on ABC's The Mike Wallace Interview *television program in September 1957. Photograph used by permission of Mike Wallace and the American Broadcasting Company.*

WALLACE: Oh, I see. Well, may I ask you one last architectural question? We have just about ten seconds for an answer to this one, Mr. Wright. What do you think of Miss Monroe as architecture?

WRIGHT: I think Miss Monroe as architecture is extremely good architecture, and she's a very natural actress, and a very good one.

WALLACE: Thank you very . . .

WRIGHT: I don't think she was spoiled by too much training as an actress. [Are] you going to give me this book?

WALLACE: (laughter) I sincerely hope that you'd autograph it for . . .

WRIGHT: I never saw it before. How is it my publisher gave it to you and didn't show me?

WALLACE: Tomorrow night, the second part of our tribute to Frank Lloyd Wright. You'll hear Mr. Wright reflect on the nature of government, of freedom and of immortality. That's tomorrow night, again, with Frank Lloyd Wright. Mike Wallace—that's it for now.

PART TWO
The Second Interview

WALLACE: This is Mike Wallace with another television portrait in our gallery of colorful people. Last night we rebroadcast the first part of a two-part interview with the late Frank Lloyd Wright, as a tribute to a great man. You'll see the second part of this timeless interview with Frank Lloyd Wright in just one minute.

And now to our story. Mr. Wright, first of all, let me ask you this. You once said, "If I had another fifteen years to work, I could rebuild this entire country. I could change the nation." Now, would you tell me, why should you, one man, want to change the way of life of more than 170 million people?

WRIGHT: Well, have I said "change the way of life"?

WALLACE: Yes, when you say "I could rebuild this entire country, I could change the nation."

WRIGHT: I think the way of life in which . . . to which the country is committed needs that change . . .

WALLACE: In other words, you're saying . . .

WRIGHT: . . . and I think it's taking place. And I see no reason why, with intelligence, we shouldn't plan it.

WALLACE: You're saying that practically everyone in the United States is out of step except Frank Lloyd Wright.

WRIGHT: Not at all. I don't say anything of the kind. It isn't their job to build. It's mine. And I think they should have a right to look to their architects for what they should build and how they should build it.

WALLACE: As an architect, how would you like to change the way that we live?

WRIGHT: I wouldn't start to change so much the way we live as what we live in and how we live in it.

WALLACE: Yes, but you cannot differentiate what we live in from the way we live. We are what we live and where we live.

WRIGHT: We make shift in what we live in now. We don't really live in it. We don't really understand what it is to live in an *organic* building with *organic* character.

WALLACE: Well now, an *organic* building,

organic character—these are words which a mobocracy perhaps would have difficulty understanding.

WRIGHT: Well let's say *natural.* Does that suit you better?

WRIGHT: Well let's say *natural.* Does that suit you better?

WALLACE: I'm still not . . . I would like specifically to know what you mean. How would you like to change the way that we live?

WRIGHT: I would like to make it appropriate to the Declaration of Independence, to the centerline of our freedom. I'd like to have a free architecture. I'd like to have architecture that belongs where you see it standing, and was a grace to the landscape instead of a disgrace. And the letters we receive from our clients tell us how those buildings we build for them have changed the character of their whole life and their whole existence, that it's different now than it was before. Well, I'd like to do that for the country.

WALLACE: When you come to New York, as you did today, and you see . . . Did you come by air?

WRIGHT: Yes, I came by air.

WALLACE: And you see the skyline on New York, this does not excite you? This does not exalt you in any manner?

WRIGHT: Quite so.

WALLACE: It does not?

WRIGHT: Does not. Because it never was planned. It's all a race for rent, and it is a great monument, I think, to the power of money and greed, trying to substitute money for ideas. I don't see an idea in the whole thing anywhere, do you? Where is the idea in it? What's the idea?

WALLACE: The idea is obviously, it would seem to me, that a lot of people want to live together, as you point out, to make their livings, to make money, to enjoy what this large city has to offer. And I guess from time immemorial people have flocked, more or less, to one spot, to exchange ideas as well as goods.

WRIGHT: But, my dear Mike, there was justification for that, when there was no other means of communication than by personal contact. That's when the plan for this city you're living in now originated. It originated back there in the Middle Ages when the only way you could have a culture, the only way you could get social distinction or any education from it, was by ganging up.

WALLACE: But you're still willing . . .

WRIGHT: If our modern improvements—what shall we call them, advantages?—are advantageous, we can't get it here in the city any more.

WALLACE: All right. Under those circumstances. Let's move to some specific opinions. In one of your books, *Frank Lloyd Wright on Architecture,* you wrote: "We can escape literature nowhere, and its entire fabric is drenched with sex. Newspapers recklessly smear sex everywhere. Every magazine has its nauseating ritual of the girl cover. The he and she novel is omnipresent."

WRIGHT: Yes.

WALLACE: What's wrong with sex, Mr. Wright?

WRIGHT: Nothing.

WALLACE: Then why do you write what you said?

WRIGHT: It would be wrong with you, rather than sex.

WALLACE: (laughter) Why do you write what you say?

WRIGHT: I believe in it. I think that's true, and I

think that it is because we don't have religion, we don't have an architecture, we don't have an art of our own. We have no culture of our own, that society is drenched as it is, from the bottom up, instead of getting something from the belt up.

WALLACE: Well, we're a young culture. We're a young country.

WRIGHT: We're not a culture. We're only a civilization.

WALLACE: All right. We're a *young* civilization, and it takes time to develop a tradition.

WRIGHT: I don't think we're too young, because civilization was going a long time with everybody that ever got here.

WALLACE: But how do you account for the fact? Let's go to motives, let's go to understandings of why. If . . .

WRIGHT: Why what?

WALLACE: Why we are so preoccupied, as you point out, not with above but with below the belt?

WRIGHT: I can't tell you that.

WALLACE: Haven't you ever thought about it?

WRIGHT: No.

WALLACE: You're just commenting upon the fact and not trying to find out the reason.

WRIGHT: I'm not particularly interested in that feature of human character or nature. I think I'll have to leave the upper region of the pantaloons to the people themselves. I've never been particularly interested in it.

WALLACE: In what way, if any, has your attitude toward sex changed over the course of the past sixty, seventy years?

WRIGHT: I don't think I ever had an attitude toward it. I don't think I've manifested an attitude toward it. I've taken it in my stride for what it was worth, and it seems to me that's the way to take it.

WALLACE: Let's turn to your political views. After a visit to Soviet Russia, back in 1936–37, you wrote the following in a publication called *Soviet Russia Today:* "I saw something in the glimpse I had of the Russian people themselves which makes me smile in anticipation." This was twenty years ago.

WRIGHT: Yes.

WALLACE: "The Russian spirit."

WRIGHT: Right.

WALLACE: You said, "I felt it in the air, saw it as a kind of aura about the wholesome maleness of the men and the femaleness of her women."

WRIGHT: Good.

WALLACE: "Freedom already affects these people unconsciously. A kind of heroism is surely growing up in the world in the Soviet Union."

WRIGHT: I think so.

WALLACE: You still feel that way?

WRIGHT: I still feel that way. And when I came home and wrote that in my *Autobiography,* Alexander Woollcott, do you remember him?

WALLACE: I do.

WRIGHT: Alexander was a good friend of our friend the President.

WALLACE: Roosevelt?

WRIGHT: Roosevelt. And Alec told me that the President had read what I had wrote, and he said: "My sentiments exactly."

WALLACE: Well, now, you are an individualist. You certainly believe in freedom, you cherish it . . .

WRIGHT: Yes.

WALLACE: . . . therefore, how can you explain this enthusiasm for a country which even then, and certainly now, has instituted thought control by terror, political purges, by blood, suppression of intellectuals?

WRIGHT: Do you ever dissociate government and people?

WALLACE: Frankly . . . You're putting this question to me personally?

WRIGHT: Yes.

WALLACE: I find it very difficult to dissociate governments and people.

WRIGHT: I don't find it difficult. I find that government can be a kind of gangsterism, and is, in Russia—and is likely to be here, if we don't take care of ourselves pretty carefully—a kind of gangsterism, and instead of being something from the bottom up, it's something from the top down, again.

WALLACE: But the people have to stand still for it.

WRIGHT: No. I don't think they do. I think the people are unaware of all these things that are happening to them. I don't think they've appraised them at their true value.

WALLACE: Don't governments grow out of people, Mr. Wright?

WRIGHT: It should, but it doesn't. It hasn't in Russia. And it hasn't here, particularly, lately. It doesn't grow out of the people's knowledge of what's good for them and what is the *nature* of the thing they're in. They're without the intelligence Thomas Jefferson thought would be ours, in a democracy. We haven't manifested it. We can see now mediocrity rising into high places. We can see how Jefferson's unwillingness to qualify the vote has resulted in this mediocrity rising into high places.

WALLACE: But we are responsible, aren't we?

WRIGHT: We are responsible ourselves, but we don't wake up to the responsibility. We don't take it. Where in this . . . where do you know a group of men or women who are consciously aware, politically we'll say, of the principles which were declared by the Declaration of Independence, and the responsibility for the development of a conscience that it places upon them? You don't find it; it's very rare. It doesn't manifest in the street, it doesn't manifest in the movies, it doesn't manifest . . . sometimes in the theater we see little of it.

WALLACE: Well, then, in the days that have gone by since our Declaration of Independence, we've gone to the dickens in a handbasket but *somebody* has been responsible and evidently the people *have* to be responsible. When I say the people, the mob, whomever—people don't arrive at being President or Senator or Mayor unless they're elected.

WRIGHT: It's perfectly true. But there will be no turn for the better until the people awaken to the *nature* of the thing that has them in thrall. But this matter is not a matter for a tinker. It's a matter of something that must be grown. And I don't see it growing, as Thomas Jefferson thought it would grow, by education. I think education has been lax in all this thing. I believe we haven't gone to school to learn about ourselves, we haven't gone to school to learn the *nature* of things, and until *nature* study is the basis of our education, we will continue to be in danger of Communism, of all the -isms and the -istics and the -ites you can name.

WALLACE: Well, what's wrong with Communism? You just . . .

WRIGHT: Oh, Communism is utterly, from my standpoint, wrong. I'm an individualist. Known all over the world as such.

WALLACE: You love the people of Russia but you do not love their government?

WRIGHT: That's right. I despise their government and said so. I haven't heard a word from Russia all these years. And it would make them laugh in Russia if they ever heard of it—I don't suppose they have—that I've been accused of Communistic sympathies in my own country.

WALLACE: Mr. Wright, suppose you were approached by one of your students, one of your apprentices, say . . .

WRIGHT: Yes.

WALLACE: . . . who felt pessimistic about his future, because of the hydrogen bomb, the threat of war, the world's general insecurity; and he came to you and said: "Mr. Wright, help me to understand, give me something to live by." What could you tell him?

WRIGHT: That's what they're all asking me. And that's what I'm telling them, every Sunday morning, and all the time they're working with me. I don't put a line on the drawing board that the answer isn't there. And they're there for the way of life we live which is the answer too to this very question you're asking. That's why these youngsters come to me from all over the world.

WALLACE: And the answer is?

WRIGHT: The answer is within yourself, within the *nature* of the thing that you yourself represent, as yourself. And Jesus said it, I think, when he said: "The Kingdom of God is within you." That's where architecture lies. That's where humanity lies. That's where the future we're going to have lies. If we're ever going to amount to anything, it's there now, and all we have to do is to develop it.

WALLACE: Mr. Wright, you . . .

WRIGHT: Now I don't call that the mob. I call that human nature and I call that humanity. Now, humanity to me is not a mob. The mob is the degeneration of humanity. The mob is humanity going the wrong way.

WALLACE: You have faith in youth. You have no faith in the mob. Yet youth becomes adult and turns into a mob, or do I misunderstand?

WRIGHT: Yes it may. But that's our misfortune, and that's because they are not properly educated and don't have an opportunity to go right instead of left.

WALLACE: You write, at some small length anyway, in your latest book, *A Testament,* published by Horizon Press—you write about your religious ideas. I understand that you attend no church?

WRIGHT: I attend the greatest of all churches.

WALLACE: Which is?

WRIGHT: And I put a capital N on *Nature* and call it my church and that's my church.

WALLACE: Your attitude toward organized religion is one of . . .

WRIGHT: That's what enables me to build churches for other people.

WALLACE: Well, this I do want to understand.

WRIGHT: If I belonged to any one church, they couldn't ask me to build a church for them. But because my church is elemental, fundamental, I can build for anybody a church.

WALLACE: What do you think of church architecture in the United States?

WRIGHT: I think it's, of course, a great shame.

WALLACE: Because it improperly reflects the idea of religion?

WRIGHT: Because it is a parrot and monkey

reflection, and no reflection of religion.

WALLACE: Let's go to your . . .

WRIGHT: Is that a little bit too fantastic?

WALLACE: No, no, as a matter of fact, no one has asked me, but I heartily agree.

WRIGHT: I can take that to the universities, and take it to the kind of atmosphere in which they administer education to the young, and get exactly the same failure.

WALLACE: Well now, wait, wait—I said that I heartily agree, and yet something immediately comes to mind. When I walk into St. Patrick's Cathedral, and I am not Catholic, but when I walk into St. Patrick's Cathedral, here in New York City, I am enveloped in a feeling of reverence.

WRIGHT: Sure it isn't an inferiority complex?

WALLACE: Just because the building is big and I'm small, you mean?

WRIGHT: Yes.

WALLACE: . . . mmm, I think not.

WRIGHT: I hope not.

WALLACE: You feel nothing when you go into St. Patrick's?

WRIGHT: Regret.

WALLACE: Regret?

WRIGHT: Regret.

WALLACE: Because of what? Because . . . ?

WRIGHT: Because it isn't a thing that really represents the spirit of independence and the sovereignty of the individual, which I feel should be represented in our edifices devoted to culture.

WALLACE: When you go out into a big forest, with towering pines, and this almost a feeling of awe that frequently you do get in the presence of nature . . .

WRIGHT: Yes.

WALLACE: . . . do you not then feel insignificant? Do you not feel small, in the same sense that I feel small and insignificance?

WRIGHT: On the contrary, I feel large. I feel enlarged and encouraged, intensified, more powerful.

WALLACE: Let's go . . .

WRIGHT: And that's because—why?—because in the one instance you're inspired by an artificiality contrary to *nature*. Am I clear?

WALLACE: You are clear, although I must say that I don't agree, because whatever inspires, whatever inspires a feeling of reverence, a feeling of goodness, a feeling of understanding—not understanding—that's a bad word.

WRIGHT: Oh, no, now you're on dangerous grounds.

WALLACE: Not understanding, I say is good for the insides, is good for the soul.

WRIGHT: No, it may be very bad, very bad. Our natures are now so warped in so many directions, we are so conditioned by education, we have no longer any straight, true, clean reactions, that we can trust; and we have to be pretty wise and careful what it is we give up to, what it is we admire, what it is we are inspired by. I daresay that the stevedore is inspired by the prostitute whom he seeks. I daresay that all these things may be good, so far as they go, because they are necessary. But I wouldn't say that they're what should be. I wouldn't say that they were ideal.

WALLACE: Mr. Wright, there's a good deal of talk about the function of the American press. And the press is popular in some circles, unpopular in others. In just a moment, I would like your opinion of the American press and we'll get Mr. Wright's answer in just one minute.

Now then, Mr. Wright, what is your opinion of the American press?

WRIGHT: I think the American press, once upon a time, was characterized by individuals, great ones, strong men, men with great purpose, strong prejudices of course, but also strong loyalties and convictions. Today, I can't see that there is much trend in what we call the newspaper world—no, that isn't the word. What's the word? What is the word for this letterpress Goliath? . . .

WALLACE: Communications industry?

WRIGHT: . . . which the whole country lives now, in the newspaper? Everywhere you go, their noses are in something to read.

WALLACE: Yes.

WRIGHT: Well, how is it we became so literate all at once? How is it that we are fed, spoonfed, everything, from A to Z, by reading this and reading that, by this newspaper, that newspaper, this magazine, that one? We don't seem to have any life at all except by reading something. We learn nothing except by reading. What brought this about? I don't know.

WALLACE: Well, certainly you're not against eclectic reading?

WRIGHT: To a certain extent I am, yes. I think you should not read spasmodically. I don't think you should read just for the sake of reading, either. I think if you're going to read, you should read something that'll feed you, build you up, strengthen you and be what you need to know.

WALLACE: What magazines do you read?

WRIGHT: Almost none.

WALLACE: Truly?

WRIGHT: Truly.

WALLACE: Then what are the few that you do?

WRIGHT: *Time* is the one which I get most out of, for a long time. I used to get the news from *Time*. But I don't think lately that I've needed it, and I don't think I've read it much lately. I don't feel that I need to get anything of that sort.

WALLACE: You don't feel that you need the news? You don't feel that you have to be . . .

WRIGHT: Only the general drift . . .

WALLACE: I see.

WRIGHT: . . . and the main substance of it. The particularities, no.

WALLACE: Do you think that you are any less rebellious, less of a radical in your art and life, than you were a quarter of a century ago, Mr. Wright?

WRIGHT: Rather more so—only more quiet about it. (laughter)

WALLACE: To what do you attribute your . . . ?

WRIGHT: Warren McArthur, a very good friend of mine, once said to me, "Frank, here, you don't have to paint your shirt front red and stand out in the street and holler about this," he said. And I began to think it over, and I think he's right. It is. You don't have to push hard or talk loud or in any way get up to defend what you believe in. If it is right and if it is good and if it is sound, it will defend you, if you give it a chance. You don't have to push it. I've never pushed myself. I've never turned over my hand to get a client during my life. I have never sought publicity of any kind. I've yielded to it, because Lloyd Lewis came to me once and when I was rolling the reporters downhill in a kerosene barrel and doing all those things to get rid of them. "Frank," he said, "these boys have to live. Don't you understand that you're bringing all this down on yourself just because you haven't got the wit to be kind to them and to see that they have to live just as well as you do, and they're sent out here to get something, and if they don't get it, they may get fired." He said, "It takes all kinds, Frank, to make a world." (laughter) And so I began to give. Here I am, giving again.

WALLACE: Yes, you are and I want you to give, if you will, the answer to just one more question.

WRIGHT: Go ahead.

WALLACE: Are you afraid of death?

WRIGHT: Not at all. Walt Whitman has the guard on that; if you want to consult him, read him. Death is a great friend.

WALLACE: Do you believe in your personal mortality?

WRIGHT: Yes, insofar as I am immortal, I will be immortal. To me "young" has no meaning. It's something you can do nothing about, nothing at all. But youth is a quality, and if you have it, you never lose it. And when they put you into the box, that's your immortality.

WALLACE: Mr. Wright, I thank you for spending this half hour with us.

WRIGHT: Well, you're welcome. I hope it has been of some interest . . .

WALLACE: It has indeed.

WRIGHT: . . . to whoever's listening, but I don't know. (slight laughter)

WALLACE: At the end of that interview, one of

Frank Lloyd Wright's last, we asked him, in view of his age, whether he believed in immortality. Mr. Wright said, "Insofar as I am immortal, I will be immortal." That answer was perhaps Frank Lloyd Wright's most fitting epitaph. Mike Wallace—that's it for now.

Wright: ". . .insofar as I am immortal, I will be immortal." Frank Lloyd Wright as he appeared on ABC's The Mike Wallace Interview *television program in September 1957. Photograph used by permission of Mike Wallace and the American Broadcasting Company.*

18 The Last Interview

A superior teacher is one who is both an introvert and an extrovert. An introvert because he must be alone when he is learning and improving, and challenging himself with new problems. An extrovert because he must have the ability to be communicative.

Frank Lloyd Wright's final interview was conducted by Louise Elliott Rago at Taliesin West on Friday, April 3, 1959. Louise Elliott Rago was a teacher of art at the Weatley School at East Williston, Long Island, New York and was also a graduate student, at that time, in the Department of Art Education at New York University. In Wright's last formal conversation he talked, once again, on education and the artist. Frank Lloyd Wright died on April 9, 1959.

Before the Last Interview

These are Rago's thoughts before her conversation with Wright:

I was overjoyed. I was to have an audience with Frank Lloyd Wright, king of modern architecture. Architecture is known as the queen of the arts. What would I say? What would I do? My first impulse was to go to the library twenty-four hours before the interview, to learn all *about this Buddha-like*

Edited and reprinted by permission of *School Arts* from Louise Elliott Rago's "Spirit of the Desert— Frank Lloyd Wright's Last Interview: Why People Create," *School Arts,* Vol. 58, No. 10, June 1959, pp. 27–30.

genius who had amazed the world. Certainly Wright is to art and architecture, I thought, as George Bernard Shaw is to literature. I then reconciled myself with the fact that it would take years, and possibly a lifetime, to understand Wright's credo on art, architecture, and the creative man. Even though Frank Lloyd Wright was truly American and his art represents significantly the American way of life, he was not readily accepted until after he was discovered by the Germans in 1910. Robert Frost, too, was first appreciated in England, not here. Wright laughed like a schoolboy at the irony in the suggestion that he was appreciated first by Europeans, while Americans are constantly fighting for freedom of expression, individuality, and the dignity of man.

I am sure all of you can visualize an idyllic earthy paradise—a Shangri-la. Wright's desert home several miles from "nowhere" gives one the impression of being out at sea. The reflection of varied warm, earthy colors results in this misleading illusion. I could only think of a mirage. But no, I actually was here—to talk with the most uncommon man of the century. When Dr. Harry Wood, chairman of the art department at Arizona State University, introduced me, Mr. Wright bowed very graciously, but then quipped: "Oh! No! Not another interview." I immediately attempted to regain my ground by informing him that this would be most unorthodox because I was really not a writer but a teacher—an art teacher; and that I wanted to ask him a few questions about his reactions to teaching and to education, and primarily art education.

Intuitively I felt a warm, harmonious rapport when Mr. Wright smiled and his blue eyes brightened, and he said, "You know my mother was a teacher. The future of the world lies in the young. A creative teacher is the finest we have humanly." Mr. Wright commented that teachers should automatically maintain significant social status comparable to that in Europe. This recognition, however, should be attained—not through sheer force—but by the teacher himself exemplifying all the attributes of a good teacher.

The Conversation

RAGO: Since we are discussing the importance of *good* teaching and *good* teachers, Mr. Wright, what would you say are the criteria of a *good* teacher? This, of course, would apply to all teachers, not only art teachers.

WRIGHT: First and foremost a *good* teacher should be an artist and a truly original and creative person. This person should possess genuine qualities of humanness. Too many teachers are constantly talking *down* to their

Social Critic of the Twentieth Century

pupils. A teacher has a ready-made opportunity to elevate the standards of the young, if he would only grasp this opportunity. A superior teacher is one who is both an introvert and an extrovert. An introvert because he must be alone when he is learning and improving, and challenging himself with new problems. An extrovert because he must have the ability to be communicative. He must always be willing to give information and to give of himself, and never fear that his students will surpass him. The most inspirational teacher will challenge and allow his students to surpass him.

RAGO: As an art teacher in a public school, I am very curious to know when you feel a child should begin to learn about art.

WRIGHT: It's a natural, right from an early age. The child's garden is missing in America today. All teachers should study and learn Plato, and then take it on to the children. A child should begin to work with materials just as soon as he is able to hold a ball. By holding a ball, a child gets a sense of the universe and there is a closeness to God. The ball or sphere leads the child to other geometric shapes; the cone, the triangle, the cylinder. Now he is on the threshold of nature herself. When the child begins to work with materials, and begins to create, this is the beginning of the child's getting off on both feet. A new world is opened to him.

RAGO: We have often heard people say, Mr. Wright, that a certain piece of art work has a spiritual quality. It apparently means something different for different people. Would you like to comment on this and give us your views?

WRIGHT: There would be no great art unless it possessed a spiritual quality. If there were no spiritual quality in architecture, it would just be plain lumber. Design to the artist is like drinking water—design is necessary for the artist to breathe. Sometimes you merely enjoy design, and sometimes it has a definite purpose. They are all right if they are the right thing at the right time. Anyone in the art field realizes the full intent of making a plan, a drawing or a sketch—this is not to be taken lightly as far as the artist is concerned.

Frank Lloyd Wright circa late 1950s. Photograph by Obma Studio, courtesy of The Frank Lloyd Wright Memorial Foundation.

It is all over when the boys and girls get to the university. The curriculum in the high schools does not afford the student enough opportunity for creative expression. What's a *curriculum*? To derive *curriculum* from the Latin would mean that it simply was a racetrack. High school should be a busy and intensive period in boys' and girls' lives, but they race through without learning anything worthwhile—just as if they were out on the *track*. Education has been tramped on. Only a few qualified minds should go to the university—only those minds that wish to be troubled. Abolish the university. All open-minded vision has been narrowed down to what a few people want—the Regentry. Those who want to learn will go ahead on their own. Universities today are merely devices for building an iron-bound conformity to a society which destroys its creative thinkers.

RAGO: There seems to be so much controversial talk about the nonconformist—the "beatnik" . . .

WRIGHT: We need nonconformity, but the nonconformist must conform, also. It's the nonconformist, of course, who rises above the masses. We should not be too concerned with the grand average; we should be more concerned with the person who rises above this. The common man is the grand average. We cannot turn our future to the grand average . . . The Masses. I believe the 'M' in 'The Masses' should be shifted to the article to make 'Them Asses.' (Wright laughs slightly) You know, 'Vox Populi.'

There is no room for a creative mind in the cities because there is no contact with nature. There is no contact with other creatures or protoplasm. It's a great pity that the word *nature* has been so degraded. The 'N' in *nature* should be capitalized. Everything we are ever going to have, or see or be lies in *nature*.

Rago's Afterthoughts

I felt that I had imposed on this generous, gentle, spiritual man, who was so willing to share with others. A thought flashed through my mind—how could anyone think him irascible, flamboyant, crotchety, caustic, bizzare? I had heard this type comment. I could only see all that was positive in him. For me he represented goodness; particularly in his affection for young people and his love for the world.

It was partly the atmosphere, I am sure, that lent such magic to his words. We sat in the tiny oriental throne room, with its open wall and its furniture designed by Mr. Wright. Looking out on the green grass and the golden sun of the open patio added importance to his discussion of nature. The writings of Lao-tse and Henry Thoreau (both of these men having been lovers of nature) were among his favorite works. As Dr. Wood and I left this beloved Taliesin West we could hear him stroking the piano in his great living room.

314

Social Critic of the Twentieth Century

Frank Lloyd Wright's last resting place near Taliesin, Spring Green, Wisconsin. Photograph by the editor.

I couldn't help but rejoice. How fortunate I was to have had an almost unearthly interview with this aesthetic man with the Oriental wisdom. Dr. Wood commented that Mr. Wright used to say that he did not play the piano, "The piano played him."

The Arizona sun he loved so much was dropping low over the desert that surrounds Taliesin. The giant Saguaros and the Gila Mountains were turning blue. The Greasewood was putting on a golden evening gown. At that moment I would never have guessed that Mr. Wright would go to the hospital the following evening. Less than a week later his funeral service was held in the Taliesin living room where he had led me personally. Mine was the last interview he gave.

Epilogue

QUESTIONER: There are very few of us that will be architects. What can those of us who are not do to promote change to an *organic* architecture?

WRIGHT: Well, those of you who are not going to be architects are lucky. You are going to be waited on by those of us who are. All we ask of you is to know architecture when you see it—to know the good from the bad. It is up to you for our sakes—the sake of the architect. I am an architect and the truth is that there is not much use in being an architect without you fellows. We are working for you. We want you to see and feel the truth, the integrity, the beauty of what we do. We ask for it. Otherwise what are we? After all, you are the boss of the situation—you fellows who aren't architects!

Extracted and edited from a talk given to the Society for Contemporary American Art by Frank Lloyd Wright on October 5, 1948 at Orchestra Hall in Chicago, Illinois.

Index

Index

Partridge, Charlotte, 3, 4, 6, 9
Pasadena, California, *see* Millard, George Madison "La Miniatura"
    Residence
Patrick, George, 105, 106, 109, 112, 114, 116
Pattern, *99, 100,* 217
    in design, 116
    in nature, 97–98
    see also Nature pattern
Patterson, Alicia, 245–248, 250–253
Payne, Thomas, 179
Peace, 285
Pei, I. M. (architect), *see* Apartment Helix Project; Mile-High Center
Pennsylvania, *see* Elkins Park; Ohiopyle; Philadelphia; Pittsburgh
"People, Yes, The," (Sandburg poem), 245, 246, 247
Pfeiffer, Annie Merner Chapel (Lakeland, Florida), *29*
Philadelphia, Pennsylvania, 215, 233, 292. *See also* Gimbel Brothers
Philadelphia Enquirer (newspaper), 296
Phillips, H. I., 251, 295
Philosophy, 61
    in architecture, 76–77
"The Philosophy of an Architect" (WTTW-Chicago television
    program), 75–89
Phoenix, Arizona, *see* Arizona Biltmore Hotel; Wright, David
    Residence
Picasso, Pablo, 263, 295–296
Pierre Hotel (New York, New York), 287
Pilgrims, 71
Pittsburgh, Pennsylvania, 8, 223. *See also* Pittsburgh Community
    Center Projects
Pittsburgh Community Center Projects (Pittsburgh, Pennsylvania),
    125
Plan factory, 61
Plastic (as a construction material), 219, 220
Plastic continuity, 21. *See also* Continuity
Plato, 313
Plaza Hotel (New York, New York), 65, 245, 287
Poetry, 197, 245, 246, 254, 263
Poets, 116, 196–197, 217–218, 227. *See also* Architects (as poets)
Political views, 305
Politicians, 83, 161, 228, 276–277
Popular opinion, 63
Porter, Andrew T. "Tanyderi" Residence (Spring Green, Wisconsin),
    44, *85, 157*
Post and beam construction, 47
Pound, Ezra, 250–251
Prairie, 34, 55, 60
    Western, 179
Prairie house, 255
Prairie School tradition, 169
Prefabrication, 101, 102
    American System Ready-Cut, *103*

    Marshall Erdman Company, *103*
    Usonian Automatic, *102*
Presley, Elvis, 300
Press, 14. *See also* American press
Price, Harold C., Sr. ("Hal"), 3, 23, 114
Price, Harold C. Sr., Price Company Tower (Bartlesville, Oklahoma),
    23, *25,* 114, 135, *136,* 143, *146, 147,* 149–150, *150, 151,* 209,
    214, 237
Price, Lucien, 251
Price Tower, *see* Price, Harold C. Sr., Price Company Tower
Primitive civilizations, 72
Principle, 77, 163, 176–177, 233
    democratic, 155, 162
Production, 132
Professionalism, 8
Professors, 169, 180
Proportion, 101
Public housing, 129
Public relations, 296
Public Service Company of Oklahoma, *146*
Public service corporations (utility companies), 178
Pyramids (Egyptian), 158

Quantitiy production, 201
Queens, New York, 286

Racine, Wisconsin, 3, 14, 17. *See also* Johnson, S. C. and Son
    Administration Building; Johnson Wax Research and
    Development Tower
Radio, 130, 232
Rago, Louise Elliott, 311–315
Railway stations, 259–260
Ranch house, 21, 181–182
RCA Building (New York, New York), 281
Real estate, 202
    investors, 187
Realtors, 128, 129, 130, 232
Recentralization, 142
Redding, Connecticut, 17. *See also* Loeb, Gerald M., Residence
    Project
Regents (of Universities), 169, 180
Rehabilitation (of the city), 133
Religion, 74, 89, 292, 294, 305
Renaissance architecture, 21, 176, 288
Repose, 97, 127, 180
Republic, 127
Restaurants, 105–116
    European, 112, 113
    French, 113
    planning of, 106
    United States, 106, 112

Universities, 72, 86, 161, 169, 177, 180, 208, 235, 314. *See also* Harvard University; University of Arkansas-Fayetteville; University of California-Berkeley; University of Oklahoma-Norman; University of Wisconsin-Madison; Yale University

University of Arkansas-Fayetteville (Fayetteville, Arkansas), 229

University of California-Berkeley (Berkeley, California), 185, 229

University of Oklahoma-Norman (Norman, Oklahoma), 169–170, 175

   School of Architecture of, 169–170

University of Wisconsin-Madison (Madison, Wisconsin), 12, 30, 33, 217

Urban, Joe, 287

Urbanism, 202

Usonia, 96, 119

Usonia, No. 1, *see* Herbert Jacobs First Residence

Usonian Automatic Concrete Block, *102*. *See also* Modular concrete block

Usonian city, *see* Broadacre City Project

Usonian freedom, 125

Usonian houses, 23, *24*, *25*, 96

Usonian style, 96, 124

Uxmal, 138

Venice, Italy, 240. *See also* Academy of Fine Arts; Maria della Salute, Santa

Venus (planet), 261

Villages, 182

   small, 202

Violence, 86

Virginia, 173

Wainwright Building (St. Louis, Missouri), 34, *35*

Waldorf Hotel (New York, New York), 287

Wales, 188, 215

Wallace, Sir Alfred, 160

Wallace, Mike, 238, 291–292, 294–296, 298–310

Wanamaker's (New York, New York), 60

War, 124, 277–278, 294. *See also* World War I, World War II, Korean War

Warriors, *see* Soldiers

Washington, D.C., 128, 260, 276. *See also* Capitol, The; Jefferson Memorial; Lincoln Memorial; Washington Monument

Washington, George, 179, 267

Washington Monument (Washington, D.C.), 267, *268*

Wasmuth Portfolios, *see Ausgeführte Bauten und Entwürfe von Frank Lloyd Wright*; and *Frank Lloyd Wright: Ausgeführte Bauten*

Wauwatosa, Wisconsin, *see* Annunciation Greek Orthodox Church

Way of All Fresh, The (Butler), 96

Weatley School (East Williston, New York), 311

Webb and Knapp Incorporated 8, 135. *See also* Zeckendorf, William, Sr.

Welsh, 14

   ancestry of F. L. Wright, 43, 44, 247

   Triads, 248

Western North Carolina Council of Architects, 245

WGBH-FM Radio (Boston), 65

"What Are the Airwaves Saying" (*AIA Journal*), 128–133

Whitehead, Alfred North, 251

"White Horse Girl and the Blue Wind Boy" (Sandburg poem), 246

Whitman, Walt, 155, 179, 218, 260, 261, 277, 310

Willey, Malcolm E. Residence (Minneapolis, Minnesota), 96, *97*

Williams, John J., 236–237

Wind Point, Wisconsin, *see* Johnson, Herbert F. "Wingspread" Residence

Winslow, William H. Residence (River Forest, Illinois), *22*

Wisconsin, 37, 44, 245. *See also* Dousman; Iowa County; Madison; Milwaukee; Racine; Richland Center; Seattle; Shorewood Hills; Spring Green; Wauwatosa; Wind Point

Wisconsin Indians, 43

Wisconsin River, *106*, *110*, *111*

Wisdom (Oriental), 315

Wisdom: A Conversation with Frank Lloyd Wright (NBC television program), 31–56, *32*, *36*, *37*, *43*, 240

Wisdom: Conversations with Elder Wise Men of Our Day (book), 31

Women, 277–278, 281, 284–286

   of America, 285

   as President of the U.S., 284–285

   as voters, 284

Wood, 60, 84, *85*, 209

Wood, Dr. Harry, 312, 314–315

Woollcott, Alexander, 305

Work (as a condition of learning), 211

World War I, 270

World War II, 129

World's Columbian Exposition (Chicago, Illinois), 209, 256

WRCA-TV (Washington, D.C.), 134

Wright, Anna Lloyd Jones (F. L. Wright's mother), 11, 12, 33, 37, *68*, 188, 215, 279, 312

Wright, Catherine Dorothy (F. L. Wright's daughter), *13*, 278

Wright, Catherine Lee Clark Tobin (F. L. Wright's first wife), 12

Wright, Rev. David (F. L. Wright's paternal grandfather), 215

Wright, David (F. L. Wright's son), 3, 12, *13*, 14, 91, 92, 102, 104

Wright, David Residence (Phoenix, Arizona), *91–92*

Wright, Frances, (F. L. Wright's daughter), *13*

Wright, Frank Lloyd:

   age of, 172

   as amateur, 186

   as Bernard Maybeck Lecturer, 185

   birthdate, 70

   birthplace, *13*